THE
COLORADO

The *ion*

THE COLORADO MOUNTAIN CLUB PRESS
GOLDEN, COLORADO

Published by The Colorado Mountain Club Press.
710 10th Street, Suite 200, Golden, CO 80401
(303) 279-3080 1 (800) 633-4417
email: cmcoffice@cmc.org & website: http://www.cmc.org/cmc

Text copyright 2002 by Colorado Trail Foundation.
Copyright 2002 by Colorado Mountain Club Press.
Manufactured in the United States.
Managing Editor for CMC Press: Terry Root.
Graphics Design and Maps: Steve Meyers and Terry Root.
Text Layout: Lyn Berry.
Proofing: Linda Grey and Susan M. Junkin.
Project Liaison for CTF: Merle McDonald.
GPS Data: courtesy of Jerry Brown, Bear Creek Survey Service, Inc.
Front cover photo: Lime Creek, CT Segment 25 by Aaron Locander.
Front cover inset photo: Crossing Tenmile Range, CT Segment 7 by Rick Tronvig.
Facing page photo: Tarn near Eldorado Lake, CT Segment 24 by Aaron Locander.

The Colorado Trail: The Official Guide, 6th Edition
  by The Colorado Trail Foundation
  with contributions by Hugo Ferchau, David Gaskill, Gudy Gaskill, Denise R. Mutschler, Peter D. Rowland and as noted elsewhere in the text.
Library of Congress Control Number: 2002113481
ISBN # 0-9671466-6-6

Warning: Although there has been a major effort to make the trail descriptions in this book as accurate as possible, some discrepancies may exist between the text and the lay of the trail in the field. Therefore, extreme care should be taken when following any of the routes described in this book. This book is not intended to be instructional in nature but rather a guide for users of The Colorado Trail who already have the requisite training, experience and knowledge. In addition, there may be differences in the way certain individuals interpret the trail descriptions beyond that intended. Before you begin an extended trek, or even a short hike, on The Colorado Trail, all users need to be fully capable of independent backcountry mountaineering and orienteering techniques and precautions. Proper clothing and equipment are essential. Failure to have the necessary knowledge, equipment and conditioning will subject users of The Colorado Trail to extreme physical danger, injury or death. Some routes described in this book have changed and others will change; hazards described may have expanded and new hazards may have formed since the book's publication. Each user of The Colorado Trail is responsible and liable for all costs which may be incurred if a rescue is necessary. The State of Colorado pays the cost of rescuing anyone in possession of a valid Colorado fishing license, hunting license or hiking certificate.

A portion of all proceeds from the sale of this guide goes to benefit the Colorado Trail Foundation, helping to fund their efforts to educate the public and to build and maintain the Colorado Trail for you and future generations.

⚠ TABLE OF CONTENTS

For ease of navigating *The Colorado Trail, The Official Guidebook*, sections of the guide are organized by the colors shown.

Marshall Pass to San Luis Pass (Seg. 16-20)

San Luis Pass to Junction Creek (Seg. 21-28)

Reference

C olorado! Who could ever forget the azure blue sky, the color deepening as the day draws to an end? This is heaven underfoot!
— Gudy Gaskill

FOREWORD ⚠

by GUDY GASKILL

Colorado! The name rolls off the tongue and brings to mind visual images of red rock walls, cascading waterfalls, lofty peaks, alpine meadows bedecked with wildflowers, and a unique outdoor lifestyle. This lifestyle has created a state of vigorous, healthy, and robust men and women, who flock to the mountains to practice their climbing and mountain biking skills in the summer and a multitude of snow sports in the winter. They live sincerely, work longer, and play harder. It is truly a magnificent state.

I have traveled all over the world, climbed and hiked in many different climates and environments, but each time as the plane brings me safely down to terra firma, my mind always comes back to the same question. Why did I ever leave Colorado? Colorado is home, a big friendly state with such a variety of scenery. Who could ever forget the azure blue sky, the color deepening as the day draws to an end, the spectacular cumulus clouds that billow up before the afternoon showers, and the show of golds, oranges, and crimsons in the sky on a late summer evening? Who could forget the tunnel of golden aspen, with a treasure of gold coins covering the fragrant earth on a crisp autumn day? Or the brilliance of ice crystals, shimmering a million colors in the early morning sun? This is heaven underfoot!

The Colorado Trail, a wilderness path designed to traverse some of the most scenic areas of the Rockies and the Continental Divide, is a unique experience for both body and soul. This revised guidebook to the trail describes all the wonders and beauty that you will see along the Colorado Trail. It chronicles the trees, flora, and fauna that you will encounter along the way. It will stir your imagination with the geological observations, creating a desire to know more of the area's ancient history and the powers of nature that formed this landscape. The Colorado Trail has also become a living history lesson, as it relates the tales of its earliest inhabitants, from Indians to turn-of-the-century miners and railroad barons. This guidebook makes the trail an educational reality.

We have received many wonderful letters from trail users from all over the world. The peace, solitude, and beauty have given us all a new look at our place on the earth. The Colorado Trail has changed many lives. Our daughter, Polly, who just recently came off the trail, wrote these words in one of her journal entries: "I walk the spine of rocks around the curve of the mountains. Awareness vibrates — colors, textures of plants radiate from the earth with vibrancy and life. Rock gardens of immense beauty gift my eyes. Tufts of shimmering bird feathers alight on rough bark. Rusted lichen paint the granite, life's green light dances on the ground. The smell of nature's perfume rises from the earth. The sound and touch of changing wind breathe against every hair on my body. Aliveness. Gratitude."

That is the effect the trail has on body and soul. That is the Colorado Trail!

Eldorado Lake, Segment 24.

GUDY GASKILL AND THE COLORADO TRAIL

The Colorado Trail is a continuous, recreational trail that crosses Colorado for 468 miles from Denver to Durango. The trail passes through seven national forests and six wilderness areas, traverses five major river systems and penetrates eight of the state's mountain ranges. What makes the trail even more impressive is that it was created through a massive volunteer effort involving literally thousands of dedicated people.

The CT is administered through an unusual joint venture involving the private non-profit sector, represented by the Colorado Trail Foundation, and the public sector, by the US Forest Service. Because of this special relationship, the trail has been built and maintained largely through donated funds for just a small fraction of the cost that would otherwise have come out of taxpayers' pockets.

Conceived in 1973 by the Forest Service, the trail was to fill a void in a growing segment of outdoor users — individuals and families who wanted a walk in the woods and enjoy the out of doors, but didn't want the extremes of a wilderness experience. In 1974, a meeting of several focus groups was organized to brainstorm and develop a plan. The Colorado Mountain Trails Foundation was formed with 3 main goals: 1) to develop a main trail between Denver and Durango, and provide access trails and loops to points of interest off the main trail; 2) to provide educational opportunities for schools, universities, and organizations in an outdoor, linear classroom setting; and 3) provide for public involvement, awareness, and appreciation of resource management, and to encourage self-development through participation in the voluntary construction, maintenance and management of the trail.

The agreement between the foundation and the Forest Service marked the beginning of a continuing relationship, with both entities agreeing on cooperation in all aspects of building and maintaining the Colorado Trail. The Forest Service mostly cleared the way and provided technical assistance and personnel, and the foundation supplied the gear and organized the volunteers. Unfortunately, many obstacles faced the project, including lack of focus and drive, and cuts in the Forest Service budgets. But then in the early 1980s the Colorado Mountain Club's Trail and Hut Committee decided to make building the CT a priority. The CMC committee was headed up by Gudy Gaskill, who became the trail's champion. This priority by the Trail and Hut Committee became an important turning point for the future of the Colorado Trail.

Once a few CMC volunteer crews had been fielded, Gudy realized that the trail could be built by volunteers for roughly $500 per mile — a realistic cost to be borne by a volunteer-staffed, non-profit organization. The project enjoyed an important boost in 1986 when then Governor Lamm offered his support. Lamm's interest sparked renewed cooperation between the State of Colorado and the Forest Service. That same year Gudy established a new non-profit organization, the Colorado Trail Foundation, to take over the responsibility of building the trail from the overworked and singularly focused CMC Trail and Huts Committee. The progress of the trail's volunteers during the summers of 1986 and 1987 was truly remarkable, completing

Gudy Gaskill

nearly 60 miles of trail on six Forest Service districts. By the end of summer 1987, the Colorado Trail was functionally linked and open for business between Denver and Durango, although much work remained in improving older tread and re-routing many stretches off existing roads. As the Colorado Trail has grown and matured since then, it would seem that the original goals for a premier, scenic trail envisioned by the Forest Service have been fulfilled. The CT today has comfortable tread for the casual day hiker, but also provides plenty of challenges for backpackers intent on completing the entire length.

The Colorado Trail swells with the richness of long-lasting partnerships. Indeed, the real heroes are Gudy and her thousands of volunteers who provided the painstaking manual labor to hack out a trail from the mountainside. Led by the persistent and dedicated Gudy, the volunteers expanded far beyond the small original band of CMCers, now to include people from all corners of the planet. The stories behind these volunteers are many, but the commonality between all seems to be the satisfaction derived from having contributed to a tangible natural resource which will remain a legacy for generations. A legacy which will feed the quest for adventure and precipitate the special dimension of life imparted by the spirit of the outdoors.

(Excerpted from "The Colorado Trail, A Story of Partnerships" by Belinda Wiman, *Colorado Trail Foundation Tread Lines*, Spring 1994.)

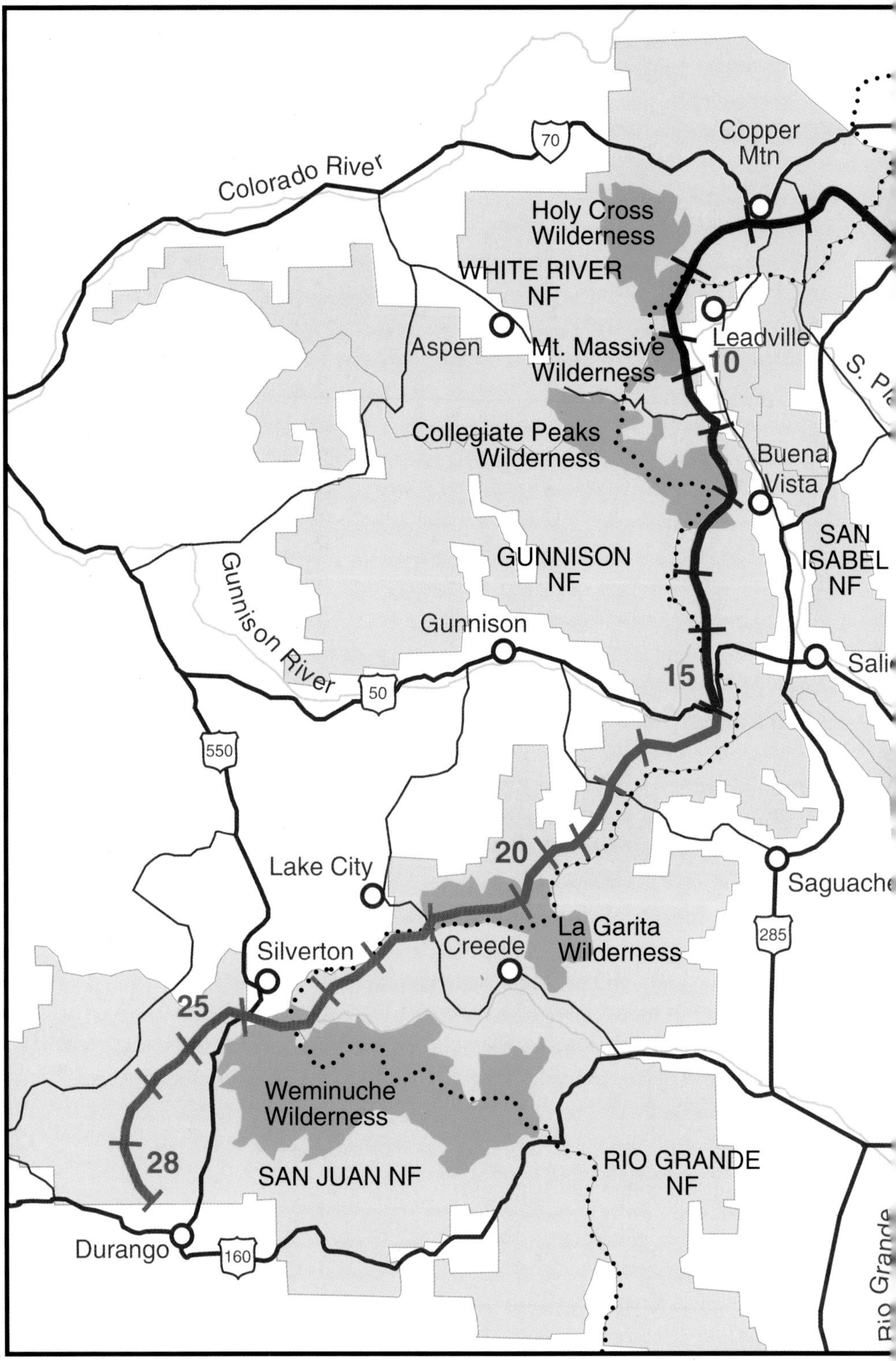

Copper
Mtn

70

Colorado River

Holy Cross
Wilderness

WHITE RIVER
NF

Leadville

Aspen

Mt. Massive
Wilderness

10

Collegiate Peaks
Wilderness

Buena
Vista

SAN
ISABEL
NF

S. Pl

Gunnison River

GUNNISON
NF

Gunnison

Sali

50

15

550

20

Lake City

Saguache

La Garita
Wilderness

285

Silverton

Creede

25

Weminuche
Wilderness

28

SAN JUAN NF

RIO GRANDE
NF

Durango

160

Rio Grande

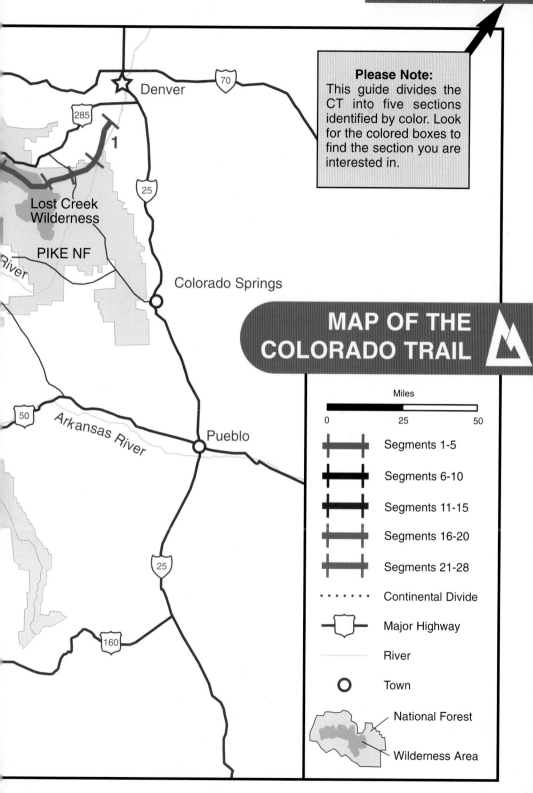

Please Note:
This guide divides the CT into five sections identified by color. Look for the colored boxes to find the section you are interested in.

Denver

Lost Creek Wilderness

PIKE NF

Colorado Springs

Arkansas River

Pueblo

MAP OF THE COLORADO TRAIL

Miles

| 0 | 25 | 50 |

Segments 1-5

Segments 6-10

Segments 11-15

Segments 16-20

Segments 21-28

Continental Divide

Major Highway

River

O   Town

National Forest

Wilderness Area

HOW TO USE THIS GUIDE

The 28 segments that make up the Colorado Trail each represent a chapter in this guide. The average length of a segment is 17 miles, although actual distances vary from 11 to 29 miles. Most individual segments could conceivably be completed by day hikers with light loads, although some might make for a very long day. Backpackers with heavy packs could conceivably take many days to cover some of the longer segments. Those going from end to end might take two months to complete the entire distance, assuming they will hike about 9 miles per day, with one day off per week for side trips or relaxation. A map on page 10-11 shows the entire length of the CT, plus major highways, towns, and wilderness areas along the route.

"Introduction" Page

Each chapter begins with an *introduction* page containing important information summarizing that segment. The start and end points, plus distance and approximate elevation gain, are shown in a box, along with a photograph taken along that segment. The elevation gain is the sum of major ascending portions and is a general indicator of how much extra effort will be required to deal with the ascent.

Be sure to check out *Gudy's Tips*, useful inside information about that segment from the champion of the Colorado Trail, Gudy Gaskill. No one knows the CT better. Use the handy *Trip Log* to jot down reminders or the latest news on closures or re-routes obtained from the Colorado Trail Foundation website or by calling the CTF office.

About This Segment

The next major section provides general information, interesting facts, and local history. Especially important here for long-distance hikers are the indications of where water and camping are available. Mountain bikers will receive a heads-up on whether a detour is required (or recommended) for that segment.

Trailhead/Access Points

Instructions for reaching the trailheads and trail access points are given in this section. All the segments described in this guide begin and end at points accessible by vehicle. Many have additional trail access points within the segment. Generally, *trailhead* refers to an official access point with a parking area, which sometimes can be primitive and skimpy. *Trail access* refers to a point where the trail crosses or approaches a road but where no official parking is provided. One of the priorities in the next few years is to increase and improve the number of trailheads on the Colorado Trail. In the meantime, be careful where you park your car.

A camp along Pole Creek, Segment 23.

Maps and Jurisdiction

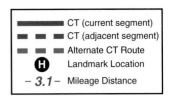

This section is a list of available maps that cover each segment. The first is a *vicinity map*, based on United States Forest Service (USFS) maps, useful for general orientation purposes. These maps are reproduced in this guide, with page numbers leading you to them. Each map shows the CT segment in red, with adjacent segments dashed. Alternative trails to the main line of the CT are shown in blue and dashed as well. Key *landmark locations* are also shown here, with distances between them indicated.

In the bottom right corner of each *vicinity map* page, a *trail profile* shows the ups and downs encountered along that segment, including a graphic display of the steepness of individual portions and the position of the *landmark locations*. A chart in the bottom left corner summarizes these *landmark locations*. The altitude and distance of these locations from both the start of the segment and the Denver start of the CT are indicated, along with GPS coordinates designating the Latitude and Longitude. If you are entering these coordiantes by hand into your GPS unit, set the unit to coordinate format (D.ddd) and NAD27 CONUS datum.

For more precise orienteering purposes, The Colorado Trail Foundation (CTF) offers their *Official Colorado Trail GIS Reference Map Series* on CD ROM, including viewing software showing the CT positioned precisely on topographic maps, plus GPS generated data.

United States Geological Survey (USGS) topographic maps are listed next in the *Maps and Jurisdiction* section. These are the most detailed maps available, at a scale of 1:24,000. However, nearly 50 maps are required to cover the entire CT. Finally, *Trails Illustrated* brand maps are also available that encompass nearly all of the CT. These maps are of a smaller scale than the USGS topos but are "field-ready," being water proof and tear-resistant.

The appropriate USFS Ranger Districts are listed under *Jurisdiction*. Contact addresses for these are provided on page 263.

Supplies, Services and Accommodations

A short paragraph describes supply points and services nearby to the CT. For major supply points, a town or city map is included that pinpoints services such as grocery stores, showers, post offices, and laundries. It should be noted that for some remote segments of the CT, no convenient points of supply are available.

Trail Description

The trail descriptions are laid out progressing from Denver to Durango. The descriptions indicate the distance of recognizable landmarks (indicated in bold) from the beginning of the trail segment. Accompanying the mileage count, in parentheses, is the altitude of that landmark. These mileages were obtained using a "rolotape" device in the field, are much more accurate than mileages generated by measuring distances on maps and are reasonably close to mileages generated by sophisticated GPS measurements.

Mountain Bicycle Detour

Cyclists are not allowed to travel the CT where it traverses a designated wilderness area and should likewise avoid other segments where terrain dictates it. This section describes mandatory and recommended detours. A map is provided to show the general orientation for these.

Global Positioning System

Besides the GPS coordinates listed for selected *landmark locations* on the *vicinity maps*, you'll find over 800 more GPS positions on page 268 of this guide. This data was generated through a unique project begun in 1999 with the CTF and Jerry Brown of Bear Creek Survey Service of Durango, CO. Using a Trimble Pathfinder Pro XRS professional grade GPS unit, Brown was able to collect positions at about every six feet along the trail, producing a precise map of the CT well beyond anything achieved on previous mapping efforts. The section beginning on page 268 lists positions roughly every mile along the trail, plus positions for readily recognizable trail features like trail and road junctions, stream crossings and the like.

And There's More

Additional *information* boxes provide interesting facts or useful information for specific segments, in order to help you get the most out of your CT experience.

Indicates **helpful tips** for CT hikers, plus highlights other hikes or climbs in this segment.

Indicates a **viewing opportunity** in this segment, such as interesting places or wildlife.

Indicates information for **mountain bikers**, including required or optional detours in this segment.

Indicates the normal condition of **access roads**. The vehicle pointing right (east) is the access at the start. The vehicle pointing left (west) is the access at the end of this segment.

  Paved or graded dirt access road

  Rough, dirt access road

  4-wheel drive access road

Indicates the likely availability of **water** for this segment during late summer.

  Plentiful water sources

  Scattered water sources

  Water is difficult to obtain

Indicates the suitability of using a **mountain bike** for this segment.

  Suitable for mountain bikes

  Recommended detour

  Mandatory detour

HIKING
THE COLORADO TRAIL

The Colorado Trail assumes varying characteristics as it meanders through eight mountain ranges with dissimilar topographic and geologic features. For its entire 468 miles, the trail imposes diverse demands on its users, and their ability to adjust to those changing demands determines how much they will enjoy their trek. There is always something along the way to challenge some and intimidate others.

As with other trails in the state, the Colorado Trail is not developed to the point that it can be followed blindly. Nor should it be, especially in the many wilderness areas through which it passes. This guide assumes that all users of the Colorado Trail are familiar with basic backcountry techniques, precautions and orienteering skills. For those who are not, organizations such as the Colorado Mountain Club hold regular sessions to acquaint neophytes with these virtues before they venture out on the trail.

Planning a Hike on the CT

Probably only a very few of the total number of those hiking the Colorado Trail will do so straight through, from one end to the other. A more realistic and certainly less taxing plan would be to travel segment by segment, in either day hike or backpack fashion, and take advantage of the various side trips and explorations available along the main trail corridor.

When planning a hike, keep in mind that portions of the trail below 9500 feet generally are accessible from May to October, depending on weather extremes and the orientation of the trail. Above 9500 feet, the hiking season can be dramatically shorter, again depending on the trail location and the amount of snowfall.

One of the main considerations in planning a hike for early summer is lingering snow. If you intend to sample different segments of the trail as you feel inspired, then you can visit a given area whenever conditions are best. Long-distance trekkers, however, cannot be choosy about avoiding a snowed-in section if it happens to lie in their path. Many high crests and ridges are likely to be laden with snow until early July, especially on their north sides. Crossing any snowfield is risky and should be done only with adequate mountaineering experience.

Those planning a terminus-to-terminus trek should consider that, if they start at the eastern end, it is approximately 70 miles before they top out at timberline on Georgia Pass. If they begin at the western end, however, timberline comes in approximately 20 miles at Kennebec Pass. Thus, a trek starting at Denver and progressing to Durango could begin earlier. In any event, setting out from Denver before the third week of June, or from Durango before the first week of July, would generally be impractical because of the hazards of lingering snowfields.

Backpacking through an aspen grove below Mount Shavano, Segment 14.

The logistics of returning to your starting point for longer distance trekkers can be troublesome and should not be overlooked until the last minute. Several towns along the way are served by regular bus routes, although this service has been drastically reduced in recent years, and is subject to change from season to season. Denver and Durango have been connected by regular airline service in the past, again subject to changing schedules. Check airline and bus availability, and obtain passage, well in advance of your trek, and do not assume that schedules as quoted will remain from season to season (or even in the same season). Those taking airline passage into Denver may want to investigate express van service from Denver International to the various resorts in Summit County (Breckenridge, Frisco, Copper Mountain) and catch the CT there. In the past, the metro Denver intra-urban bus service, the Regional Transportation District, has provided limited weekday service to near Waterton Canyon and the eastern terminus of the CT (currently listed as the 75X Martin/Waterton Express). You can also hop in a cab to get to the beginning of the CT in Waterton Canyon, but this service is much more expensive than hitching a ride on the RTD. Those wishing to take advantage of railroad passenger service may do so by planning a hike around the Durango and Silverton RR narrow gauge line, which runs daily during the summer between the two towns. For information on fares and schedules, write the Durango and Silverton Railroad, 479 Main Avenue, Durango, CO 81301.

Day hikers have less complicated options from which to choose. They can either walk as far as they wish and then retrace their steps to their starting point, arrange a car shuttle between trail access points, or split the group and swap car keys with the other party hiking in the opposite direction. Another option is to take advantage of many side trails which connect to the Colorado Trail and then loop back to the starting point.

Whether you are day hiking or backpacking, the increased isolation from civilization south of US-50 can be intimidating. Therefore, it would be worthwhile to prepare one's psyche for this portion, and have a compatible companion along with whom all outstanding differences have been resolved. This part of the Colorado Trail is less visited than other portions of the route, and in places is more of a challenge to follow. In addition, the high route through the San Juans, which parallels the crest of the Continental Divide, may very likely be blanketed with snowfields until mid-July. This compounds the area's isolation from civilization and heightens the need for hikers to keep a steady head and possess good mountaineering and orienteering skills.

Contrary to some overblown stories, wild animals are not likely to molest you during your trip. A clean camp is your best insurance against marauding animals. Wild animals are generally not crazed and are after food, not you. The most important factor is to keep food secured and out of your tent. Mosquitoes are the wilderness occupants you are most likely to encounter, and they too are looking for a meal, so bring repellent. An occasional flock of domestic sheep is likely to be encountered, especially in the San Juans. If you find yourself part of the flock, the shepherd's advice is to leash your pets to prevent a chaotic stampede, and to avoid eye contact with the animals lest they interpret your stares as a prelude to attack, thus also precipitating a stampede.

Based on their own experiences and preferences, different travelers will come up with slightly varying lists of supplies to have along on a backpacking trip. The essentials aside, some comments are included here to help plan a trek on the Colorado Trail.

If you are planning an extended trek, it would be impractical to carry all your food from the beginning. Unfortunately, with the exception of Copper Mountain resort (which has only very limited services), groceries and sporting good stores are located in towns which lie well off the trail. However, there are small general stores at resorts and private campgrounds nearer the trail that might serve you in a more limited way.

It is possible to pack your nonperishable meals into boxes before leaving and then mail them to yourself in care of "General Delivery" to post offices in towns where you plan to stop. Your local post office can give you tips on how to do this. Another alternative is to rely on friends or relatives to meet you with fresh supplies at access points along the trail.

Clothing, the traveler's first line of defense against the elements, deserves careful consideration. The Colorado Trail experiences extremes of mountain weather conditions, with the warmth of the less lofty elevations in the Rampart Range and lower Arkansas Valley contrasting sharply with the exposed alpine ridges of the San Juan Mountains. An appropriate combination of cotton and wool garments, including hat and gloves, plus rain gear, is essential, even though any number of these layers of clothing will probably be taking up space in your pack most of the time. It is conceivable that some garments, especially socks, will wear out in 468 miles. Special measures should be taken to replace certain items you feel might succumb to that fate. Do not overlook protection for your skin and eyes, which would include strong sun lotion, ultraviolet screening sunglasses, and a hat with brim. Consult the suggested equipment checklists provided on page 262.

Your boots and feet will take a beating on the trail. And even though there are some sections that might lend themselves well to the use of lightweight boots or athletic shoes, only heavier footgear will see you through the high altitude march along the Continental Divide, where snowfields and talus will be encountered. If your boots are well broken in, but not nearing the end of their life, they will likely see you through the entire trek.

Drinking water is generally readily available along the Colorado Trail, although there are a few sections where adequate supplies are as far as 20 miles apart. These require some planning and foresight if you do not want to be caught at a dry camp. Unfortunately, cattle grazing is common along most of the trail, and all water, with the exception of tested potable supplies at campgrounds, should be treated or filtered to screen out protozoa that might otherwise bring your trek to an untimely halt.

Some sections of the Colorado Trail may be obscure or inadequately marked; therefore, maps and compass, as well as a knowledge of their use, should be part of every hiker's provisions. The maps in this guide are intended to schematically describe the area of each trail segment, and should be supplemented by either detailed USGS topographical maps or the Colorado Trail Foundation's *GIS Reference Map Series* on CD ROM, available from the CTF office. Forest Service maps provide additional information, such as towns, campground locations, highways and backcountry roads.

In addition to the above mentioned essentials, it is prudent to take a first-aid kit along. Even better is to have as many members of the group as possible schooled in first-aid techniques. They can be lifesavers in emergencies.

Safety on Your Trek

An experienced mountaineer will be prepared and take no unnecessary chances. Along the more isolated portions of the Colorado Trail, assistance will be many hours, even days, away. Travelers should keep the following points in mind:

Beware of the conditions. The varied terrain of the Colorado Trail puts you at risk for both hypothermia and dehydration. Plan for the possibility of each, as well as the lightning hazard of exposed ridges.

Start hiking early. You will encounter storms of varying intensity, whether they are mid-summer thunderstorms or late summer snow showers. Generally, mornings are more likely to be clear, and leaving early gives you a better chance to get to your destination and set up camp in comfort.

Travel with a companion. Backpacking or hiking alone is not recommended, even for the experienced. If you do so, make sure your itinerary is known by others and check in as often as possible.

Be in shape. Your best insurance against accidents is to be in top physical condition. Acclimatize yourself before beginning your trek, and guard against fatigue. Pushing yourself too hard in rugged terrain can be an invitation to disaster.

To activate a rescue group, contact the nearest county sheriff. See page 263 for a list of contact phone numbers for each segment. In more and more situations, counties and other jurisdictions are passing along the considerable costs incurred while conducting search and rescue to the persons involved. To protect yourself and to keep search and rescue efforts at a high standard in the future, the Colorado Trail Foundation recommends that you purchase a *Colorado Outdoor Recreation Search and Rescue* (CORSAR) card. This card establishes a fund to reimburse local sheriffs for costs incurred in search and rescue and protects the bearer against being held liable for such costs. Note that it does not reimburse individuals for medical costs. The CORSAR card costs $3 for one year and a five-year card costs $12. You can purchase the card from the CTF office. Note that if you already have a valid Colorado fishing, hunting or snowmobile, ATV, or boat registration you are already covered in this program by a surcharge on those licenses.

Trail Markings

This guide generally does not refer to trail markers and signage because they are often vandalized or stolen. Over the years, Colorado Trail markers have varied considerably. Their one common, eye-catching characteristic has been the incorporation of the trail's unique logo. Trail markers can be either triangular or diamond shaped, and may be fashioned from wood, metal or plastic. Reflective metal markers were once used extensively on the trail, but have been discontinued because of their expense and appeal to souvenir hunters. Aesthetic redwood markers have survived on isolated sections in the Saguache and Gunnison districts. Less expensive, triangular plastic markers have been used most recently.

In more remote stretches and wilderness areas, the Colorado Trail is marked by wooden posts, rock cairns and blazes on tree trunks. Some older blazes are almost completely healed over and difficult to see. Some Forest Service districts use unimpressive but practical carsonite posts to identify the route. These are long, slender slats, dark brown in color and made of a material resembling

CT Logo

fiberglass. They tend to nod conspicuously back and forth in anything but the lightest breeze. You might also encounter routes marked with blue diamonds. These identify cross-country ski routes and are not necessarily intended to mark the Colorado Trail. South of US-50, where the Colorado Trail follows along or near the crest of the Continental Divide, it coincides for long distances with the Continental Divide Trail. In these sections, you may see an occasional CDT trail marker.

Unfortunately, trail signage and markers are still being vandalized or, more likely, disappearing completely, making for obvious difficulty at critical junctions and for confirming your route. However, in regard to this activity, we are at a loss to modify the behavior of others. In addition, be aware that some CT hikers have reported difficulty in orienteering during inclement or foggy weather, which often leads to disorientations particularly where the trail tread is spotty or indistinct and trail markings sporadic.

Miscellaneous Notes

The abbreviation "FS" refers to Forest Service roads. FS-543, for example, means Forest Service Road 543. These roads can generally be traveled by conventional automobiles. If not, a "4WD" designation identifies the road as suitable for four-wheel-drive vehicles only. Keep in mind that some backcountry roads suitable for conventional automobiles can be rendered impassable during inclement weather, even to 4WD vehicles. Also, Forest Service roads, as well as county roads, often undergo changes in their numerical designation. Therefore, road numbers as given here may be incorrect from season to season as they are changed in their respective jurisdictions. Please be aware that the trail descriptions give road numbers for informational purposes only. Roads are usually not posted with their numbers in locations convenient for hikers, and these postings, like trail markers, are often missing or vandalized. Finally, be aware that from season to season existing roads can be closed off to vehicular traffic, or new roads (particularly new log roads) can appear from season to season, radically changing the trail description as presently written.

The Colorado Trail is generally a footpath, but in places it follows roads of varying quality. The trail descriptions refer to several types of roads. A "jeep track" is the lowest quality of road, and typically appears as a parallel double track or trail separated by a hump of grass. Jeep tracks usually run through meadows or tundra and can be either closed to vehicular traffic or still actively used. A "jeep road" or "log road" can likewise be closed or opened to vehicles. These may be rough, narrow and sometimes steep. The guide also refers to "old roads" which are usually long-abandoned supply routes that now more closely resemble rough, widened trails.

"Route" is a term sometimes used to describe the Colorado Trail in general. However, for stretches where the trail is so obscure that no tread is visible, "route" is used to indicate the lack of an obvious trail. A "posted route" or "cairned route" has been marked with either wooden posts or rock cairns, respectively.

Notes to the Sixth Edition

The Colorado Trail has seen a steady increase in use since it was officially dedicated in September 1987. This demand has consumed many previous editions of the guide and has kept CTF volunteers busy over the years trying to document changes in the CT due to continuing trail re-routes and improvements, as well as natural and human forces. It is surprising how quickly the extreme environment of the Rockies can alter a trail's appearance. Overgrowing vegetation, downed trees and avalanches can render the trail difficult to follow regardless of how well it was built and marked originally. Even the cumulative effects of hundreds of human and equine feet (and bicycles) on the trail have had a significant impact. Portions of the Colorado Trail have been altered by these continuing forces, not to mention ongoing trail construction and maintenance, with the possible consequence of rendering sections of this guide obsolete from season to season.

The unexpected level of trail use has produced some surprises. For one, the flurry of feet on the trail (not to mention hard-working trail maintenance volunteers) is, in many places, producing a more established route. The down side is that introspective backpackers may be chagrined at the increased traffic. A best effort has been made to keep the trail descriptions accurate in this guide. When we are made aware of trail changes as they are described in this edition, that information will be posted on the Colorado Trail Foundation website: www.coloradotrail.org. Or contact the CTF at 710 10th Street #210, Golden, CO 80401. Phone 303-384-3729 #113.

Cycling the Colorado Trail

Mountain bicycles, sometimes called fat tire bikes, are becoming more popular year by year and will be encountered increasingly on the Colorado Trail. They are not, however, allowed in wilderness areas. This guide explains adequate detours for mountain bicycles around the six wilderness areas through which the official route passes. In addition to these mandatory exclusions, there are areas along the trail route that cyclists might want to avoid. These stretches would most likely include the parts of the CT traversing above timberline where the terrain is particularly rough and steep, and where sensitive alpine vegetation is unusually sensitive to damage. If planning a mountain bicycle trip on the CT, it might be a good idea to contact the appropriate Forest Service district(s) to check if any further restrictions have been imposed.

Long-distance mountain bicyclists should not be disappointed by the fact that they are occasionally compelled to make detours, for the alternate routes hold as much fascination and interest as the main trail route. The detours described here use primarily 4WD roads, Forest Service roads and county roads. However, it is sometimes necessary to use busy highways where special safety precautions are advised and where extra care should be taken to make yourself visible to motorists. Safety gear is a must whether you are negotiating the trail or maneuvering through curving mountain roads with blind corners. Cattle guards, an obvious danger to bicycles, will be encountered often on Forest Service and county roads. Be aware that, in most cases, private property is immediately adjacent to county roads and highways, but is rarely marked as such.

Many sections of the CT are experiencing heavy mountain bicycle traffic, such as in the Buffalo Creek Recreation Area (Segment 3). All mountain bicyclists should follow a simple ethical code to prevent conflicts with other trail users' pre-existing rights and to preserve the physical integrity of the trail itself. Please remember to: 1, ride safely and equip yourself properly with safety gear; 2, courteously yield the trail to other users; 3, be particularly cautious around pack animals which might be terrified of your appearance and method of conveyance; and 4, ride responsibly with the knowledge that cutting switchbacks, and skidding around corners and water bars can destroy a well-designed and laboriously built trail.

The routes identified are not the only possibilities for detouring certain sections of the CT in all cases. Bicyclists might rather prefer to identify their own route using a Colorado state highway map and the appropriate Forest Service maps. These maps are also helpful with general navigation, identifying campgrounds, etc. However, if you design your bicycle itinerary on the CT, please remember that all Forest Service wilderness areas MUST be detoured.

A summary of the bicycle detours listed here are:

✔   A mandatory detour around Lost Creek Wilderness, using a series of Forest Service roads over Stoney Pass via Wellington Lake and then up the Tarryall River.

✔   A highly recommended, optional detour of the alpine route over the Tenmile Range, using the Tenmile Bike Path.

✔   A mandatory bypass around Holy Cross and Mount Massive Wilderness areas using Forest Service roads and a section of US-24.

✔   A mandatory detour around Collegiate Peaks Wilderness using county roads and a section of US-24.

✔   An optional detour around Raspberry Gulch using county roads.

✔   A mandatory detour around the La Garita Wilderness using a section of Colorado Hwy-149 and Forest Service road over Los Piños Pass.

✔   A highly recommended detour around Coney Summit using section of Colorado Hwy-149, county roads and Forest Service roads.

✔   A mandatory bypass around the Weminuche Wilderness using US-550 and Forest Service roads.

✔   An optional detour around the Junction Creek gorge using a Forest Service road.

Cities and Post Offices

The Colorado Trail passes close to several towns and villages. A short synopsis of services that may be expected in those cities (population data: *1998 State Demographer*) and the approximate distance to these cities from various trail locations given as part of the description of each trail segment. Airline and bus service schedules are not included because they tend to change from season to season. Additional information can usually be obtained by contacting the Chamber of Commerce for the various communities. Some of these communities are very small and services may be limited or may change from season to season as described here. If you intend to send a package to yourself in care of General Delivery, it would be wise to contact that post office in advance to determine business hours and availability of that service.

Regulations and Backcountry Ethics

The Colorado Trail lies almost entirely on National Forest lands. In some areas, the trail route uses rights-of-way and easements across or adjacent to private property and patented mining claims. Negotiations for certain easements are still under way. Keep in mind that rights-of-way can be withdrawn by owners if problems associated with their use arise. Please respect any private property and no trespassing postings. Remember also that federal law protects cultural and historic sites on public lands, such as old cabins, mines and Indian sites. These historic, cultural assets are important to us all as a society, and are not meant to be scavenged for personal gain or enjoyment.

Forest Service occupancy regulations are primarily designed to limit wear and tear in fragile wilderness areas. However, some heavily used, non-wilderness areas, such as the Buffalo and Jefferson Creek Recreation Areas, also have certain restrictions. Within wilderness areas, groups must be limited in size, camps and tethered pack animals are not permitted within a certain distance of lakes and streams, and pets must be kept on a leash. Check with the Forest Service in advance of your outing to determine the specific restrictions of the area you will be visiting.

Wilderness Area Regulations

Colorado has 36 designated wilderness areas, encompassing over 3 million acres. The Wilderness Act of 1964 prohibits logging, mining, permanent structures, commercial enterprises, and motorized and mechanical transport (including bicycles) in these protected areas. The CT passes through six wilderness areas, including **Lost Creek, Holy Cross, Mt. Massive, Collegiate Peaks, La Garita, and Weminuche**.

Trekkers can minimize impact on these pristine and spectacular places by adhering to the *Leave No Trace* principles outlined on page 266, and by following these general rules governing wilderness areas: 1. Camp at least 100 feet from lakes and streams. 2. Use a stove rather than building a fire. 3. Bury human waste six inches deep and 200 feet from water sources. Pack out toilet paper. 5. All dogs must be leashed (or are prohibited in some areas). 6. Pack out your trash. 7. Mountain biking is prohibited.

Each wilderness area will also have specific rules that apply to that area. Check with the appropriate Forest Service office (see page 263) for additional regulations that may apply.

Mt. Massive Wilderness, CT Segments 10 & 11.

Beyond such imposed regulations, all users of the backcountry have a responsibility to maintain the pristine conditions of our national forests as they find them. Refrain from cutting switchbacks and other practices which lead to trail erosion. Use existing campsites where possible, and resist the temptation to develop new ones by rearranging rocks for fire rings or digging drainage channels. Use a backpacker's gas stove for your cooking, and limit the use of social campfires. Before starting your trek, check with the Forest Service for the current forest fire danger, which can sometimes be extreme, and any restrictions on campfires. Walking and talking softly is in tune with the backcountry code and increases your overall awareness of the wilderness. A list of contact addresses for Forest Service offices is provided on page 263.

COLORADO TRAIL HERITAGE

The heritage of the Colorado Trail in many ways is a reflection of the unique history of the mountain West. The entire length of the trail was created, at least in part, by linking newly built tread to numerous existing, and sometimes historically significant, roads and trails. Because of this, we can consider the trail's tradition as going back far beyond the mid-1970s when Gudy Gaskill and her first trail crews were heading to the hills. The route of the trail today has been influenced by these long forgotten Indian trails, ghost towns, and abandoned mine roads and narrow gauge railroad grades. In addition, more contemporary obstacles such as logging areas, water projects, and ski resorts have had consequences to the trail's route.

The result has been a route that not only emphasizes the incredible natural beauty of the state but also highlights the imposing impact over time that we have made upon the land. Such a legacy might be the Colorado Trail's most valuable if it influences coming generations to look upon our social and cultural values from the perspective of past, present and future, and in recognition of our successes and failures. In this respect, the trail has a subtle message to transmit, one that not all will be receptive to. Each trail segment covers this legacy in detail, which observes the following themes:

The Indians

Some sections of the Colorado Trail we cover today were first used by Indians, who traveled the fertile mountain parks of Colorado for generations to hunt and to fight amongst themselves for those hunting grounds. In the process, they created many trails, some of which we still pass over, totally unaware of their long departed spirits.

The Utes, the mountain people, are probably the best known of the Indian tribes in Colorado because of the skirmishes between them and white settlers. These battles eventually saw the Utes exiled to a small corner of the southwest part of the state. Prior to an 1863 treaty made with the Utah Tabeguache Band, the Utes had laid claim for centuries to most of the mountainous areas of the state. The 1863 treaty, however, limited them to a reservation whose boundaries followed the Continental Divide on the east and south, the Colorado and Roaring Fork Rivers on the north, and the Uncompahgre River on the west. Soon, the Utes would be restricted even further as pressure from an ever increasing flood of migrating Easterners and mining entrepreneurs persuaded the government to move them farther west in 1868 to a reservation in western Colorado bounded by the 107th meridian. Two agencies were set up to distribute goods and food to the Indians. One was to the north on the White

Old mining shack above the treeline and along Elk Creek, Segment 24.

River and one was to the east on Los Piños Creek at the foot of the Utes' ancestral Continental Divide passage over Cochetopa Pass.

The promise of profitable mining in the San Juan Mountains resulted in a council at the Los Piños agency in 1872, at which the government attempted to persuade the Utes to turn over even more of their reservation. The following year Felix Brunot, with the help of Otto Mears, persuaded the Utes to turn over nearly four million acres in what was to become the rich San Juan mining district around present-day Silverton. This infamous agreement came to be known as the Brunot Treaty. In the end, the White River Utes and the Uncompahgre Utes were driven out of Colorado to a reservation in Utah. The southern Ute bands were removed to two small reservations in southern Colorado bordering New Mexico.

Chief Ouray, who had attempted to save his Indian nation by cooperating with the government, witnessed the tragic decline of the Ute people whose important contributions and culture are nearly invisible today. However, several towering mountain peaks in the southern Sawatch Range and an important pass in the Cochetopa Hills have immortalized the memory of these banished mountain people.

Early Explorers and Expeditions

The Spanish for centuries had been well entrenched in the regions south of present-day Colorado, but they had little if any knowledge of the region to be traversed by the Colorado Trail until Fathers Escalante and Dominguez, during their expedition of 1776, viewed the western San Juan country. The friars' ramblings took them on a roundabout tour of western Colorado and eastern Utah, and they described the La Plata and San Miguel Mountains northwest of Durango as well as many future tourist destinations. Escalante and Dominguez never made it to California, as they had hoped, but their adventure helped New Mexico Governor Juan Bautista de Anza when he visited the eastern San Juan Mountains, the Cochetopa Hills and the San Luis Valley three years later.

De Anza led an army north from Santa Fe in pursuit of a Comanche band that was terrorizing Spanish colonists, and thereby became the first European to enter the central portion of the Southern Rockies. Along the way de Anza noticed that the Rio Grande had its beginnings on the eastern flank of the San Juans, not far to the north as previously had been assumed. He was also the first white man to lay eyes on the ancient Continental Divide crossing known to the Utes as "Buffalo Gate," or Cochetopa. He correctly deduced that further west, beyond the ridges seen from the San Luis Valley, flowed the headwaters of the western San Juan rivers described by Father Escalante. De Anza continued north to Poncha Pass, descended into the Arkansas Valley near today's Salida, and viewed the skyscraping Sawatch Range.

In the adventurous half century between 1813 and 1863, expeditions in the American West were sponsored by the War Department's newly formed Corps of Topographical Engineers. Major Steven Long's 1820 expedition, which skirted the east slope of the Rampart Range, was organized under the auspices of the Corps. Long's group was timid about penetrating the Rockies, but they did struggle a few miles up Platte Canyon, which was destined to become the eastern trailhead of the Colorado Trail. The group then headed south, where the party's botanist, Edwin James, discovered the blue columbine, Colorado's state flower.

Later expeditions, led by Captain John Charles Fremont, probed the La Garita Mountains, South Park and the upper Arkansas River Valley. Fremont, the son-in-law of influential Senator Thomas Hart Benton, conducted several expeditions into the Rockies for the Corps. He is probably best known in Colorado for the disaster which struck his expedition during the winter of 1848-49 in the rugged La Garita Mountains.

In 1852, Congress authorized the Corps to conduct preliminary transcontinental railroad surveys through the Rockies. Captain John W. Gunnison explored what seemed to be the only logical route in Colorado, that is, over Sangre de Cristo Pass, across the San Luis Valley and over Cochetopa Pass. Unfortunately, the river drainage west of Cochetopa Pass cut down into the impregnable gorge of the Black Canyon. Even more unfortunately, Gunnison and seven others in the party were killed later that summer in Utah, by a band of Piutes out to avenge the murder of their chief's father by a group of uprooted settlers. The transcontinental railroad was eventually built through Wyoming. As a further reminder of the tragic end of the Gunnison expedition, Cochetopa Pass has remained a rather minor Continental Divide passage, and today is a serene landmark on the Colorado Trail.

The Great Surveys

After the Civil War, the most significant of the Colorado Surveys were led by Ferdinand Hayden and Lieutenant George Wheeler. By 1869, Hayden had lobbied Congress sufficiently to fund his civilian United States Geological Surveys of the Territories. During the three summers between 1873 and 1875, the Hayden Survey covered most of Colorado's high country, climbing and naming many of its summits which were used as triangulation points. Hayden skillfully staffed his teams with competent topographers, geologists and experts in fields ranging from anthropology to paleontology. After a decade of exploring and preparing invaluable maps and reports, the Hayden Survey came to an end in 1879 with the creation of the United States Geological Survey.

The Wheeler Survey, unlike Hayden's civilian expedition, was sponsored by the War Department and concentrated mainly on topographic features. Its premature demise in 1878, before the completion of its work, was at least in part the result of intense competition among the surveys. As a result, Wheeler never gained the prominence that Hayden did. Both of these great surveys, however, provided maps and valuable information which guided railroad builders and prospectors and led to further taming of the mountains. Many of the mountains we view today from the CT were named by these survey teams.

Early Entrepreneurs

The Colorado Trail meanders through a wide band of territory, known popularly as the Mineral Belt, which begins west of Boulder and trends southwesterly to Silverton. The riches of this region supported some of Colorado's most rip-roaring boom towns of old. These towns were eventually connected by a web of stage roads, trails and railroads, some of which remain as parts of the Colorado Trail today.

Exploring our mining heritage in the San Juans.

An early route for prospectors was pointed out by Fremont in 1844. Prior to the Civil War, a group of southerners used the route which became known as Georgia Pass. These miners panned their way to prosperity near the headwaters of the Swan River, today a Continental Divide crossing on the CT.

At the same time the Fiftyniners were digging their first placers in the Swan River, prospectors were filtering into California Gulch near the headwaters of the Arkansas River. A rich placer boom in the 1860s was responsible for the brief appearances of the towns of Oro, Granite and Dayton. But the real boom had to wait until 1878 when miners uncovered silver deposits concealed in lead carbonate, which gave the rejuvenated camp its new name of Leadville. For a short time, the satellite communities of Kokomo and Robinson in the Tenmile Mining District competed with Leadville for prominence in the area. This historic district is now submerged deep below an immense tailing pond visible from Elk Ridge near Kokomo Pass on the CT.

Lieutenant Charles Baker, who tired of the Yankee company in California Gulch, followed the Continental Divide south into the San Juans. His party panned unsuccessfully for gold around Bakers Park, even though it meant trespassing on the Ute reservation. Being a true confederate, Baker took a brief leave from prospecting to fight in the Civil War. He then returned to southwestern Colorado, where he was killed by Indians. The area was still technically closed to Anglos, but other encroaching prospectors uncovered rich mineral deposits there. When the Brunot Treaty removed the Utes in 1873, Bakers Park boomed with the production of silver and received its new name of Silverton. Eventually, a railroad was built into town, and it remains as a historic crossing on the CT today.

Toll Roads and Railroads

Clever little Otto Mears built roads out of the San Luis Valley along routes that had been pioneered by the Utes and earlier explorers. Mears' objective, in which he was quite successful, was to maintain toll booths and freighting companies to supply the boom towns with goods he produced in the valley. His first enterprise was to build a road north over Poncha Pass to the placers on the upper Arkansas River. Mears next teamed up with Enos Hotchkiss to build the Saguache-San Juan toll road via Cochetopa Pass and Los Piños agency in 1874. Originally intended to go up the Lake Fork, over Cinnamon Pass, and then down into Silverton, that stretch of road was delayed when Hotchkiss discovered the Golden Fleece mine while building a road near Lake City.

Mears did more than build toll roads. As the San Juan produced more minerals, he developed an interconnecting network of narrow gauge railroads to serve them. The most prominent was the Rio Grande Southern, whose 168 twisting miles of track between Durango and Ridgway passed some of the Rocky Mountain's most stunning scenery.

Perhaps most persistent of the mountain railroads was the Denver and Rio Grande. In 1870, General William Jackson Palmer incorporated the D&RG and planned to build his railroad from Denver to Mexico City. But plans changed and Palmer's railroad, using narrow gauge track and equipment that could climb steeper grades and turn tighter corners, became Colorado's premier railroad. The small cars and locomotives were soon puffing over passes and into mining communities to the cheers of the citizenry. Today the CT visits the old grade of the D&RG at Tennessee Pass, Marshall Pass, and in the Animas River canyon.

Spurring the D&RG on were competing mountain railroads such as Governor John Evans' Denver, South Park and Pacific and the Colorado Midland. The DSP&P was constructed in the 1870s from Denver up Platte Canyon to Kenosha Pass. From there, one branch continued across South Park to Leadville and Gunnison via the legendary Alpine Tunnel. The other branch ascended the Continental Divide at Boreas Pass to serve Breckenridge and the Tenmile Mining District. You will use the route of the DSP&P at the trail's eastern terminus in Waterton Canyon, and you will cross its route at Chalk Creek and Kenosha Pass.

The more ambitious standard gauge Colorado Midland was built by a feisty easterner named John J. Hagerman, who came to Colorado to die of tuberculosis, but instead lived to build a railroad. The Midland was a well respected, although short lived, railroad that linked the silver mines at Aspen to the eastern slope via Leadville and the breathtaking 11,528-foot Hagerman Tunnel on the craggy north shoulder of Mount Massive.

The prosperity of the late 1800s in Colorado was based largely on the mining of silver, and by 1893 the value of silver production exceeded that of gold by nearly four to one. Thus the silver camps of the San Juans, Leadville and the Tenmile District were in a precarious state when the Sherman Silver Purchase Act was repealed that same year and the nation moved toward a monetary system based on the gold standard. The battle over the monetary standard caused wrenching agony and displacements nationwide, and was at least partly to blame for the Panic of 1893. Silver-mining districts across Colorado went into a collapse from which they never fully recovered. Fortunately, for the overall economy of the state, some of the mining districts also had rich veins of gold that sustained them, but life would never be quite the same with the passing of Colorado's silver era.

Modern Development

A perplexing ore penetrating the slopes of 13,555-foot Bartlett Mountain at the head of Tenmile Creek on the Continental Divide baffled early day prospectors until specialists at the Colorado School of Mines identified the mineral as molybdenum. The claim, named Climax because of the loftiness of its location, was not developed until 1911, when its value as an alloy of steel was realized. The mine has been a mainstay of the upper Arkansas Valley economy ever since. Unfortunately, the prosperity of the mine has resulted in the incremental shaving away of the mountain whose digested remains now clog the headwaters of Tenmile Creek. These ignominious tailing ponds are visible from Elk Pass on the CT.

Other Colorado valleys have likewise disappeared, not buried under mine tailings but drowned under thousands of acre-feet of water. Denver began damming waterways as early as 1890, building the Castlewood Dam on Cherry Creek in that year and Cheeseman Dam on the South Platte River in 1905. In addition, east slope water districts cast longing eyes west of the Continental Divide. They laid ambitious plans to siphon off significant flows from the Colorado River watershed and transport the runoff to thirsty cities using an intricate system of diversion points, tunnels and reservoirs.

The most prominent water project along the Colorado Trail today is the Fryingpan-Arkansas diversion system, known locally as the Pan-Ark. This complex system diverts 69,200 acre-feet of water per year from the west slope's Fryingpan River, a tributary of the Colorado, to the Arkansas River using a network of six reservoirs, 16 diversion structures and ten tunnels. The Pan-Ark project was begun in the 1960s to shore up east slope municipalities and agricultural water users. Summit County's Dillon Reservoir, named for the little community it flooded, and 23-mile-long Roberts Tunnel comprise a system that funnels excess flow from the Blue River eastward into the headwaters of the North Fork of the South Platte River, eventually to reemerge at faucets all over Denver.

Dillon Reservoir, besides supplying water for Denver, also is a center for summer water sports in one of the state's most highly developed, year-round recreation areas. Once an active mining region, Summit County typifies the metamorphosis which has taken place in Colorado's mountain communities. The county's economy now revolves around its appeal as a glamorous vacation destination which focuses on the many posh ski resorts in the surrounding area.

Many of these ski resorts had their beginnings in the Army installation at Camp Hale from 1942 to 1945 which dramatically emphasized Colorado's potential as a winter recreation area. The training that the troops received at the Rocky Mountain outpost was not lost upon the men of the 10th Mountain Division. Many of them returned to Colorado after the war to fulfill their dreams of elegant ski resorts and to help the state develop its reputation as the nation's premier winter wonderland. The ruins of Camp Hale now rank as one of the state's most recent and unusual ghost sites, and now a destination on the Colorado Trail.

The latest development proposed along the Colorado Trail is Two Forks Dam and Reservoir, which would inundate scenic Platte Canyon southwest of Denver. If built, Two Forks Reservoir would be larger than Dillon Reservoir and would drown several miles of the trail in the craggy canyon. The question of Two Forks, which set off battles between development and environmental interests for nearly a decade, was at least temporarily resolved in 1990 when EPA chief William Reilly vetoed the project as then proposed.

Balancing the demands of an economically booming state with an unparalleled natural setting and a dynamic tourism industry is no small task. And if the past is indeed prologue to the future, then development is destined to build on development. However, this trend will not continue without a price. That price includes visual deterioration, loss of wildlife habitat and the loss of once peaceful mountain settings so important to our holistic rejuvenation. Still, despite all the development, many isolated niches remain seemingly untouched by the imposing hand of humans. The 468 miles of the Colorado Trail highlight the continuing history of a remarkable state, and if trekkers can keep it all in perspective, it can be quite an experience.

Gaines Gulch, Segment 28 (pg. 34).

There is no question that the natural history of this region is the prize, the reward for the effort made in hiking the CT. This opportunity to observe the Rocky Mountain ecosystem also underscores the need to walk, not run, while making one's tour of the trail.

— Dr. Hugo A. Ferchau

NATURAL HISTORY OF THE COLORADO TRAIL

by Hugo A. Ferchau
Thornton Professor of Botany, Western State College

This brief look at Rocky Mountain ecology is intended for those who wish to enjoy the Colorado Trail country but have previously had no contact with it, as well as for locals who have only rarely ventured into its vastness. Veterans of these wilds could probably write an equally good account of the inhabitants of the open spaces. Regardless, there is no question that the natural history of this region is the prize, the reward for the effort made in hiking the trail. This opportunity to observe the Rocky Mountain ecosystem also underscores the need to walk, not run, while making one's daily tour on the trail. In ten years of leading groups of students through the Rockies, it has been my experience that hikers who reach camp two hours before the rest can rarely relate any interesting observations. They might as well have worked out in a gym. To get the most out of your sojourn on the Colorado Trail, take the time to look, to sit, to let nature present itself to you, and to soak up all that it has to offer — you may pass this way but once.

Observing Wildlife

For some reason, we commonly use the term "wildlife" to refer only to animals. Plants, evidently, are considered to be somewhat trapped or tamed, or at least subdued. There is less drama associated with plants because we can prepare for our encounters with them, whereas animals tend to take us by surprise — they are there all of a sudden and gone all of a sudden. As a botanist, I must recognize that most people would rather talk about a bear than about the bearberry.

The native fauna of the Rockies may readily be viewed from the Colorado Trail. At this point, I should make a digression concerning the domestic dog. Some hikers feel the hiking experience is not complete without their dog. To be sure, when a backpacker is on the trail alone, companionship is pleasant. When hiking in a group, however, a dog can be a nuisance. If you are interested in being a part of the surrounding ecosystem, your dog (which is not a part of that ecosystem) should be left at home.

But back to the question of those birds, bees, and the larger and more impressive animals you may encounter. Having been over most of the Colorado Trail, I cannot think of a single day's hike which did not reveal much of the Rocky Mountain fauna. By the same token, I have seen students hide for days without seeing a single animal. This apparent contradiction can be explained by the fact that native animals are not in a zoo. They have learned behavior and instincts which assure them of avoiding threatening outsiders, such as hikers. You must meet the animals on their own terms. Several general rules may be followed. Dawn and dusk are when animals tend to be

Bighorn Sheep, La Garita Wilderness.

most active. Animals require water regularly. Many animals will learn to ignore you if you are part of the scenery, which means being relatively quiet and still. Do not try to see all of the fauna in a single sitting. Obtain some of the local texts and become familiar with the behavior of the animal or group of animals you wish to observe, and make a conscious effort to make the observations. You will probably have the most success with birds. Also, do not discount what might be considered the less dramatic animals, such as the small nocturnal rodents. A log to sit on at night and a flashlight will often allow you some captivating moments. Rising early in the morning and getting on the trail ahead of the group can also increase your chances of seeing wildlife.

Early season hikers should note that fawning of deer and calving of elk occur in June. Try to avoid being disruptive if traveling during this time of year.

Some hikers may be fearful of encountering wildlife, but there is little need for worry. After taking students into the Rockies for more than ten years, we have never been attacked by anything. I have seen mountain lion and bear at reasonable distances, and I am sure they have observed me from distances which, were they known, would have excited me. I have seen bear droppings on the trail on a cold morning that were so fresh the steam was still rising off them. My wife woke up from a nap one afternoon, and there were fresh bear claw marks on a tree over her head. Good judgment will discourage you from being molested. An animal seeks food, not your company. If you have no food in your presence, you will generally not be bothered. If you choose to keep food, even nuts or a candy bar, in your tent, you may wake up at night to find a hole cut in the floor and confront the steely eyes of a mouse or pack rat. After arriving in camp, place your food away from the sleeping area— 75 to 100 yards is a good distance.

The highly variable topography of the central Rocky Mountains provides for a kaleidoscopic variety of vegetation. The accompanying diagrams give some indications of the vegetation types encountered on the Colorado Trail, as well as their relationships to each other. Note that the zones are not defined by elevation alone, but depend also on local climatic factors. In the field, of course, matters can be even more complicated. In areas that have been disturbed, for example, as by fire or logging, different types of vegetation will exist in different relationships. Diagram 1 (page 38) shows the relationships between various plant communities in a "climax" situation, that is, in an ecologically stable, undisturbed environment. When the land has been disturbed, the plants proceed through a "succession" phase before eventually evolving back into a climax state. Diagram 2 (page 39) shows the relationships between various types of vegetation during succession. Because of the severe climate and short growing season in the Rockies, successional vegetation patterns may persist for more than a hundred years. In addition, a single hillside may be covered with successional vegetation in one place and climax vegetation in another.

Riparian Vegetation: This is the vegetation found along streambanks, and it plays a variety of important roles, such as controlling erosion and providing cover and feed for wildlife. On the western slope, lower elevation streambanks are dominated by assorted cottonwood trees, alder, maple and red-osier dogwood. With increasing elevation the cottonwoods become less evident, while the shrubs persist, eventually being dominated by willows. On the eastern slope, the cottonwoods are not as evident but, as on the western slope, a mixture of shrubs prevails, becoming increasingly dominated by willows at higher elevations.

Despite what appears to be very aggressive growth by riparian species, they are among the most sensitive to human activity. And because of their proximity to water, they are typically among the most threatened and endangered.

Sagebrush: The sagebrush, the cold desert scrubland of the Rockies, can be found from low to surprisingly high elevations. It is interspersed with grasses, and is the primary grazing land of central and western Colorado. It is also quite dry, with little water available for hikers; ranchers typically maintain water supplies in stock tanks for their cattle, but those supplies are definitely not recommended for humans. During the day, this environment can become quite hot, while at night even summertime temperatures can drop to near freezing. During June, watch out for ticks.

Scrub Oak and Piñon-Juniper Woodland: This dryland plant community is most evident along the Colorado Trail where it climbs through the foothills above Denver. It will also be seen occasionally at higher elevations, on the driest and most stressed sites, until near Kenosha Pass. Junipers tend to be widely spaced, with grasses interspersed in between, while the scrub oak tends to be clumped together so closely as to be almost impenetrable. This sort of vegetation makes for good game habitat, and hikers should be prepared for deer to pop up most anywhere, particularly in early June. In late summer, the scrub oak/piñon-juniper woodland is prone to wildfire, which can move rapidly through the dry terrain. Such fires are often started by lightning strikes, and occasionally by hikers, who are reminded to pay attention to their campfires.

Ponderosa Pine: This is the lowest elevation timber tree. Because of its good lumber quality and proximity to civilization, it has been the most extensively cut. Thus you may see large, old ponderosa stumps among woodland vegetation, indicating a logged ponderosa forest where the tall pines have not yet returned. These long needled pines tend to grow well spaced, with grasses flourishing between trees. As a result, ranchers like to graze their stock among the ponderosa, particularly in early spring. On the eastern slope, ponderosa pine is found on less stressed south facing hillsides. On the western slope, it is the tree one encounters above the open, arid countryside of the sagebrush community.

Douglas Fir: This predominant tree is not to be confused with the giant firs of the Pacific Northwest, though it is related to them. Here in the Rockies, we have the runts of the litter. The Douglas fir occupies moist, cool sites. On the eastern slope it is found on the slopes opposite the ponderosa pine, and on the western slope it grows

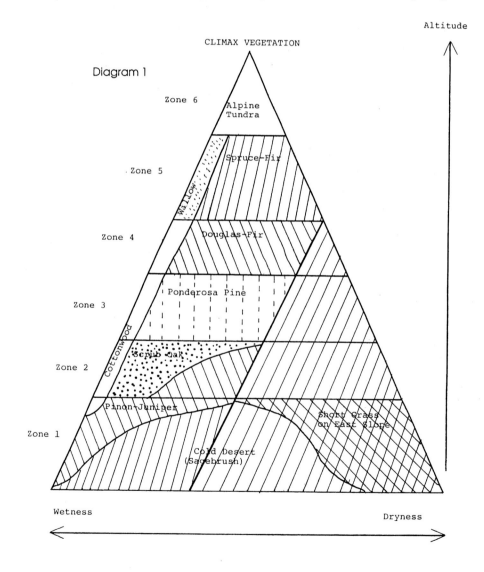

above the level of the ponderosa. In either case, as a result of the moister environment and shorter growing season, Douglas fir trees tend to grow closer together, with little ground cover underneath. Much of both the eastern and western slopes is Douglas fir habitat, but because it is also the type most likely to be burned, much of that habitat is occupied by successional vegetation. Hikers, again, should remember to be careful with fire.

Spruce-Fir Forest: This, the highest elevation forest, is composed of Engelmann spruce and subalpine fir. Because of the late snowmelt, moist summertime conditions and early snowfall, this vegetation type has been least altered by fire. Many of the spruce-fir forest in the Rockies are as much as 400 years old. These dense forests tend to contain many fallen logs, which can be a real deterrent to hiking. The logs are typically moist, and hikers walking over them may be surprised when the bark slips off and they lose their footing. Ground cover may be lacking, and

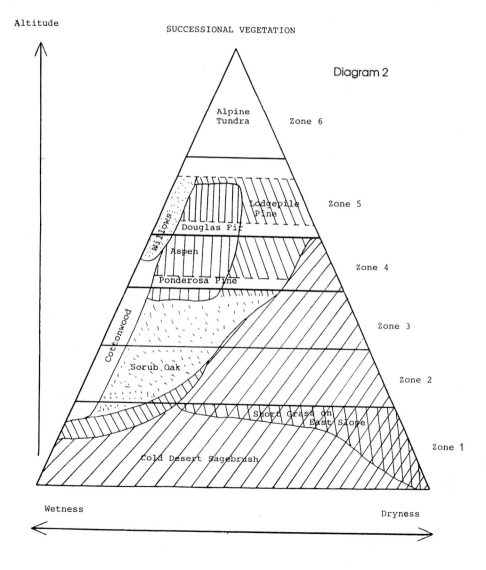

Altitude

SUCCESSIONAL VEGETATION

Diagram 2

Alpine
Tundra — Zone 6

Lodgepole Pine — Zone 5

Willows

Douglas Fir

Aspen — Zone 4

Ponderosa Pine

Cottonwood — Zone 3

Scrub Oak — Zone 2

Short Grass on East Slope

Cold Desert Sagebrush — Zone 1

Wetness

Dryness

Indian paintbrush in alpine meadows of the La Plata Mountains.

a thick humus layer may be present.

As one approaches timberline, the spruce-fir stands tend to be more open. The trees are clustered, with grasses and beautiful wildflowers interspersed between them. These tree clusters provide refuges for elk during the night. At the timberline itself, the trees are bushlike, weatherbeaten and windshorn. They often grow in very dense clumps which can provide an ideal refuge for hikers. Winds of 50 mph can whistle by virtually unnoticed while you sit in a clump of timberline trees. Animals are aware of this, too, and thus, while waiting out a storm, you may have the pleasure of observing a great deal of small mammal activity.

Lodgepole Pine and Aspen: These are ordinarily successional species which can occupy a given site for up to 200 years. The lodgepole pine often succeeds disturbed Douglas fir and spruce-fir communities and grows on the driest sites. Its seeds are opened by fire, and a wildfire will cause the deposition of thousands of seeds—and, a few years later, the appearance of many dense stands of seedlings and saplings. These pine stands are often referred to as "horsehair." There is virtually no ground cover in the deep shade beneath the saplings, and competition is fierce between the closely spaced trees. The dryness of the site encourages repeated fires.

The aspen occupies moister sites. A clump of aspen among lodgepole pines suggests a potential source of water. Aspen reproduce from root suckers, and any ground disturbance, such as a fire, causes a multitude of saplings to appear. On drier sites, aspen is typically interspersed with Thurber fescue, a large bunchgrass. In moderately moist sites the ground cover will consist of a multitude of grasses, forbs and shrubs. Wet site aspen often has a ground cover dominated by bracken fern. Aspen groves can be attractive for camping, but during June and July may be infested with troublesome insects.

Alpine Tundra: Though it strikes many people as odd, the tundra can be likened to a desert because it enjoys only minimal precipitation. During the winter, fierce winds prevent snow from accumulating anywhere except in depressions. During the summer, the snowmelt drains quickly off the steeper slopes, leaving the vegetation there to depend for survival on regular afternoon showers. Despite the harsh conditions, the alpine tundra is quite diverse, and includes such different environments as meadows, boulder fields, fell fields, talus and both temporary and permanent ponds. The cushion-like meadows are a favorite site for elk herds. The boulder fields provide homes for pikas, marmots and other animals, and the protected spaces between the boulders can produce some of the most beautiful wildflowers. The fell fields are windswept sites from which virtually all mineral soil has been blown away, leaving behind a "pavement" which, despite its austerity, may have some interesting plants. The talus fields consist of loose rock; they also host some interesting plants and animals. The ponds often teem with invertebrates and can provide good sites for observing the fascinating bird known as the ptarmigan.

Hugo Ferchau was a dedicated supporter of the CT from its early days until his untimely death in 1994. As a professor of biology and botany at Western State College in Gunnison, his experience and passion for the outdoors benefitted the CT, with his participation on the CTF board, as well as tutoring students in wilderness sessions on the CT.

GEOLOGY ALONG THE COLORADO TRAIL

by Denise R. Mutschler and David L. Gaskill

To venture along the Colorado Trail is to catch a glimpse of Colorado's history, a great deal of which is linked to the extraction of mineral wealth. For more than a hundred years Colorado towns have prospered and declined according to the fortunes of the mining industry. A far earlier history, however, is that of the land through which the trail passes. Much of the natural beauty of Colorado can be attributed to the geologic forces that have shaped the varied landscapes of this Rocky Mountain state.

In eastern Colorado lies the westernmost edge of the Great Plains, a rolling landscape that abruptly gives way to mountains at an altitude of about 5000 feet. Underlying the plains are interlayered beds of a variety of rocks: shale, sandstone, conglomerate, limestone, coal, and volcanic ash. These beds vary in age from the geologically recent to as much as 570 million years old. In the Denver Basin (see Figure 1) this 13,000-foot-thick sequence of sediments lies above a still older Precambrian basement consisting of crystalline granitic and metamorphic rocks. Geologists learn much about the earth by "reading" the rocks, and they postulate a history here that dates back 1.8 billion years.

Some of the sedimentary rocks are visible along the Front Range, where they have been bent, broken, and brought to the surface by the forces that pushed the mountains upward. Most notable are the Fountain Sandstone flatirons, which make up the Red Rocks amphitheater and other points of interest, and the hogbacks of the Dakota and Morrison formations seen from Interstate 70. This dramatic meeting of plains and mountains provides a fine setting for the Colorado Trail as it begins its winding course through the ranges and valleys of western Colorado.

At the start, the trail moves westward across the Front Range, the core of which is made of basement rocks that have been uplifted again and again during the past 330 million years. In many places the older rocks — schists, gneisses, quartzites, marbles, and metamorphosed volcanics — have been intruded by younger granitic bodies, such as the Pikes Peak batholith.

West of the Front Range, the Colorado Trail passes to the north of South Park, a wide basin underlain by sedimentary rocks like those of the plains. These rocks were intruded by mineralized stocks of granodiorite porphyry during a mountain-building period known as the Laramide Orogeny, which occurred 40 to 70 million years ago.

The trail continues through part of the Breckenridge mining district, a region famous for its gold. The largest gold nugget ever discovered in Colorado was found here and can be seen today at Denver's Museum of Natural History. The mining of

Eroded formations of metamorphosed volcanics near Snow Mesa, Segment 21.

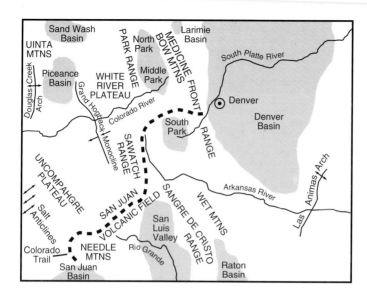

Figure 1: Geological structures underlying the Colorado Trail.

gold and silver was Colorado's principal industry in the late 1800s, when placer gold in streambeds lured eager prospectors into the mountains in search of source veins and lodes. Today we recognize far more diversity in the state's mineral wealth: limestone, sand, gravel, building stone, lead, molybdenum, zinc, coal, oil (including oil shale), and natural gas. One more commodity ought to be acknowledged—snow! Obviously, the winter sports industry depends on this annual accumulation in the mountains; less obvious, perhaps, but incredibly important, is the fact that each year as the snowpack melts, water is stored in forest soils, alluvium, and porous rocks, ready to supply the needs of every living thing.

The trail goes up and over the Tenmile Range, a block of uplifted, ancient metamorphic rocks. Beyond Copper Mountain it passes through an area of layered rocks that have been intruded by quartz monzonite and granodiorite porphyry dikes and sills. It crosses a 20-million-year-old rhyolite near Camp Hale and goes on to Tennessee Pass and the gold-bearing strata of the Cambrian, Devonian, Mississippian, and Pennsylvanian periods.

South of the pass, ancient gneisses and schists (1.7 billion years old) are cut by silver-producing veins of the St. Kevin-Sugar Loaf mining district. Early Indians once extracted turquoise from deposits in this area. The trail skirts Turquoise Reservoir on a 1.4-billion-year-old granite batholith and crosses moraines left behind by now-extinct Sawatch glaciers. At one time glaciers dammed the Arkansas River, forcing it to carve out a new channel on the east side of the valley.

The upper Arkansas Valley, part of the long, north-south Rio Grande rift, is bounded by a steplike series of parallel faults on the east and by the Sawatch fault zone on the west, along which many hot springs are located. One of these springs is at Mount Princeton, where the trail passes the Chalk Cliffs, a hydrothermally altered part of a 30-million-year-old quartz monzonite batholith. Farther south, near the summit of Mount Antero, aquamarine (beryl), topaz, garnet, and other rare minerals are found. Topaz and garnet are also found in the valley near the town of Nathrop.

Southwest of Marshall Pass is the San Juan Volcanic Field, a point of considerable geologic interest. Between 35 and 22 million years ago, this area was the scene of violent eruptions from many enormous craters. These craters, or calderas, are the present-day sites of such gold and silver mining camps as Creede, Silverton, and Lake City. Layers of volcanic rock from both passive and explosive eruptions cover the area to a depth of thousands of feet. Younger volcanic rocks, about 3.5 million years old, are also present.

Along the north flank of the Needle Mountains uplift, the trail passes through spectacular Precambrian terrain in the Grenadier Range. This includes upthrust beds of quartzite, slate, and phyllite. An erosional nonconformity between 1.4-billion-year-old Precambrian rocks and an overlying layer of quartzite represents a gap in time of about 600 million years.

Beyond Molas Lake the trail works upward through successively younger sedimentary rock layers. Some of these are different from the rock units found in eastern Colorado. Others, such as the Dakota, Morrison, Entrada, and Leadville formations, are equivalent to formations found elsewhere. The Mancos Shale of western Colorado, for instance, was deposited in the same sea as the Pierre Shale of eastern Colorado, but the western rocks are older than the eastern ones. This is because the ancient sea gradually migrated eastward, altering both the time and place of deposition.

The ridge south of Grizzly Peak consists of clays and marlstones of the Morrison Formation (well known as a source of dinosaur bones) and also of the ancient beach and lagoon deposits that comprise the Dakota Sandstone. These are intruded by igneous rocks in the form of dikes, sills, and laccoliths. From this divide, the trail affords splendid views of the area's mountain ranges: the San Miguel, the San Juan, the La Plata, and the Needles.

Heading southward to the La Plata Mountains, the trail crosses red shales, siltstones, mudstones, grits, and conglomerates. The La Plata Range consists of sedimentary rocks that were domed up during the Laramide Orogeny by the intrusions of sills, laccolith, and stocks. The dome was subsequently dissected by erosional forces and is the location of a mining district that has produced gold and silver-bearing telluride, ruby silver, copper, and lead ores since 1873.

The trail continues to wend its way southward to Junction Creek and descends by way of successive younger strata to arrive at the trail's southern terminus — Junction Creek Trailhead outside of Durango.

More extensive descriptions of The Colorado Trail's geology can be found in U.S. Geological Survey publications, including the *Geological Map of Colorado*. USGS publications are available by mail from the USGS Branch of Distribution, P. O. Box 25286, Denver, CO 80225; or over the counter from USGS Map Sales, Denver Federal Center, Building 810, Lakewood, CO. Free, non-technical pamphlets from other agencies include such topics as: *Mountain and Plains, Denver's Geological Setting; Landforms of the United States; Volcanoes of the United States; Earthquakes; Geologic Map; Portraits of the Earth; Geologic Time; Prospecting; Collecting Rocks;* and many others. **A further source of information is the Colorado Geological Survey, 1313 Sherman Street, Room 715, Denver, CO 80203.**

Segment 1
Kassler to
South Platte Canyon

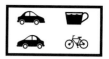

Distance: 15.4 miles
Elevation Gain: approx 2160 ft

The old railroad grade, and present Water Board road, through Platte Canyon.

Gudy's Tip

"A broken toggle or cotter pin may be difficult to replace along the trail, as sporting goods stores are far apart. Make sure your backpack is in excellent condition before setting off."

Trip Log

Date: _____ Notes: _____

_____

_____

_____

_____

About This Segment

On your way to Waterton Canyon from the east, notice the hogbacks leaning against the ancient core of the Rampart Range. With little imagination it is possible to visualize these leftover sedimentary rocks crumpling and eroding away through the eons as the Rampart Range forced its way up from below. Beyond the initial sedimentary layers at the outlet of the canyon, the gorge narrows and reveals its 1.6-billion-year-old metamorphic walls.

Although this canyon was no doubt visited by many Indians and was briefly explored by the Long Expedition of 1820, it was not permanently disrupted until 1877 when territorial governor John Evans built his Denver South Park and Pacific Railroad up the Platte on its way to exploit Colorado's mineral belt. The canyon has known little peace since, and endured a major change in the early 1980s when work began on Strontia Springs Dam. And for years the possibility of the immense Two Forks dam and reservoir just upstream from Strontia Springs threatened the canyon of the South Platte. However, in 1990, EPA chief William Reilly vetoed Two Forks on environmental grounds after a 10-year-long study. Had Two Forks been built, it would have inundated a significant portion of the CT in the western end of this segment, and would have required a lengthy trail reroute around the massive reservoir. Although the Platte River canyon and the CT are safe for now from Two Forks, some say that the careful legal language used by Reilly in rejecting the proposed configuration of Two Forks left open the possibility of a future, differently designed Two Forks dam and reservoir in the canyon. Time will tell.

Additional Trail Information: Colorado Trail trekkers sometimes complain about the first 6.2 miles of the CT on the Water Board road up Platte Canyon from the Waterton Canyon Trailhead. Admittedly, this highly used recreation area on a hot summer afternoon can be a discouraging initial experience on the CT, even with the craggy scenery of the canyon as inspiration. However, the canyon takes on a different personality in the pleasant, early morning hours before the crowds appear. Cool breezes sweep the canyon with the fragrant scent of the forests above and nearby riparian vegetation. At this hour, the canyon appears to be your personal domain. You may even be lucky enough to see the local bighorn sheep herd grazing near the river before the multitudes frighten them to the steep slopes high in the canyon.

Even so, many would consider the aesthetic trail experience to begin beyond mile 6.2, as the CT leaves the Water Board road behind above Strontia Springs Dam. This segment is particularly popular with mountain cyclists. Loaded-down backpackers need to be prepared for the columns of bikers that will be speeding by them, especially on the narrow trail section beyond mile 6.2.

CT trekkers must abide by the Denver Water Board regulations along the first 6.2-mile section in Waterton Canyon; these include no dogs or camping. Camping beyond mile 6.2 is challenging because of the terrain, but there are flat spots in a few locations. Water is usually available in Bear Creek and its side drainages for most of the season; if not, the shoreline of Strontia Springs Reservoir is not too far below. If Two Forks Dam is ever built, this access might be closed during its construction.

Trailhead/Access Points

Kassler-Waterton Canyon Trailhead: There are several routes to the trailhead at Waterton Canyon. Least confusing is to take I-25 south from Denver through the suburbs to Colorado Hwy-470. Travel west on Hwy-470 12.5 miles to Hwy-121 (Wadsworth Blvd). Go south (left) on Colorado Hwy-121 for 4.5 miles to where the road officially ends at the entrance to the Lockheed-Martin plant. Turn left off of Hwy-121 and onto a side road marked as "Waterton Canyon." Continue 0.3 mile, following the signs to the large trailhead parking area.

Douglas CO RD-97: See Segment 2.

Supplies, Services and Accommodations

Denver and its southern suburbs have the full array of services expected in a metropolitan area.

Maps and Jurisdiction

USFS map: Pike National Forest, see pages 50-51.
USGS Quadrangle maps: Kassler, Platte Canyon.
Trails Illustrated map: # 135.

Jurisdiction: South Platte Ranger District, Pike NF.

Trail Description

From the Waterton Canyon Trailhead parking area at the old Kassler water treatment plant, begin your Colorado Trail adventure up Platte Canyon on the old railroad grade, now the wide gravel Water Board road. Be advised that the first 6.2 miles of this segment are signed "Closed 1/2 hour before sunrise and after sunset." Plan your start accordingly. Isolated cottonwoods along the banks of the Platte River provide shade on warm summer days. At 5520 feet above sea level, this point is the lowest anywhere along the route of the CT, and serves as a gateway from the eastern plains grasslands to the foothills life zone. Immediately above the shadows of the cottonwoods, the dry rocky slopes of the canyon support little more than yucca, gambel oak and juniper. Higher up on the cooler, moister mountain slopes, dark patches of ponderosa pine and Douglas fir are visible.

Pass Strontia Springs Dam at **mile 5.8** (5800), leave the river behind, and continue straight ahead (south) on the dirt road, which steadily steepens. Not too far from the dam, just behind the caretaker's house, avoid the left fork that connects to Roxborough Park. The public must exit the road at a switchback to the right, 0.3 mile beyond the dam. Here, a short, dead-end spur road to the left (south) leads to a portal of multicolored metamorphic boulders at **mile 6.2** (5920), and the start of your aesthetic trail experience. A sign here reads "Colorado Trail #1776, Bear Creek - 1.6, South Platte Townsite - 10.0."

The comfortable trail switchbacks up through a shady Douglas fir forest, offering intermittent glimpses to the north of the rocky summit called Turkshead.

From the saddle at **mile 7.3** (6560), a side trail goes east via Stevens and Mill Gulches to the summit of Carpenter Peak within Roxborough State Park. Please note that bicycles and equestrians are not allowed in the park, and it is open for day use only. Descend from the saddle and cross Bear Creek at **mile 8.0** (6200). Bear Creek is the last reliable point for water until you again reach the South Platte River approximately 8.0 miles beyond.

A barely visible path can be seen descending alongside the creek here. This was an old logging road built by C. A. Deane, who had a sawmill at the confluence of Bear Creek and the South Platte River. Besides providing ties to the DSP&PRR during its construction, Deane later expanded his profitable operation by adding a hotel and the whistle stop became known as Deansbury. This historic junction is now submerged by Strontia Springs reservoir.

Continue 0.1 mile on the CT to the crossing of West Bear Creek. At **mile 9.0** (6640) the CT shares its route with Motorcycle Trail #692 for 0.5 mile, until just after the final crossing of West Bear Creek. Here the trail diverges from the motorcycle trail and proceeds uphill and to the right. Ascend another 0.6 mile to the ridge at **mile 10.1** (7200), where the motorcycle trail crosses the CT a final time. The trail continues a climb in and out of several side drainages to its high point on the northern exposed slope of Platte Canyon. Rock outcrops provide convenient perches for rest stops, from which the reservoir below and the foothills to the north and west can be viewed.

At **mile 13.0** (7280) the trail rounds an elevated valley and passes along a ridge, then begins a switchbacking descent into the valley. Pass below what would have been the shoreline of the vetoed Two Forks Reservoir, then join up with Douglas Co Rd-97 at **mile 15.4** (6120), where this trail segment comes to an end. A widened roadway here provides plentiful parking for this recently marked trailhead point. This road was originally graded for the DSP&PRR Nighthawk Branch. The historic South Platte townsite is 0.7 mile north where the boarded-up South Platte Hotel recalls memories of another era. No services are available here. The trail continues directly across the road, immediately crossing the South Platte River on the Gudy Gaskill Bridge, longest footbridge anywhere on the CT.

Viewing Bighorn Sheep

The Rocky Mountain Bighorn Sheep, selected as the state mammal, is a fitting symbol of Colorado. With their massive curving horns, rams present a majestic silhouette that matches the grandeur of their rugged surroundings. Waterton Canyon is home to a band of bighorn that have been increasingly threatened by encroaching human activities.

Bighorn are susceptible to lungworm and associated pneumonia, the spread of which is apparently facilitated by persistent crowding by visitors, causing unobservable stress in the animals. Also, traditional routes to salt licks, important to meet the animal's mineral requirements, may be cut off. The construction of the Strontia Springs Dam in the 1980s severely impacted the Waterton band, which has recovered somewhat since.

The sheep can often be spotted by visitors, sometimes moving right down to the road. CT users should not harry, startle, or attempt to feed the animals.

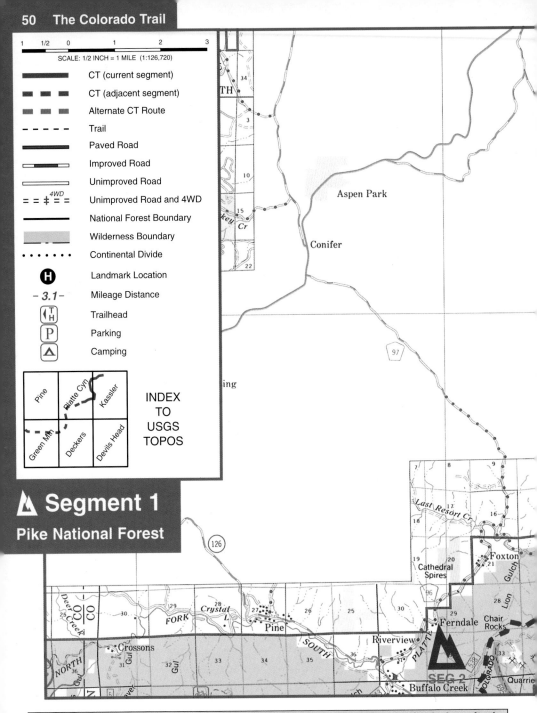

SCALE: 1/2 INCH = 1 MILE (1:126,720)	
CT (current segment)	
CT (adjacent segment)	
Alternate CT Route	
Trail	
Paved Road	
Improved Road	
Unimproved Road	
Unimproved Road and 4WD	
National Forest Boundary	
Wilderness Boundary	
Continental Divide	
H Landmark Location	
– *3.1* – Mileage Distance	
Trailhead	
Parking	
Camping	

INDEX TO USGS TOPOS

▲ Segment 1
Pike National Forest

Landmark Location	Mileage	From Denver	Elevation	Latitude	Longitude
Ⓐ Waterton Canyon Trailhead	0.0	0.0	5520	39.491279	-105.094465
Ⓑ Strontia Springs Dam	5.8	5.8	5800	39.434733	-105.122310
Ⓒ Bear Creek	8.0	8.0	6200	39.419539	-105.123802
Ⓓ Ridge above West Bear Creek	10.2	10.2	7200	39.405819	-105.152325
Ⓔ Douglas Co Rd-97	15.4	15.4	6120	39.400372	-105.167174

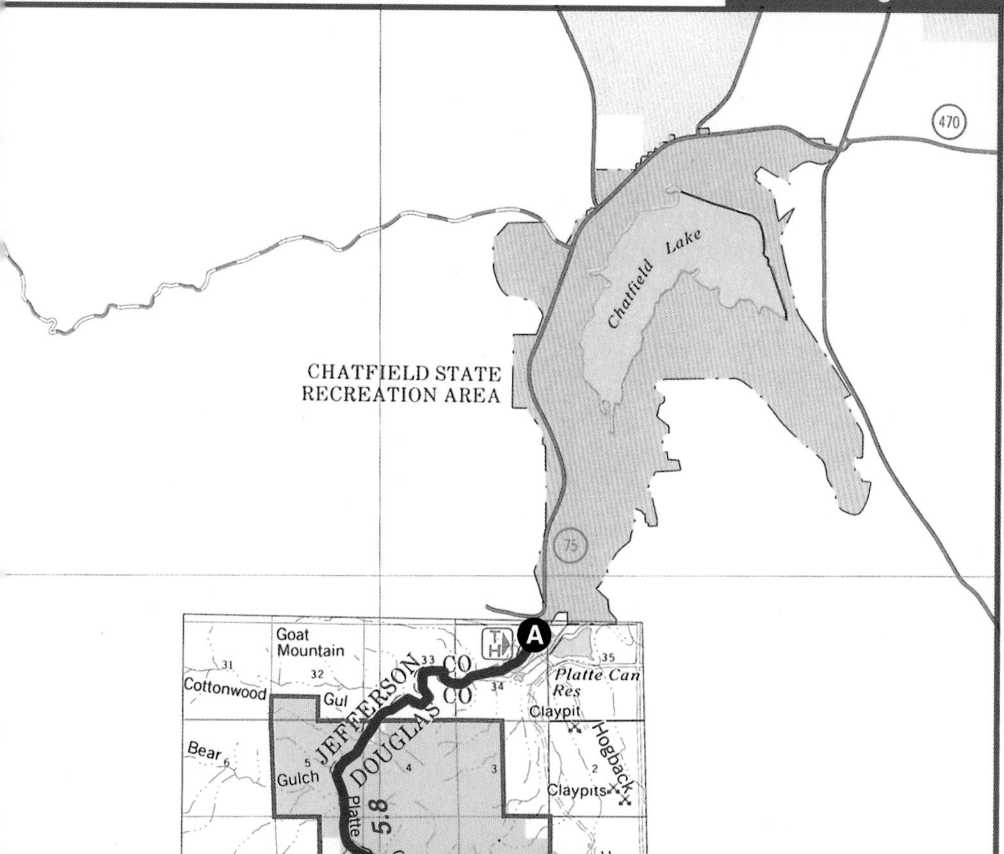

CHATFIELD STATE
RECREATION AREA

Chatfield Lake

470

75

Goat
Mountain

JEFFERSON CO
DOUGLAS CO

Cottonwood
Gul

Claypit

Platte Can
Res

Hogback

Claypits

Bear
Gulch

Platte

5.8

RIVER

Canyon

Mill

SEG 1

Turkshead
Peak
7775

Willow Cr

Sheep

Mtn

Strontia
Springs
Reservoir

Canyon

2.2

Roxborough Park

Carpenter
Peak

ROXBOROUGH
STATE PARK

Dome
Rock

96

Gaging
Stations

South Platte

Platte

5.2

Bear

Stevens

Gulch

2.2

4WD

Hogback

Willow

TRAIL

Eagle
Rock

Russell Ridge

Russ

Creek

D

Thomas
Hill

Pine
Nook

Bennett
Mountain

Elevation x 1000

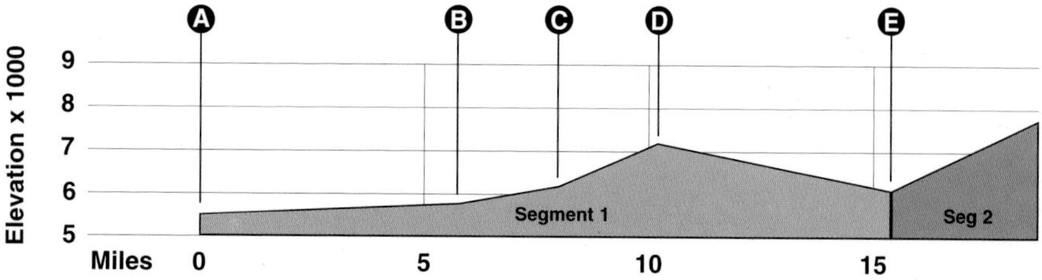

9

8

7

6

5

A   B   C   D   E

Segment 1   Seg 2

Miles   0   5   10   15

Segment 2
South Platte Canyon to Colorado Trailhead FS-550

Distance: 10.8 miles
Elevation Gain: approx 2200 ft

Hiking through Buffalo Creek burn area, Top of The World ridge.

Gudy's Tip

"When you reach the South Platte River, fill up on water as it is a long, dry climb to Top-of-the-World ridge. There is emergency water at the fire station, a short distance from where the trail crosses County Rd-126."

Trip Log

Date: _____ Notes: _____

_____

_____

_____

_____

About This Segment

In the spring of 1996, the disastrous Buffalo Creek fire consumed some 12,000 acres of forest in the middle and western sections of this segment. Later that summer, torrential downpours flooded the area, viciously eroding sections of the trail left unprotected by vegetation, and washing out the bridge crossing at South Platte townsite on the pre-existing route of the CT. Since that time, a new bridge has been constructed 0.7 miles upstream from South Platte townsite at the beginning of this segment, and a new section of trail has been built detouring the washed out old bridge crossing. However, large sections of the trail are still affected by the burned-out forest and continuing trail erosion.

During its heyday, South Platte town, just downstream from the new trail crossing on the county road, saw many trains pass the confluence of the South Platte River and its North Fork. Today the shuttered South Platte Hotel serves as a lone reminder of that age. If the Two Forks dam and reservoir project is ever resurrected, it will submerge this historic junction and a large portion of the CT, as well as significant portions of the canyon which is popular with anglers, kayakers, hikers and rock climbers.

This trail segment makes the transition from the Rampart Range to the Kenosha Mountains, and all along are splendid examples of the rounded outcrops of the Pikes Peak batholith, outcrops which take on dramatic, fortress-like appearances. The pink coloration of this billion-year-old granite is disguised by the green and black lichens which grow profusely on it.

This segment ends at the Colorado Trailhead on FS-550 near its intersection with Jefferson Co Rd-126 approximately 4.3 miles south of Buffalo Creek town.

Additional Trail Information: The now-exposed trail through the burned-out forest can be extremely hot on sunny summer afternoons. And, unfortunately, the CT route in this segment, except along the South Platte River at the outset, is completely without water. Even the burned-out Top-of-the-World Campground (now closed by the FS until further notice) is waterless, so pack plenty if you wish to make use of the many potential campsites along the way. After you pass the Platte River at the outset of this segment, you will not encounter reliable water sources until well into Segment 3. Because of the low elevation and the now shadelessness of most of the way, it is best to traverse this segment in early morning before the afternoon sun bears down on you.

This segment parallels, and crosses at its mid-point, FS-538, now closed due to the fire damage. Side roads and trails leading from this Forest Service road intersect the CT often, sometimes at confusing and poorly marked junctions, so be attentive. Enhanced, forest-less views from the burned-out Top-of-the-World ridge, which the trail traverses on its east side, are the highlight of this section.

Trailhead/Access Points

Douglas Co Rd-97 Trailhead: Travel approximately 32 miles west from Denver on US-285 to Pine Junction. Go left (south) on Pine Valley Road (Jefferson Co Rd-126), following the signs to Pine and Buffalo Creek. Continue on Rd-126 for 9.4 miles to the outskirts of Buffalo Creek. Turn left onto Jefferson Co Rd-96, which parallels the North Fork 10.6 miles to the boarded-up South Platte Hotel at the South Platte townsite. Continue over the bridge where the road becomes Douglas Co Rd-97 and go 0.7 mile further to a widened spot in the road. The long footbridge crossing the river identifies this spot. This trailhead is also accessible from US-24 at Woodland Park by traveling north on Colorado Hwy-67 to Deckers. Continue down the Platte River on Douglas Co Rd-67 and Rd-97 approximately 13.5 miles to the trailhead.

Colorado Trailhead on FS-550: See Segment 3.

Maps and Jurisdiction

USFS map: Pike National Forest, see pages 56-57.
USGS Quadrangle maps: Platte Canyon, Deckers.
Trails Illustrated map: # 135.

Jurisdiction: South Platte Ranger District, Pike NF.

Trail Description

From the trailhead parking area, immediately cross the South Platte River on this long, sturdy footbridge, the longest on the entire CT. Please note that this crossing provides the last reliable water for almost 13 miles. On the opposite bank, you will immediately descend to the level of the river and wrap back under the bridge. The trail follows the river upstream (southeast) for a few hundred feet at the base of impressive cliffs before it begins an ascent on the mountainside. Ascend steadily through nine switchbacks to **mile 0.9** (6600) where you will pick up the route of an old quarry road. These old abandoned roads lace the mountainsides, and can make following the trail difficult at times. Traces of the burn are increasingly evident as you gain elevation, and the trail may at times appear to melt into the barren, scorched, gravelly

Groceries/Post Office	Buffalo Creek Services	
J. W. Green Mercantile Co	**Distance From CT:**	
17706 County Rd 96		3.2 miles
(303) 838-5587	**Elevation:**	6,750
	Zip Code:	80425
Medical	**Area Code:**	303
Park County Health Center		
Hwy 285 (in Bailey)		
(303) 838-7653		

Supplies, Services and Accommodations

Buffalo Creek town, approximately 3.2 miles north on Jefferson County Road 126 from the trail at mile 9.5, was once a whistle stop on the DSP&PRR. It survives with a few cabins, a small general store (very unique!), a pay phone, and a Forest Service work center.

soil. In 0.3 mile the CT leaves the old quarry road and ascends a burned-out ridge to the west, after which it briefly levels out.

The trail then continues an ascent steadily through the burned-out forest to **mile 2.5** (7120) where a large outcrop of pink Pikes Peak granite could make a lazy afternoon's destination. This point affords views of Pikes Peak, Devil's Head, Platte Canyon, and the denuded ridges that resulted from the Buffalo Creek fire. Sections of the trail that pass through the burn area to this point have experienced severe erosion, and the lack of shade in this once-dense forest would make this ascent extremely uncomfortable on a warm summer afternoon.

Continue your ascent north of Raleigh Peak through a Douglas fir forest to a ridge at **mile 4.6** (7760), where Chair Rocks are visible to the west. Descend from the ridge to a dry gully, then ascend to **mile 5.5** (7760) and FS-538 at a three-corner intersection. The trail continues ahead (south) on the opposite side of the road and heads through a mostly ponderosa forest with an occasional juniper. The CT continues to bear south, paralleling FS-538 and crossing several old, abandoned roads — some

Arnold Haak hiking through Segment 2 of the CT.

which now serve as secondary trails from the Forest Service road into the many side canyons below. Take care not to wander off the main trail at these many intersections which may not be well marked. Approximately 1 mile beyond the FS road crossing, you will re-enter the burn area. One unintended consequence of the denuded forest are the enhanced views. From this section along the Top-of-the-World ridge, striking vistas to the east justify a pace slow enough to allow you to fully appreciate Raleigh Peak, Long Scraggy, and Pikes Peak's rarely seen northwest profile.

Pass the short unmarked side trail up to the now closed and burned Top-of-the-World Campground at **mile 7.2** (7680). If you have a few minutes to spare, ascend the short distance to the appropriately named campground, where a 360-degree panorama reveals the Pikes Peak massif, the entire Rampart Range and the southern end of the Front Range. Also visible to the west are the Kenosha Mountains and Windy Peak, where you will be headed if you stay on the trail.

South of the campground, the trail continues through the burned-out forest in and out of several shallow gullies. At **mile 9.1** (7520) the trail skirts the edge of the burned area and heads in a more westerly direction. Continue to Jefferson Co Rd-126 at **mile 9.5** (7600). The town of Buffalo Creek with its small general store is approximately 3.2 miles north from this point. Also to the right, and just a short side trip along the road, is a fire station where emergency drinking water may be obtained from a faucet behind the building. Be sure to turn off the water and do not linger on the fire station property. The trail turns left (south) and parallels the highway for 0.3 mile, crossing two side roads on the way. Carefully cross to the opposite side of the highway to a closed Forest Service access road. Continue approximately 200 feet up the access road to an old sand quarry, then turn left (south-southwest) on the trail. Continue on the trail to the end of this segment at **mile 10.8** (7840) at the parking area of Colorado Trailhead on FS-550.

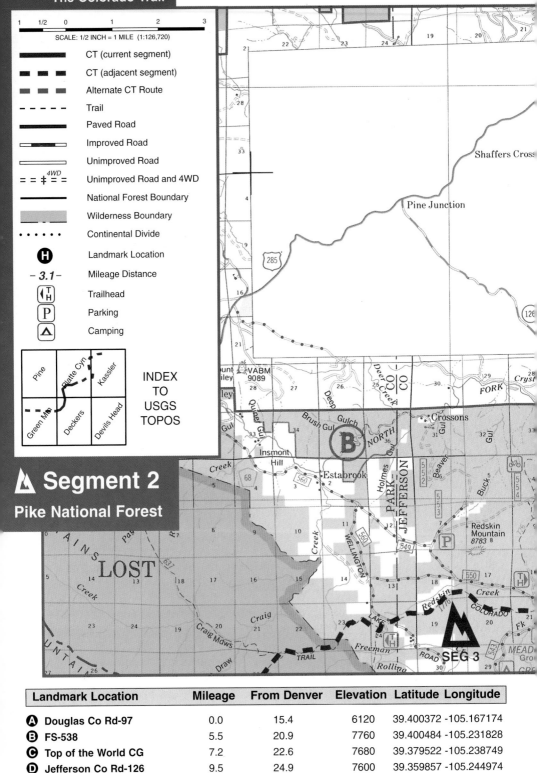

The Colorado Trail

SCALE: 1/2 INCH = 1 MILE (1:126,720)

——	CT (current segment)
– – –	CT (adjacent segment)
– – –	Alternate CT Route
- - - -	Trail
——	Paved Road
▭▬▭	Improved Road
▭▭	Unimproved Road
= = ‡ = =	Unimproved Road and 4WD
——	National Forest Boundary
	Wilderness Boundary
· · · · ·	Continental Divide
H	Landmark Location
– 3.1 –	Mileage Distance
T/H	Trailhead
P	Parking
△	Camping

INDEX TO USGS TOPOS

Pine · Platte Cyn · Kassler
Green Mtn · Deckers · Devils Head

▲ Segment 2

Pike National Forest

Landmark Location	Mileage	From Denver	Elevation	Latitude Longitude
Ⓐ Douglas Co Rd-97	0.0	15.4	6120	39.400372 -105.167174
Ⓑ FS-538	5.5	20.9	7760	39.400484 -105.231828
Ⓒ Top of the World CG	7.2	22.6	7680	39.379522 -105.238749
Ⓓ Jefferson Co Rd-126	9.5	24.9	7600	39.359857 -105.244974
Ⓔ Trailhead Parking Area	10.8	26.2	7840	39.345191 -105.257273

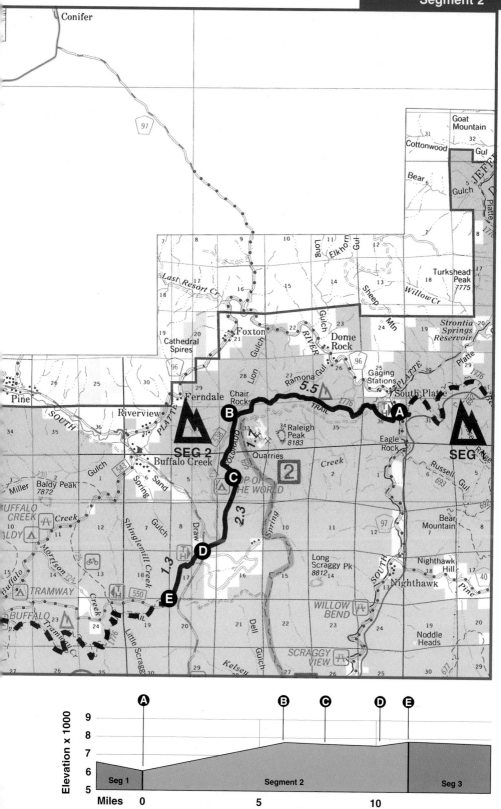

Segment 3
Colorado Trailhead FS-550 to FS-560 (Wellington Lake Road)

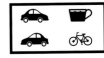

The CT passing through Buffalo Campground.

Distance: 12.1 miles
Elevation Gain: approx 1520 ft

Gudy's Tip

"The trailhead on FS-550 now charges a parking fee, so plan for that. While you can still park for free out along the highway, that is likely to end soon with postings of "no parking" by the county."

Trip Log

Date: _____ Notes: _____

_____

_____

_____

_____

About This Segment

Unlike the previous sunny, dry segment, this segment crosses several streams in a dense, cool forest and provides many potential campsites, including the Forest Service's Buffalo Campground, for those wanting a taste of civilization. (Meadows Group Campground is available through reservation only.) You will pass through the heavily used Buffalo Creek Recreation Area in this segment, which has some restrictions placed on its use.

The original trail just west of Tramway Creek was obliterated years ago by logging activity but has since been rebuilt by the Forest Service. The new tread winds above the logged area, at times just skirting it and providing views to the north.

A small trailhead parking area is provided at this segment's end where the CT crosses FS-560. Mountain bicyclists continuing west of this segment should note that they need to exit this described route at the crossing of FS-543 to detour around Lost Creek Wilderness (refer to the Mountain Bicycle Detour in the Segment 4 description).

Additional Trail Information: The area through which the CT passes west of Rd-126 is a mountain bicyclist's paradise. Recognizing this, the Forest Service has provided these users with many marked routes. Several of these mountain bicycle routes use portions of the CT as part of their links or loops. Therefore, hikers, equestrians and animal packers should be aware in advance to expect heavier than normal mountain bicycle traffic in this segment, especially on weekends. In addition, so as to not wander onto one of the many side trails, keep alert and verify your position from time to time to stay on the CT route.

Trailhead/Access Points

Colorado Trailhead on FS-550: Travel approximately 32 miles west from Denver on US 285 to Pine Junction. Go left (south) on Pine Valley Road (Jefferson County Road 126) and follow the signs to Pine and Buffalo Creek. Continue from Buffalo Creek south on Jefferson Co Rd-126 approximately 4.3 miles and go right (west) on FS-550. Drive barely 0.1 mile to the trailhead parking area on the north side of the road. The trail grazes the cul-de-sac turnaround at the end of the trailhead. There is now a $4.00 per day fee charged for parking at this popular trailhead, due to heavy maintenance requirements and the need to provide patrols against vandalism.

Buffalo Trailhead on FS-550: There is a mid-point trail access point at Buffalo Trailhead near Meadows Group Campground. To access, continue west on FS-550 approximately 5 miles. The trail crosses through the campground just up from the trailhead parking area. You can use the trailhead, but Meadows Group Campground is available only by reservation.

FS-543 Trailhead: See Segment 4.

Supplies, Services and Accommodations

Available at Buffalo Creek, see Segment 2; and at Bailey, see Segment 4.

Maps and Jurisdiction

USFS map: Pike National Forest, see pages 62-63.
USGS Quadrangle maps: Deckers, Green Mountain, Windy Peak.
Trails Illustrated maps: # 105 and 135.

Jurisdiction: South Platte Ranger District, Pike NF.

Trail Description

From the trailhead, follow the trail west, and then south, as it curves around an impressive and massive granite outcrop to the crossing of FS-550 at **mile 0.6** (7840). Beyond FS-550, the trail traverses through ponderosa and Douglas fir forests to **mile 1.7** (7800), where it assumes a more southerly bearing into the canyon of Morrison Creek. The Shinglemill bicycle path descends at right here. Pass under a huge mass of granite blocks on the steeply descending north ridge of Little Scraggy Peak and continue to **mile 2.8** (7760), where the trail seems to end at a jeep road. Bear to the right on the road, cross over the creek, and in a few steps leave the road as the trail resumes at left and ascends 0.2 mile to the crest of the ridge. An old ridge road, which is reverting to nature at its own deliberate pace, crosses the trail at right angles here. Before continuing, study the massive granite outcroppings across the valley to the east. Can you identify the peculiar formation that has been unofficially named "Cantilever Rock" from its descriptive shape?

Descend from the ridge and cross a small tributary of Morrison Creek on an earthen bridge. Head up the west side of this tributary to **mile 3.7** (7960), where a sharp right will take you out of this particular gulch and into a gentle traverse in and out of several other side gullies. The CT joins and descends an old road beginning at **mile 4.5** (8000) and crosses Tramway Creek 0.5 mile further on.

On the north side of a clearing at **mile 5.4** (7680), the CT picks up again at a sharp left as the old road continues a descent ahead as the Tramway bicycle path. The trail then traverses to **mile 5.9** (7600), where it forks; the left fork is the Green Mountain bicycle path, and the right fork keeps you on the CT. From the fork, the trail continues a general traverse with periodic descents as it winds in and out of small gullies forested with ponderosa pine and Douglas fir. In about 0.5 mile, a short side trail descends at right through a shallow gully to Buffalo Campground. An expansive logged-over area is visible below from time to time. The trail descends and crosses an old log road at **mile 7.7** (7560). This road continues to the west as the other connecting end of the Green Mountain bicycle path. From the old log road crossing, continue 0.2 mile to a stream crossing and a gentle rise to Meadows Group Campground. The Buffalo Trailhead parking area is just down the road.

The CT, Buffalo Creek and FS-543 converge at **mile 8.2** (7400). The trail ascends steeply at times 0.7 mile west of FS-543 to a broad, rounded ridge. The Castle's granite bulwark is visible to the south through a ponderosa forest. On the ascent, be careful not to prick yourself on the nearby yuccas, plants whose leaves were once woven into moccasins by the Indians and whose roots were pounded into soap.

The trail crosses the Buffalo Creek Gun Club Road at **mile 9.7** (7920), then continues generally west on a gentle ascent. Descend into a small gully at **mile 11.8** (8160), where you may notice the crossing with an old forgotten road. The trail then ascends a bit and drops down to the crossing of FS-560. A parking area is provided here at the end of this segment at **mile 12.1** (8280).

Mountain Biking Etiquette on the CT

With close proximity to the major metropolitan areas of Denver and Colorado Springs, CT Segments 1, 2, & 3 are heavily used, not just by hikers but also by equestrians and mountain bicylists, leading to potential conflicts among users. Cyclists in particular have been singled out for criticism by some for the impact they have on trails and on other users. The International Mountain Bicycling Association (IMBA) offers these etiquette guidelines for cyclists when using public trails like the CT:

Encountering Hikers: Hikers have the right-of-way, so slow down, stop or pull aside. When approaching from the rear, slow down and let them know you are there.

Encountering Equestrians: Never assume the equestrian is aware of your presence or in control of the horse. If approaching from the front, always stop and let them pass. If coming from behind, slow to their speed and ask permission to pass slowly or walk your bike around.

Ride Softly: Don't degrade the trail by your ride. Avoid riding on wet days or when the trail is fragile. Carry your bike around all soft spots and walk around puddles to avoid any widening of them.

Slow Down: Excessive speed is the single most common complaint from others. Be prepared to stop when going around corners. Don't skid or "brake slide."

Stay on Existing Trails: Never take shortcuts on tight turns or switchbacks. Stay on established trails and respect trail closures.

The Forest Service has designated a network of cycling trails on and around Segment 3 of the CT.

For more information on biking in the Pike National Forest, contact the South Platte Ranger District. For information on IMBA, visit their website at www.imba.com/ or phone (303) 545-9011.

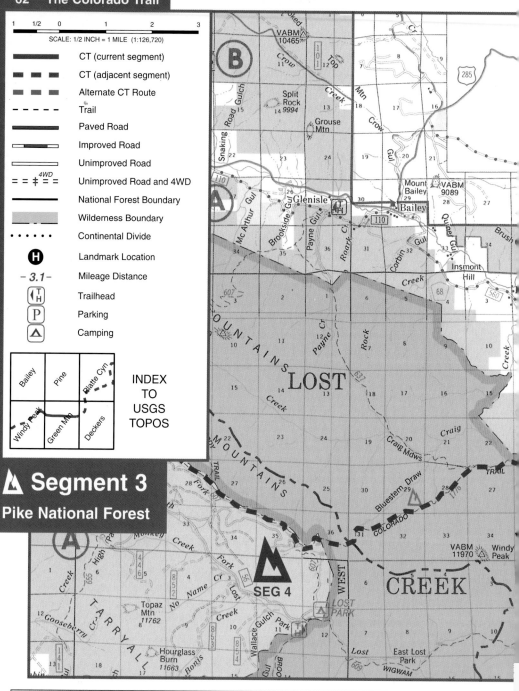

Legend

	CT (current segment)
	CT (adjacent segment)
	Alternate CT Route
	Trail
	Paved Road
	Improved Road
	Unimproved Road
	Unimproved Road and 4WD
	National Forest Boundary
	Wilderness Boundary
	Continental Divide
H	Landmark Location
– 3.1 –	Mileage Distance
TH	Trailhead
P	Parking
△	Camping

SCALE: 1/2 INCH = 1 MILE (1:126,720)

INDEX TO USGS TOPOS

Bailey | Pine | Platte Cyn
Windy Peak | Green Mtn | Deckers

Segment 3
Pike National Forest

Landmark Location	Mileage	From Denver	Elevation	Latitude	Longitude
A Colorado Trailhead	0.0	26.2	7840	39.345191	-105.257273
B FS-550	0.6	26.8	7840	39.342642	-105.265029
C FS-543	8.2	34.4	7400	39.339912	-105.340854
D FS-560	12.1	38.3	8280	39.338414	-105.400605

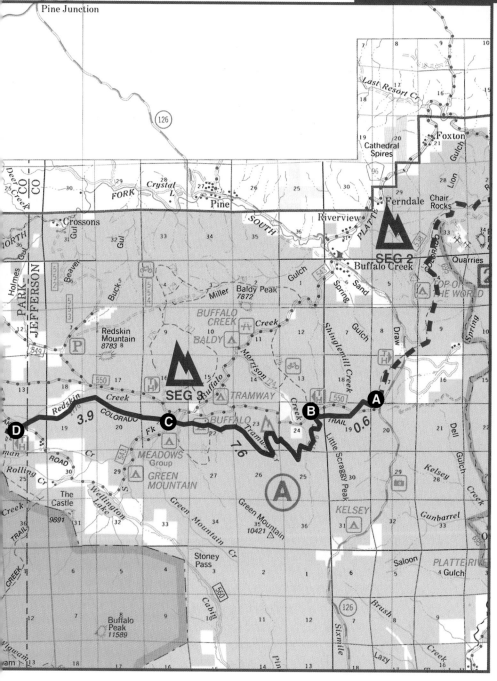

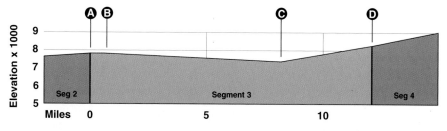

Segment 4
FS-560 (Wellington Lake Road) to Long Gulch

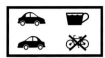

Deer jaw found in Lost Creek Wilderness.

Distance: 16.2 miles
Elevation Gain: approx 2840 ft

Gudy's Tip

"Segments 1 through 3, and then again in Segment 5, see heavy use by day-hikers and cyclists. You'll find peace and solitude in the Lost Creek Wilderness."

Trip Log

Date: _____ Notes: _____

_____

_____

_____

_____

About This Segment

If traveling westbound, you will gain a lot of elevation in this segment as you climb to the rounded ridges of the Kenosha Mountains. The exposed Precambrian crest of this range is largely hidden from view by thick lodgepole and aspen forests until you travel further west. Backpackers will find several reliable sources of water, but heavy cattle grazing may taint the supply.

Mountain cyclists are once again reminded that they must detour around the Lost Creek Wilderness, through which this segment passes (see the Mountain Bicycle Detour).

Most of this segment of the CT follows an old logging road that was built between 1885 and 1887 by W. H. Hooper for $1700. The cost was higher than expected because of several marshy stretches that needed corduroy treatment. Hooper also ran a sawmill operation in Lost Park that was eventually shut down by the Department of Interior for persistent illegalities.

Trailhead/Access Points

FS-560 Rolling Creek Trailhead: Travel west from Denver on US-285 about 39 miles to Bailey. Go left on Park Co Rd-68, which eventually ties into FS-560 (Wellington Lake Road). Continue approximately 8 miles from Bailey to where the CT crosses the road at the beginning of this segment. A small parking area is provided here.

North Fork Trailhead: This secluded wilderness portal is extremely primitive with absolutely no services, but it does provide the only direct mid-point access to the trail in this segment. Travel west from Denver on US-285 approximately 58 miles to Kenosha Pass. Continue on the highway another 3.2 miles to the turnoff marked Lost Park Road (FS-56). Turn east (left) onto the dirt road and drive 16.6 miles to FS-134. Go left on FS-134, which is a rough old log road suitable only for high-clearance vehicles. Go right at mile 1.3 and left at mile 1.5, and continue a total of 3.8 miles from the Lost Park Road to the CT in the isolated North Fork valley; this is mile 8.8 on the trail as described below.

Lost Park Campground & Trailhead: To avoid the rough drive in to the North Fork Trailhead, you can use an approach on the Brookside-McCurdy Trail from Lost Park Campground and Trailhead, an isolated but popular wilderness portal. Using the travel directions above to Lost Park Road (FS-56), follow the road 20.4 miles to its end at the campground and trailhead. From the north side of the campground, take the Brookside-McCurdy Trail north then west 1.7 miles to its intersection with the CT at the North Fork Trailhead mentioned above.

Longs Gulch Trail Access: See Segment 5.

Maps and Jurisdiction

USFS map: Pike National Forest, see pages 70-71.
USGS Quadrangle maps: Windy Peak, Topaz Mountain.
Trails Illustrated map: # 105.

Jurisdiction: South Park and South Platte Ranger Districts, Pike NF.

The town of **Bailey**, located on busy US-285 approximately 8 miles west of the Rolling Creek Trailhead using FS-560 and Park Co Rd-68, has a small business center supported by dispersed mountain residences west of Denver.

Bailey Services

Distance From CT:	
	8 miles
Elevation:	7,750
Zip Code:	80421
Area Code:	303

Supplies, Services and Accommodations

Dining	Crow's Foot	60629 Hwy 285	(303) 838-5298
	Mountain View Cafe	157 Main	(303) 838-9545
Gear	Knotty Pine	60641 Hwy 285	(303) 838-5679
Groceries	Bailey Country Store	149 Main	(303) 838-2505
Info	Chamber of Commerce	PO Box 476	
Laundry	Bailey Laundromat	Hwy 285	(303) 838-2768
Lodging	Glen Isle Resort	Hwy 285	(303) 838-5461
	Moredale Lodge	Hwy 285	(303) 838-5918
Medical	Crow Medical Center	Hwy 285	(303) 838-7653
Post Office	Bailey Post Office	24 River Rd	(303) 838-4181

Trail Description

Trail register near Lost Park.

From the Rolling Creek Trailhead parking area on FS-560, the CT ascends a Forest Service road to **mile 0.3** (8360), where a gate closes the road to vehicles. At this point, Rolling Creek Trail bends to the left and the CT leaves the road and continues to the right. Observe the wilderness regulation sign here. At **mile 0.9** (8560) the CT joins up with the old road built by Mr. Hooper and begins a steady ascent bearing generally southwest. Pass through a gate a half-mile further on and enter Lost Creek Wilderness at **mile 1.8** (9100). The wilderness boundary is marked by an inconspicuous little metal sign. In a few places it is possible to get a glimpse through the trees of Mount Evans to the north. Otherwise, because of the thick stand of lodgepole pines blanketing the area, the only vista along here is of nearby Windy Peak when it aligns itself with the swath cut for the old Hooper Road. Continue at left on the more prominent Hooper Trail where there is a fork at mile 2.3. At **mile 3.1** (9320) the Payne Creek Trail descends at right. The CT continues its ascent southwest on the old

Panorama of Lost Park.

Hooper Trail alternately passing through lodgepole and aspen forests, and crosses a small stream at **mile 4.5** (9360).

Look for the CT to detour to the left off of the old road at **mile 5.4** (9840) to avoid the marshy areas that caused Hooper to exceed his budget. The CT rejoins the Hooper Road two miles further on, well above the soggy stretch, at a 10,480-foot forested ridge. From the ridge, descend to the broad, elongated meadow of the North Fork of Lost Creek 1.1 mile beyond and exit the wilderness area. Intersect the Brookside-McCurdy Trail at the North Fork Trailhead at **mile 8.8** (10,200). If you follow the Brookside-McCurdy Trail south, it will take you in 1.7 miles to the Lost Park Campground. From this trail intersection, look for the ruins of an old sawmill to the south across the creek. Could this be the remains of Mr. Hooper's busted operation?

From this trail intersection, the CT begins a slow ascent northwest, paralleling the north side of the North Fork's broad grassy valley. A contingent of curious cattle will most likely be observing your progress. In a few places, the nearby craggy metamorphic ridge of the Kenosha Mountains comes into view.

Top the saddle at the head of the North Fork at **mile 14.2** (10,880). Here, the more obvious CT bears slightly to the left as it leaves the old Hooper Trail, which becomes faint and eroded as it descends steeply following the drainage. The CT contours west beyond the North Fork saddle for 0.2 mile where it takes a sudden turn to the south. The view west from the outcrops at this point would be a memorable location for long-distance westbound trekkers. Here, visible for the first time, is the Continental Divide to the west. The trail loses elevation quickly as it switchbacks down to a stream crossing in an area of washed-out beaver ponds at the end of this segment at **mile 16.2** (10,160). Two short spur trails on either side of the stream lead down to the popular parking area and trail access point at the end of FS-817, a short side road on the Lost Park Road in Long Gulch.

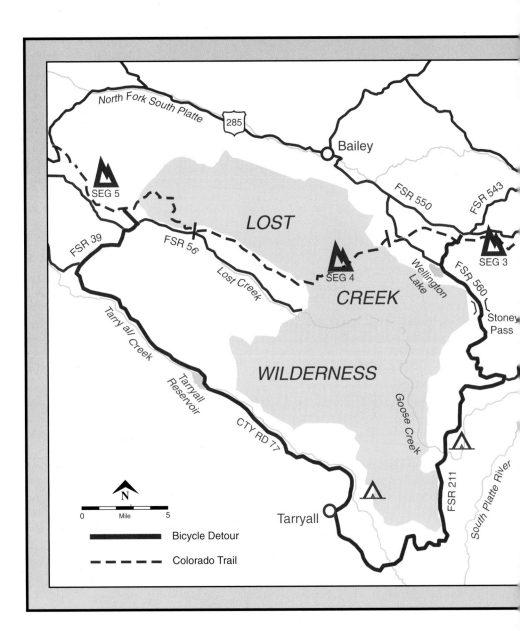

Lost Creek Wilderness Detour — *Segments 3, 4 and 5* *(Pike National Forest):* This long detour follows Forest Service and county roads around the southern perimeter of Lost Creek Wilderness. It passes several campgrounds and provides vistas of the Tarryall Mountains and the Rampart Range south to Pikes Peak. You will pass through the old mining town of Tarryall, which started life in 1896 as Puma City. The story goes that an unsociable miner, known only as Rocky Mountain Jim, grew tired of the non-stop activity in Cripple Creek and moved to the picturesque valley, where he discovered the first lode in the area. Unfortunately for Jim, many others quickly followed until the town had a population of a thousand. A more direct, but correspondingly more dangerous detour (not described here) follows FS-550 and FS-543 to Bailey and then busy, narrow, winding US-285 to the summit of Kenosha Pass.

Detour Description: Begin this detour about midway through Segment 3 where the CT crosses FS-543 at **mile 8.2** (7400). Continue west and south up FS-543 for 2.7 miles to Wellington Lake. Go left here onto FS-560 and top out 2.4 miles later at Stoney Pass (8560). Then proceed along the Forest Service road another 7 miles, passing a side road that leads to the Flying G Ranch. Go right onto FS-211 at **mile 13.6** (7470), and then go right again in another 5.4 miles, following the signs to Goose Creek Campground. Continue to **mile 35.8** (8220) and go right on paved Park Co Rd-77. Continue through Tarryall and pass the entrance to Spruce Grove Campground a few miles beyond. Pass beyond Tarryall Reservoir to **mile 63.0** (9220) and go right onto Park Co Rd-39 (FS-39), marked also as Rock Creek Hills Road. Continue north and go right (east) onto Lost Park Road (FS-56) at **mile 68.6** (9560). Pedal to **mile 70.7** (9410) and go left onto FS-133 at the sign pointing out "Colorado Trail, Rock Creek Trailhead." Regain the official CT at **mile 72.0** (9720), where it crosses the road. In the description of Segment 5, this point is mile 7.7 (9720).

Landmark Location	Mileage	From Denver	Elevation	Latitude	Longitude
Ⓐ FS-560	0.0	38.3	8280	39.338414	-105.400605
Ⓑ Lost Creek Wilderness border	1.8	40.1	9100	39.332608	-105.421574
Ⓒ Kenosha ridge	7.3	45.6	10480	39.305294	-105.491883
Ⓓ North Fork Trailhead	8.8	47.1	10200	39.306693	-105.514500
Ⓔ North Fork saddle	14.2	52.5	10880	39.346970	-105.598055
Ⓕ Long Gulch trail access	16.2	54.5	10160	39.348420	-105.615909

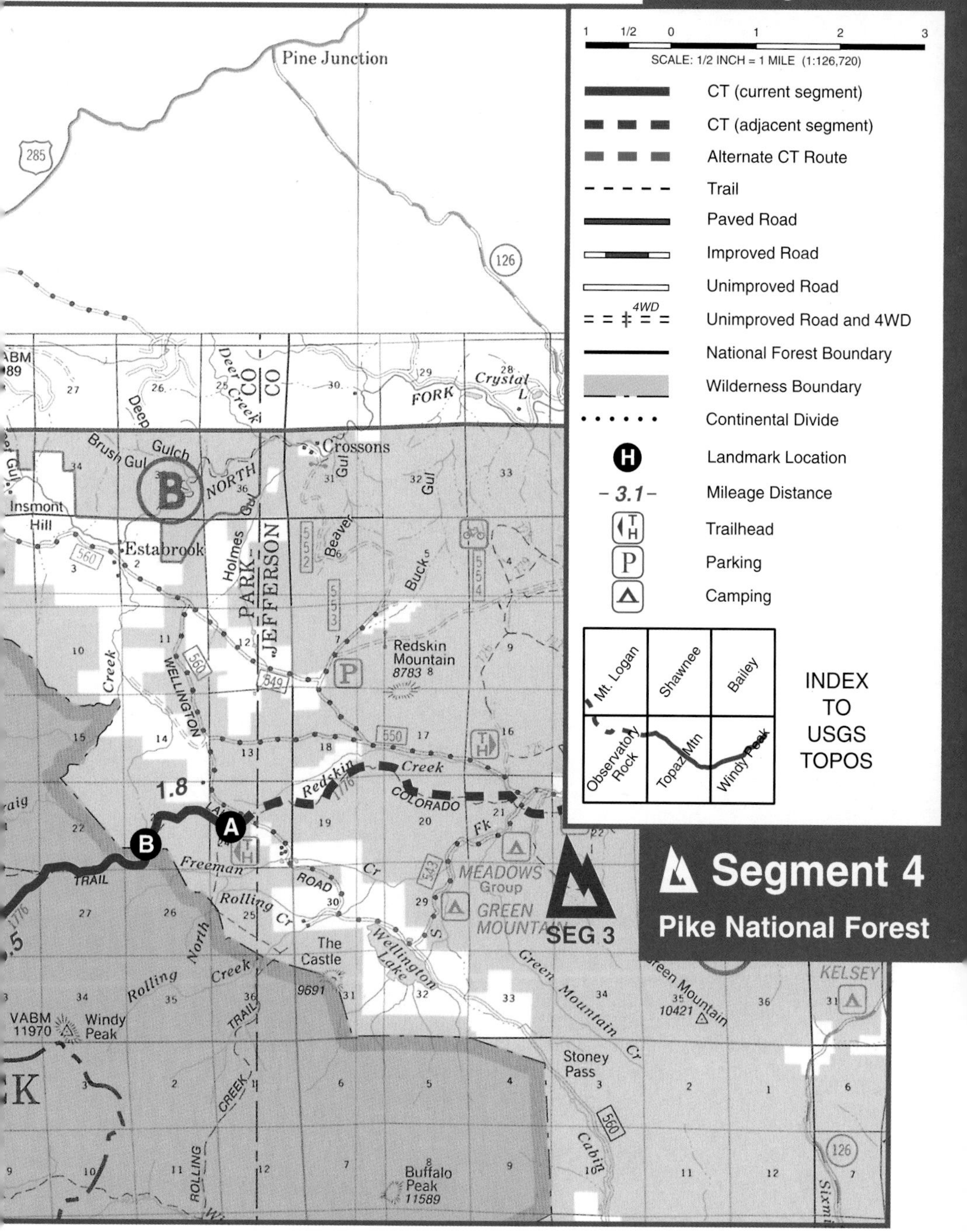

SCALE: 1/2 INCH = 1 MILE (1:126,720)

CT (current segment)	
CT (adjacent segment)	
Alternate CT Route	
Trail	
Paved Road	
Improved Road	
Unimproved Road	
Unimproved Road and 4WD	
National Forest Boundary	
Wilderness Boundary	
Continental Divide	
Landmark Location	
Mileage Distance	– 3.1 –
Trailhead	
Parking	
Camping	

INDEX
TO
USGS
TOPOS

Mt. Logan	Shawnee	Bailey
Observation Rock	Topaz Mtn	Windy Peak

Segment 4
Pike National Forest

SEG 3

Pine Junction

285

126

Crossons

Estabrook

Redskin Mountain 8783

Windy Peak
VABM 11970

The Castle 9691

MEADOWS Group

GREEN MOUNTAIN

Stoney Pass

Buffalo Peak 11589

KELSEY

Green Mountain 10421

Elevation x 1000

| 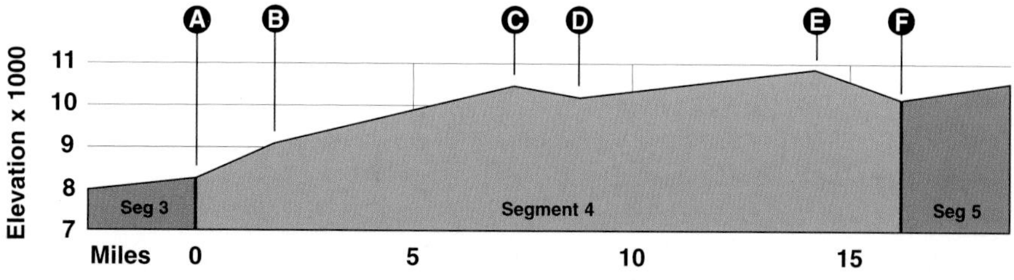 A | B | C | D | E | F |

Seg 3   Segment 4   Seg 5

Miles   0   5   10   15

Segment 5
Long Gulch to Kenosha Pass

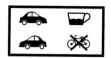

Panorama of South Park from Kenosha Pass.

Distance: 14 miles
Elevation Gain: approx 1540 ft

Gudy's Tip

"*Between Black Canyon and Kenosha Pass, stop to take in the incredible vistas of South Park and the mountainous backdrop.*"

Trip Log

Date: _____   Notes: _____

_____

_____

_____

_____

About This Segment

Grazing cattle will most likely accompany you in this segment, especially during those few times water is available in trickles at both Rock Creek and Johnson Gulch. Water can be pumped during the summer from a well located in Kenosha Campground at the end of this segment.

A popular day hike starts at the Kenosha Pass Trailhead and travels east to one of the many observation points where panoramas reveal nearby South Park and the Mosquito Range as a dramatic backdrop. This easy outing is especially rewarding in autumn when the extensive aspen forests light up the cool days with an energetic golden brilliance. Kenosha Pass is a broad open meadow, and the Denver, South Park and Pacific RR took advantage of the expanse to build a switchyard. The trailhead contains an interesting railroad interpretive display of the tracks and switchyard which were removed in the 1930s.

This segment is also popular with mountain bicyclists, up until the Rock Creek to Black Canyon stretch, which is within the Lost Creek Wilderness.

Trailhead/Access Points

Long Gulch Trail Access: Travel west from Denver on US-285 approximately 58 miles to Kenosha Pass. Continue on US-285 another 3.2 miles to the turnoff marked "Lost Park Road" (FS-56). Turn left (east) onto the dirt road and travel 11.8 miles to an inconspicuous side road which branches left and is only about 0.2 mile long. This short side road has been marked in the past as FS-817. Park your car at the end of this short road and hike up either of two connecting side trails which lead in a few hundred feet to the intersecting CT.

FS-133 Rock Creek Trailhead: This trailhead is on a rough, but not necessarily 4WD road, with large water bumps. From the travel directions above, go approximately 7.5 miles on Lost Park Road (FS-56) east from US-285 and then turn left onto FS-133, which is marked "Colorado Trail, Rock Creek." Continue up the rough road 1.3 miles to the point where the CT crosses it. The small and informal Rock Creek Trailhead here provides limited parking.

Kenosha Pass Trailhead: See Segment 6.

Supplies, Services and Accommodations

The town of **Jefferson** is approximately 4.5 miles southwest from Kenosha Pass on US-285. The Jefferson Market (719) 836-2389, a delightful old general store, provides basics and has a very small post office within (719 836-2238.)

Maps and Jurisdiction

USFS map: Pike National Forest, see pages 76-77.
USGS Quad. maps: Topaz Mountain, Observatory Rock, Mount Logan, Jefferson.
Trails Illustrated map: # 105.

Jurisdiction: South Platte and South Park Ranger Districts, Pike NF.

Trail Description

From either one of the two short access trails from the short side road off of the Lost Park Road in Long Gulch, the CT continues west, and enters Lost Creek Wilderness. Ascend to a densely forested saddle at **mile 2.1** (10,520), then descend slightly into upper Black Canyon and cross a seasonally flowing trickle, a tributary of Rock Creek. The trail descends on the north side of the canyon, winding in and out of several side drainages with intermittent flows. Cross Rock Creek at **mile 7.1** (9520), just downstream from the Rock Creek Cow Camp. Here the trail vanishes momentarily in thick, shrubby cinquefoil which may conceal the wooden-timber creek crossing.

On the west side of Rock Creek, follow the old road 0.1 mile downstream (southeast) and be alert for the trail, which veers to the right off the road and immediately enters a spruce forest. Ascend 0.1 mile and pass through a red gate, then make a sharp right turn onto another old road. Continue an ascent 0.3 mile west-northwest on the abandoned road and look for the trail to resume at left as the road begins to level out. Cross FS-133 at the Rock Creek Trailhead at **mile 7.7** (9720), then descend through a grassy clearing to Johnson Gulch and cross the tiny seasonal flow on a wooden timber at **mile 8.2** (9520).

From the Johnson Gulch stream, follow the trail about 300 feet west then south-southwest as it ascends to the lower portion of a grassy rise. The trail here barely grazes the edge of an old jeep road at left, the former trail route, which heads northwest up a shallow, dry tributary gully to Johnson Gulch. From this point, a new section of trail bears right (north-northwest to northwest) and ascends to the rounded ridge line just north of the gully bottom. Follow this new trail section as it slowly climbs northwest in an intermittent forest of aspen and bristlecone. This new route is an improvement from the original because of the ever-expanding views as you gain elevation, and for the shade the trees provide. The trail ascends to a lofty panorama point at **mile 10.0** (10,000), where South Park and the Continental Divide are visible to the west, and the Kenosha Mountains and Black Canyon to the east.

After descending through a forest of aspen, bristlecone and spruce, the trail abruptly opens into another grassy expanse at **mile 10.5** (9960). Proceed 0.2 mile north-northwest on the footpath to the base of a grassy hill. The CT ascends the southwest side of the hill, passing through stands of aspen and stately bristlecone, to **mile 11.0** (10,200), where it makes a left turn onto an old jeep road. Bear generally north to mount a broad forested ridge, and then begin a traverse generally north-northwest at about the 10,400-foot level.

Descend to a short double span over an old defunct irrigation channel at **mile 12.4** (10,240). Resume your descent in an aspen forest that shimmers with a golden glow in autumn. Go left where the trail adopts another old road at **mile 13.5** (10,080) and continue to the Kenosha Pass Trailhead on the east side of US-285 at **mile 14.0** (10,000). If you have the time and interest, take in the railroad interpretive display. To continue into Segment 6, go approximately 0.3 miles on the Forest Service road and carefully cross the busy highway, and proceed into Kenosha Pass Campground. Signs within the campground will direct you to the trail.

Lost Creek Wilderness

The name "Lost Creek" conjures up an image of an enigmatic place. And indeed, this 119,790-acre designated wilderness has a fascinating history of lost gold, vanished dreams, and hidden places.

Lost Creek begins in the open meadows of Lost Park, sandwiched between the granite knobs of the Kenosha and Tarryall Mountains. Lost Park was the scene of the last native bison killed in Colorado in 1897. From here the creek descends into a deeply etched canyon, vanishing among tumbled boulders and through underground tunnels, and reappearing nine times. The "lost" stream eventually re-emerges for good as Goose Creek at the southeast end of the wilderness.

Over a century ago, the notorious Reynolds gang terrorized nearby South Park, holding up stagecoaches and lone riders for their gold. The stories vary, but some say that the gang stashed their lost cache in Handcart Gulch, north of Kenosha Pass, while others claim it is hidden among the strange granite outcrops that dot the hills above Lost Park, a frequent hideout for the gang.

Dreamers often vanished into the recesses of Lost Creek looking for riches. Both the Lost Jackman Mine and the Indian Mine were supposed to be fabulously rich in gold; but if they ever existed at all, they are lost forever to time.

Perhaps the most ambitious scheme was an early 20th-century

Boundary sign, Lost Creek Wilderness.

attempt to build an unusual subterranean dam on Goose Creek that would have flooded a major valley to meet the water needs of Denver.

Fortunately this effort failed, and Denver citizens have benefited more by having this magnificent wilderness preserved at their doorstep. Lost Creek Wilderness was established in 1980. Despite heavy use by recreationalists, there are still some unexplored corners and hidden places in the Lost Creek. In the early 1990s, prolific peakbagger Bob Martin frequently visited the area in his quest to climb every peak in Colorado over 11,000 feet. He discovered half-a-dozen remote "eleveners" tucked away in the wilderness area without signs of a previous ascent. He reports that most were difficult scrambles, some requiring the assistance of a rope.

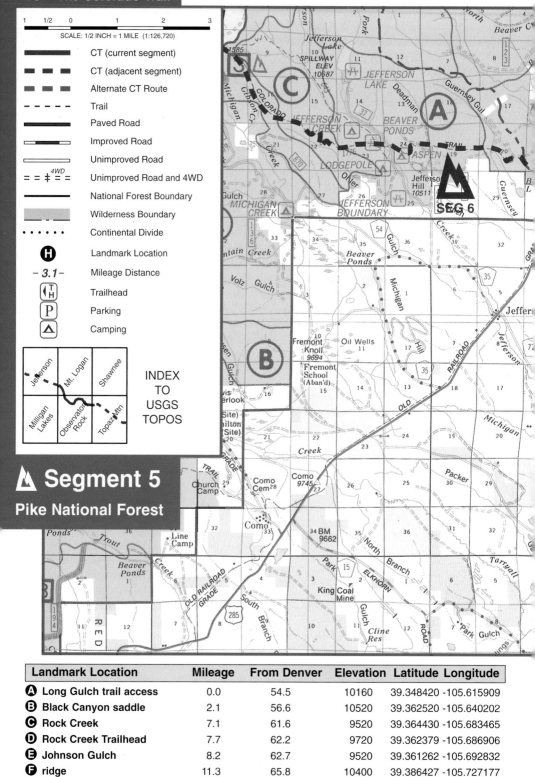

Segment 5
Pike National Forest

Landmark Location	Mileage	From Denver	Elevation	Latitude	Longitude
Ⓐ Long Gulch trail access	0.0	54.5	10160	39.348420	-105.615909
Ⓑ Black Canyon saddle	2.1	56.6	10520	39.362520	-105.640202
Ⓒ Rock Creek	7.1	61.6	9520	39.364430	-105.683465
Ⓓ Rock Creek Trailhead	7.7	62.2	9720	39.362379	-105.686906
Ⓔ Johnson Gulch	8.2	62.7	9520	39.361262	-105.692832
Ⓕ ridge	11.3	65.8	10400	39.386427	-105.727177
Ⓖ Kenosha Pass Trailhead	14.0	68.5	10000	39.412497	-105.757668

Callahan
GENEVA CREEK
Roberts Tunnel Portal
Grant
River
Webster
Platte
Gulch
Best
Santa Maria
Singleton
Smith
Boxwood Gul
Mount Blaine 12303
North Twin Cone Peak
VABM 12319
Shutetown
Foster Gulch
Gulch
Tyler
Ben
RD
RD
PLATTE
South Twin Cone Peak 12323
RIVER
Kenosha Pass
Kenosha
Cr
SOUTH
SOUTH
PLATTE
PARK
Historical Monument
COLORADO
Creek
Rock
CRAIG
Craig
PARK
TRAIL
KENOSHA
SEG 5
Clark Spring
Gulch
Snyder
Johnson
TRAIL
Black
Canyon
Wilson
Bed Spr
Lone Chimney Spr
Long
LOST
PARK
Gulch
ROAD
SEG 4
North
Coleman Spr
Robbins Spring
Willow Spring
Dunlap
Dixon Spring
Monahan
Porcupine Spring
Lee
Gulch
Gulch
Mud Spr
Mud Gulch
Creek
Ratcliff
Little
Ratcliff
Bear
Gulch
North Tarryall Peak
Beaver
Cr
High
Park
Gul
Mud Hill
Rock
Rob VABM 9193
Gul
Gulch
Rees Spr
Rees Gul
Hall
Graveyard
House
Gooseberry
Cr
Creek
Tarryall
TARRY
2.7
3.1
0.6
0.5
5.0
2.1

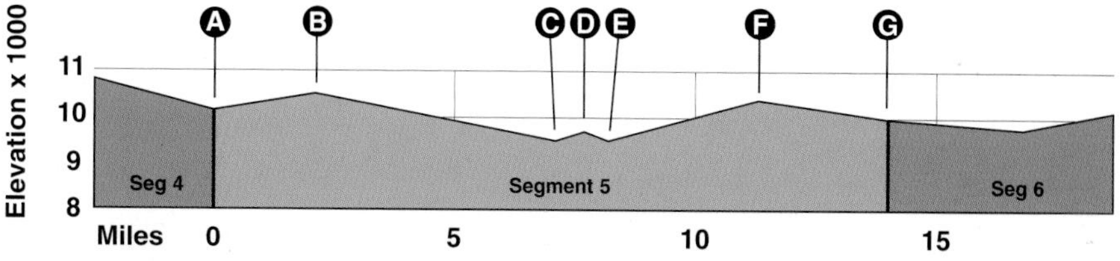
A
B
C
D
E
F
G
Elevation x 1000
11
10
9
8
Seg 4
Segment 5
Seg 6
Miles
0
5
10
15

Segment 6
Kenosha Pass to Goldhill Trailhead

Distance: 32 miles
Elevation Gain: approx 4520 ft

Sunrise on Georgia Pass.

Gudy's Tip

"If you decide to take the old, shorter CT route down the Swan River Road be forewarned that it is very dusty and unpleasant for hiking. The new official CT route is a much more enjoyable experience."

Trip Log

Date: _____ Notes: _____

_____

_____

_____

_____

About This Segment

Kenosha Pass had long served as an Indian trail into the fertile hunting grounds of South Park and was crossed by Anglo parties as early as 1830. In the mid-1840s Colonel John C. Fremont crossed the pass, and when miners began streaming into the Blue River drainage, they paralleled the old Indian trail and then veered west over Georgia Pass, approximating the route of today's CT.

In 1860, a 25-year charter was given by the Kansas Territorial Legislature to John McIntyre, Major Bradford and Judge Steke to build and maintain a toll road from Denver to California Gulch (future Leadville) using, in part, the Kenosha Pass route. The following year, a stage line began operating over the road. It was Clark Herbert, a driver for the line, who named the pass after his hometown of Kenosha, Wisconsin. Twenty years later, Governor Evans built his DSP&P Railroad over the pass. The DSP&P chugged to Breckenridge and, eventually, Gunnison.

At the same time the California Gulch stage line was being built, a group of southern miners were working Georgia Gulch west of the divide and defending their claims as others poured over Georgia Pass. The energetic town of Parkville developed at the mouth of the gulch, but mining activity was so great that by the 1880s the town had been inundated by the tailings of its own prosperity.

A more drastic means of recovering the gold was introduced in the early 1900s by Ben Stanley Revett. His efficient but destructive dredge boats did recover well-hidden gold deep within the valley bottoms, but at the same time they created enormous piles of rock which still run parallel with the Swan and Blue Rivers.

Mount Guyot (13,370 feet) is a prominent landmark in this segment and was named in honor of Princeton geography professor Arnold Guyot, who was grateful for having his name attached to a peak just a few miles south, and on the same connecting ridge, of the two fourteeners named for his well-known colleagues, John Torrey and Asa Grey. Interestingly, a "guyot" is also a geologic term denoting an underwater volcano. Colorado's Mount Guyot is neither submerged nor a volcano, but an igneous intrusion somewhere in the neighborhood of 40 to 72 million years of age, much younger than the granite knobs and metamorphic rocks of the Rampart Range and the Kenosha Mountains.

Additional Trail Information: The CT has its first crossing of the Continental Divide in this segment. You will top out about 0.5 mile east of, and 300 feet higher than, historic Georgia Pass. Water and basic Forest Service facilities are available during the summer at the campgrounds at Kenosha Pass and Jefferson Lake Road. Beyond Jefferson Lake Road and Jefferson Creek, there is no reliable water supply until the trail drops down into the headwaters of the Swan River on the west side of Georgia Pass. Camping within Jefferson Creek Recreation Area is restricted to established campgrounds only. For day hikers in this recreation area, the West Jefferson Trail provides a loop back from the CT near Georgia Pass to the valley.

The Swan River drainage, in the second half of the segment, is the site of past and present private enterprises. Many of the mining operations here are still active and a patchwork of private property exists throughout the national forest property, so please behave accordingly.

Beginning in 1988, volunteers worked on a new trail that bypassed the original CT route which followed forest service and county roads from the top of Georgia Pass at Glacier Ridge Road to Colorado Hwy-9. By summer of 2001 this new trail was finally complete from the Glacier Ridge Road to Hwy-9 near the end of this segment. The new official CT trail route, although considerably more aesthetic than the road, is significantly longer and drier than the pre-existing road route, and contains more elevation gain. If you plan a camp on the new official route in this section, you will find many flat, although waterless, sites. Conversely on the original county road route, water is always nearby in the various drainages of the Swan River, but camping in the vicinity of the road is not possible because of private property in the valley bottom.

Trailhead/Access Points

Kenosha Pass Trailhead: Travel on US-285 approximately 58 miles west from Denver to the summit of Kenosha Pass. The trail crosses the highway at Kenosha Campground, and continues through it. The Forest Service does not allow trail user parking within the campground. Parking is available at the trailhead parking area approximately 0.3 miles east of the highway on the Forest Service access road. The pass is a broad open meadow, and the Denver, South Park and Pacific RR constructed a switchyard here in the 1880s. The trailhead also contains an interesting railroad interpretive display.

Jefferson Lake Road Trail Access: From Kenosha Pass, continue on US-285 4.5 miles to Jefferson. Go right on the side road marked "Jefferson Lake Road." Drive 2.1 miles, then go right again at the sign which marks the way to Jefferson Lake. Continue 3.1 miles to where the CT crosses the road. A tenth of a mile further there is temporary parking at Beaver Ponds Picnic Ground. More permanent backpacker parking is available 0.6 mile up the road, near the entrance to Jefferson Creek Campground. The Jefferson Lake area requires a fee for auto access and campground and picnic area use.

Georgia Pass Trail Access: Using the driving directions above, from Jefferson on US-285, go right on the side road marked "Michigan Creek Road" (also marked as the Jefferson Lake Road). After 2.1 miles go straight ahead and avoid the right fork to the Jefferson Lake Recreation Area. Follow the Michigan Creek Road approximately 10 additional miles to the top of Georgia Pass. The last mile is rough and goes best with a high-clearance vehicle or 4WD vehicle. From the pass, continue 0.2 mile up the Glacier Ridge Road to the CT crossing.

Goldhill Trailhead: See Segment 7.

Maps and Jurisdiction

USFS maps: Pike and White River National Forests, see pages 84-85.
USGS Quadrangle maps: Jefferson, Boreas Pass, Keystone, Frisco.
Trails Illustrated maps: # 105, 108, and 109.

Jurisdiction: South Park Ranger District and Dillon Ranger District.

Supplies, Services and Accommodations

The town of **Jefferson** is approximately 4.5 miles southwest from Kenosha Pass on US-285. The Jefferson Market (719) 836-2389, a delightful old general store, provides basics and has a very small post office within (719 836-2238.)

Trail Description

West of US-285, the CT passes through the southern portion of Kenosha Campground. Once inside the campground, bear to the left twice, and proceed a few steps until the road passes through a gate. Notice here that the trail resumes to the right, just beyond the fence and climbs northwest through a forest of aspen and lodgepole pine. In July, the understory is thick with golden banner, paintbrush and columbine. At **mile 0.7** (10,400) the noise of US-285 disappears as the trail passes over a ridge and begins a descent through inclined meadows and aspen groves. Expansive South Park extends to the horizon, bounded to the west by the Mosquito Range, the Thirtynine Mile Mountains to the south, and the Puma Hills to the east. As you descend through the clumps of aspen trees, notice where ravenous wildlife have stripped patches of bark off the trunks.

Cross an old road at **mile 1.4** (10,280) and continue west along a minor ridge with more views of South Park. At **mile 2.3** (10,120), the trail opens into an open area of shrubby cinquefoil. The trail may be difficult to find here, but it continues west, marked by cairns that have been partially demolished by grazing cattle. Pick up a reliable trail in 0.1 mile and resume a descent in the open. Cross FS-809 at **mile 2.9** (9880) and continue ahead on the trail through a meadow of shrubby cinquefoil. Enter an aspen grove 150 feet beyond the road and then pass over Guernsey Creek, which is spanned by a huge sawn timber.

The CT exits the aspens a hundred feet beyond the creek and just north of a primitive but popular car camping spot. The trail bears west-southwest, then west in the open to **mile 3.4** (9880), where the trail begins an ascent west to west-northwest through pleasant alternating pockets of aspen and meadow. At **mile 3.8** (10,000) the trail rises to and briefly parallels an old irrigation ditch for 0.2 mile. Bear to the right off the ditch route and ascend 0.3 mile in an aspen forest to a cluster of knurled bristlecone pines where you cross FS-427. About 0.1 mile beyond cross Deadman Creek, and then continue to **mile 4.7** (10,160), where you'll go right (north-northwest) onto an old jeep road. In just 0.2 mile, as the road assumes a more westerly bearing and crosses a small stream, the trail resumes at left (south-southeast). This section of trail passes through an old logged and burned-out area that is slowly reseeding itself into a new forest. Re-enter the unharmed lodgepole forest beyond, and ascend to a saddle which extends north from Jefferson Hill at **mile 5.2** (10,200). Pass through a gate here, then descend to **mile 5.8** (10,000), where you will cross Jefferson Lake Road. Beaver Ponds Picnic Ground is only a few steps north on this road.

Continue on the CT 0.1 mile and cross Jefferson Creek on a sawn timber bridge, then begin a gradual ascent. Go right (north-northwest) on an intersecting trail at **mile 6.1** (10,000) and proceed 250 feet to where the CT resumes to the left (west). The West Jefferson Trail continues ahead here (northwest). The CT steadily gains elevation through several switchbacks that ease the ascent. At **mile 7.4** (10,400) you'll pass through an old logging area that has grown back to a mature forest, although the trail does temporarily use or cross some old grown-over log roads in the vicinity. Beyond the old logging area, the trail continues an ascent through several gentle switchbacks on the southeast side of this broad, forested ridge, an extension of the Continental Divide. At **mile 8.0** (10,680) a side trail comes in from the left and above, it is marked as a connection to the Michigan Creek Road.

At **mile 10.5** (11,400) the trail enters the krummholz zone, the interesting transition between forest and tundra. The prevailing wind pattern is immortalized in the postures of these stunted flag-trees. The trail continues into the tundra at **mile 11.1** (11,600). Here, the West Jefferson Trail takes off to the right (northeast) at a well-marked junction for a return into the valley at Jefferson Creek Campground. This side trail provides a pleasant round-trip day hike from Jefferson Creek Road. The CT continues as a sketchy tundra trail west-northwest from this junction following posts and cairns to the grassy ridge of the Continental Divide ahead.

Mount Guyot is prominent beyond the divide as a rocky cone almost due west. When you cross a jeep track in about 0.5 mile, you will be approaching a shallow saddle between two minor humps on the divide. The faint trail will align more north-northwest as you attain this shallow saddle and the crest of the Continental Divide. On the west side of the divide, continue on a rocky trail which descends north from the shallow saddle. This short, rocky trail continues 0.2 mile to the Glacier Ridge Road at **mile 11.9** (11,800).

At this point, the original and new routes of the CT diverge as mentioned in the introduction. The new trail continues north to northeast beyond the road. The original CT route descends west-southwest on the road 0.2 mile to Georgia Pass, then continues north and northwest on the 4WD road down the Swan River South Fork.

Continuing north-northeast from mile 11.9 above on the new CT route will take you across a faint section of alpine trail marked by rock cairns just below and parallel to the Glacier Ridge Road. Enter an upper limit spruce forest 0.4 mile beyond and pick up a reliable trail that bears generally north. There are outstanding views down the valley from time to time of the Tenmile and Gore Ranges. At **mile 14.8** (10,960), you will cross an old road at a right angle. Continue descending on this well-built new trail for 0.4 mile, where you will cross an old, but well-defined, trail at an angle. In another 0.5 mile, and after turning through a few switchbacks, you will pass a scummy pond to your right. Don't be tempted to get water here; the clear flowing Middle Fork is only a mile away. From the scummy pond, the trail descends to a comfortable crossing of Missouri Gulch Creek, and 150 feet north, the Swan River Middle Fork. Catch the Middle Fork Road a few steps beyond (north) at **mile 16.7** (10,160).

To continue on the trail, go right (northeast) on the road for 50 feet and look for the trail to continue at left (northwest). If you wish to continue on the new official route of the CT, skip the following description and go to the next paragraph. If, however, you wish to take the abbreviated (shorter) route to the end of this segment (particularly advised for mountain bikers), descend left (west then north, then west again) on this Swan River Road to its end at Hwy-9, approximately 8.0 miles. Carefully cross the busy highway to the paved bicycle path which parallels it and bear right (north) on the bike path. Continue approximately 0.6 mile to the end of this segment at Goldhill Trailhead parking area at the intersection of Summit Co Rd-950 and Hwy-9.

To continue on the trail beyond the Middle Fork Road, ascend to a logged ridge at **mile 17.2** (10,200), where you can survey your route from the divide to the southeast and peer down the Swan River valley to the northwest. Descend to **mile 18.9** (10,000), where you will cross the North Fork Swan River on a long section of raised turnpike trail, laboriously built to keep your feet dry in soggy areas. Please be aware that this may be your last reliable water source for the next 13 miles, if you follow the official trail route. Just before you cross the North Fork Road, the trail changes direction from generally north to west. This road crossing is your last chance to take the Swan River Road alternate route to the end of this segment (see previous paragraph above).

Continuing on the trail beyond the North Fork Road, ascend steadily to an unofficial trailhead just off the North Fork Road at **mile 19.5** (10,200). Here the trail parallels a small seasonal stream for several hundred feet, and cools the ascent on warm summer afternoons. In 0.5 mile, as the trail reorients north and continues an ascent to the ridge, it enters a sunny logged area that provides views back to Georgia Pass and Mount Guyot. At **mile 21.3** (11,040) near the upper end of another logged-over area, the trail levels out and begins a long trek to the northwest near the top of a long forested ridge between the Swan River and an elevated drainage of Keystone Gulch. Some of the ski runs and lifts of Keystone's back bowls are visible to the right (northeast). About 0.7 mile beyond, go left and ascend as the trail forks. As the trail begins a long descent in another mile go left again at a second fork. Just a few hundred feet beyond, the trail descends through a multiple series of switchbacks to a fragrant sage meadow in the dry headwaters of Muggins Gulch. At **mile 25.5** (10,000) go left (south) through the last switchback as a side trail continues north into the headwaters of Soda Creek.

For the next mile, the CT will mostly traverse near 10,000 feet on the north side of a minor summit, alternating through sunny lodgepole pine forests and sage meadows. At **mile 26.9** (9880) go right (northwest) as the trail forks in a lodgepole forest. Water may be available where the trail crosses the tiny seasonal flow in Horseshoe Gulch at **mile 28.1** (9400), but don't depend on it in dry years or near the end of summer.

Beyond Horseshoe, the trail ascends for nearly a mile to near 9800 feet, bearing generally west in forests and meadows, then begins a slow descent in a dry drainage. Shortly, busy Hwy-9 will be audible before it is visible. When you bend to the right and reorient north, the Tiger Run RV Resort will be noticeable below. A final series of switchbacks will take you down to the floodplain of the Swan River at **mile 31.3** (9200), where the trail will squeeze uncomfortably between a condominium building and a detention pond. On the south end of the pond the CT bears somewhat obscurely to the right (west) as another trail continues south around the perimeter of the condo complex. Rise briefly to a paved county road and look to the opposite side for the trail to begin again on a sturdy bridge at the edge of the wide gravel shoulder. Continue west on the trail for 0.25 mile until it drops to the level of the same paved county road which it parallels for another 0.1 mile on the gravel shoulder to a bus stop on Hwy-9. Carefully cross the busy highway and pick up the paved bicycle path on the opposite side. Go right (north) on the bicycle path 0.2 mile to **mile 32.0** (9200) where this segment ends at Goldhill Trailhead parking area at the intersection of Summit Co Rd-950 and Hwy-9.

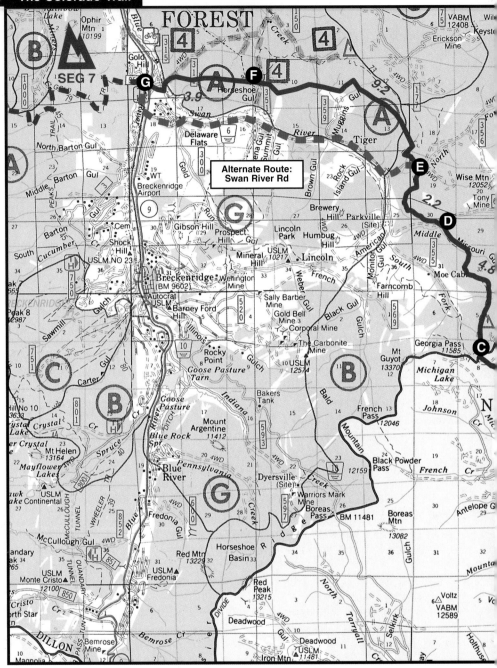

Landmark Location	Mileage	From Denver	Elevation	Latitude Longitude
Ⓐ Kenosha Pass Trailhead	0.0	68.5	10000	39.412497 -105.757668
Ⓑ Jefferson Lake Road	5.8	74.3	10000	39.429614 -105.844415
Ⓒ Glacier Ridge Road	11.9	80.4	11800	39.461113 -105.909660
Ⓓ Middle Fork Swan River	16.7	85.2	10160	39.497819 -105.925079
Ⓔ North Fork Swan River	18.9	87.4	10000	39.516570 -105.934040
Ⓕ Horseshoe Gulch	28.1	96.6	9400	39.536282 -105.998621
Ⓖ Goldhill Trailhead	32.0	100.5	9200	39.541222 -106.041571

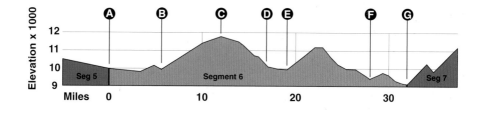

SCALE: 1/2 INCH = 1 MILE (1:126,720)

CT (current segment)
CT (adjacent segment)
Alternate CT Route
Trail
Paved Road
Improved Road
Unimproved Road
Unimproved Road and 4WD
National Forest Boundary
Wilderness Boundary
Continental Divide
H Landmark Location
– 3.1 – Mileage Distance
Trailhead
Parking
Camping

INDEX TO USGS TOPOS

| Frisco | Keystone | Montezuma |
| Breckenridge | Boreas Pass | Jefferson |

▲ **Segment 6**
White River & Pike NF

White River NF Map

Pike NF Map

SEG 5

PIKE
NATIONAL FOREST

Elevation x 1000

12
11
10
9

Seg 5   Segment 6   Seg 7

Miles   0   10   20   30

Segment 7
Goldhill Trailhead to Copper Mountain

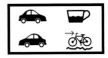

Distance: 12.5 miles
Elevation Gain: approx 3600 ft

Hikers on the CT approach the crest of the Tenmile Range.

Gudy's Tip

"The hanging glacial valley at 11,000 feet in the Tenmile Range supports a huge colony of pikas."

Trip Log

Date: _____ Notes: _____
_____
_____
_____
_____

About This Segment

This portion of the CT, which makes its way over the Tenmile Range, is steep and strenuous. The alpine section has a sketchy trail and has not been well marked in the past. The steep, alpine mountainsides here will challenge even the seasoned hiker, and inclined snowfields may linger well into July. Suitable real estate for setting up a campsite may be mostly elusive; however, the stretch along Miners Creek offers nearby water and occasional flat spots. The logging roads and clear-cuts which intercept the trail in several places along the first 2 miles make the going a little confusing, and the blue diamond markers on tree trunks in the initial portion of this segment identify cross-country ski trails and not necessarily the CT.

Mountain bicyclists may not want to attempt this section, but instead use the detour around the Tenmile Range as described in the Mountain Bicycle Detour below. Less experienced hikers may also want to consider this detour, which follows the Tenmile Bike Path to Frisco and up Tenmile Canyon to Wheeler Flats Trailhead near Copper Mountain.

The alpine tundra traversed along the crest of the Tenmile Range is exquisitely carpeted with foliage in late July and early August and provides a scenic foreground for these ancient metamorphic summits. This linear mountain range connects the southern end of the Gore Range with the northern end of the Mosquito Range. It is named for the creek on its western boundary and is known for its sequentially numbered peaks.

Trailhead/Access Points

A mid-segment trail access point on Miners Creek, reached via Frisco and Rainbow Lake (beginning on Summit Co Rd-1004), is mentioned here only in passing because it is extremely rough and rocky, even for 4WD vehicles.

Goldhill Trailhead: Travel west from Denver approximately 73 miles on I-70 and take the Frisco/Breckenridge/Colorado Hwy-9 exit. Proceed approximately 5 miles south of Frisco on Hwy-9 toward Breckenridge. Goldhill Trailhead will be on your right (west) at the intersection with Summit Co Rd-950. There is parking for several cars here. If you are coming in from the south on Hwy-9 over Hoosier Pass, continue north approximately 4 miles beyond Breckenridge. Goldhill Trailhead will be on your left (west).

Wheeler Flats Trailhead: See Segment 8.

Maps and Jurisdiction

USFS map: White River National Forest, see pages 92-93.
USGS Quadrangle maps: Frisco, Copper Mountain, Vail Pass.
Trails Illustrated maps: # 108 and 109.

Jurisdiction: Dillon Ranger District, White River NF.

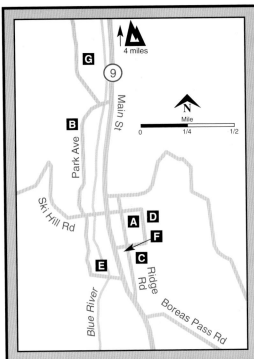

Breckenridge Services

Distance From CT:	
	4 miles
Elevation:	9,605
Zip Code:	80424
Area Code:	970

Breckenridge is approximately 4 miles south of Goldhill Trailhead on Colorado Hwy-9. Frisco has comparable services and is located approximately 5 miles northwest of the trailhead. Summit Stage provides free bus service between towns with a bus stop 100 meters south of the trailhead. Both towns are restored mining/railroad towns serving the popular Summit County resorts; so lodging and restaurants may be pricey.

Supplies, Services and Accommodations

Bus		Summit Stage		(970) 668-0999
Gear	A	Mountain Outfitters	112 S Ridge	(970) 453-2201
Groceries	B	City Market	400 N Park Ave	(970) 453-0818
Information	C	Chamber of Commerce	311 S Ridge	(970) 453-2918
Laundry	D	Village Norge	105 S French	(970) 453-2426
Lodging		Breckenridge Central Reservations		(800) 221-1091
Medical	E	Breckenridge Med. Ctr	555 S Park Ave	(970) 453-9000
Post Office	F	Breckenridge Post Office	305 S Ridge Rd	(970) 547-0347
Showers	G	Breckenridge Rec. Ctr	880 Airport Rd	(970) 453-1734

Trail Description

Begin at the convenient trailhead point just off Colorado Hwy-9. The trail starts just opposite the small, informal parking area and continues through an alternating landscape of sagebrush meadows and lodgepole forest with an understory of lupine. The trail appears to end at a confusing three-way logging road intersection at **mile 1.0** (9680), but actually it bears to the left (southwest) from this intersection. The CT steadily gains elevation in a lodgepole forest, bearing generally south to south-southwest, then takes a more westerly direction before it crosses a logging road at **mile 1.6** (9960). Continue 700 feet uphill, then bear right (north) as the trail joins another old road. Go right (north) at the intersection with another old road at **mile 1.9** (10,120). Continue 200 feet further to a clear-cut. Proceed north across the clear-cut on a short section of connector trail. In a few hundred feet, you will pick up the old road again in the forest at the opposite edge of the clear-cut. Go left (west) as the road forks again in another 250 feet. The road leads generally west and slowly takes on a more trail-like character as it ascends to a somewhat rounded, rocky summit at **mile 2.3** (10,240). A sparse lodgepole forest allows glimpses of the crest of Tenmile Peak to the west.

Descend 0.4 mile from the rocky summit and cross the last logging road. At **mile 3.2** (9920) you join up with the Peaks Trail, a popular local trail which connects Breckenridge to Frisco. Go left (south) and uphill on the Peaks Trail for 0.3 mile, then bear right (west) onto the Miners Creek Trail. The wide, rocky trail ascends to the southwest, paralleling a small tributary stream of Miners Creek for 0.6 mile, then abruptly leaves the drainage and climbs to a ridge. Traverse a steep side cut as the trail makes its way to the 4WD trail access point on Miners Creek at **mile 4.8** (10,560). Continue west from the small parking area, proceeding 200 feet to a point where you will encounter a barricade on the original trail ahead. Go right (west-northwest) here, onto a newly constructed trail, and, after a few steps, cross over Miners Creek on a bumpy corduroy bridge. The trail ascends, steeply at times, through a spruce forest, then veers southward near timberline. At **mile 5.5** (11,120), the CT breaks out momentarily into a finger of alpine tundra which reaches down from a glacial cirque on Tenmile Peak.

Ascend steeply beyond timberline to a small saddle at **mile 6.6** (11,840). From this point, a narrow, alpine footpath ascends generally south, heading for the shallow Peak 5-6 saddle ahead. Several cairns along the way on the steep mountainside confirm your route. After about a mile of this alpine section of trail, and as it climbs toward the crest of the range, the CT maneuvers steeply through several switchbacks to avoid a precipitous, rocky area ahead. Mount the Tenmile Range at **mile 7.8** (12,440) on the long, shallow saddle that connects Peaks 5 and 6. Here the sketchy trail ends, but you should follow the broad saddle south toward Peak 6, while enjoying the abundant views. Can you identify Mount of the Holy Cross far away to the west?

After a 0.5 mile walk along the saddle, the route bears slightly to the right (south-southwest) as it approaches Peak 6 and begins a steady descent on the west side of the mountain range. Pick up a faint trail as the route continues its descent on the steep mountainside. The CT bears more westerly as it approaches timberline, and becomes a better trail just inside the trees at **mile 9.6** (11,640). Continue descending for 0.4 mile to the intersection with the Wheeler Trail at **mile 10.0** (11,240). The Wheeler Trail is a trail unique to the Tenmile Range; it starts near Hoosier Pass at the south end of the range and continues to Wheeler Flats Trailhead at the end of this segment. Descend in a northerly direction on the Wheeler Trail and cross several small streams along the way. The steep terrain in this area would be a definite impediment to camping.

At the valley bottom, you will intersect an old jeep road which parallels the east side of Tenmile Creek at **mile 12.1** (9760). Continue ahead (west) and cross the creek on a historic stock bridge. On the other side, after a few steps go left (south to south-southeast) on an old jeep track. The jeep track eventually will give way to a faint trail in the forest roughly paralleling a power line. At **mile 12.5** (9800) this segment comes to an end where the trail crosses Hwy-91. There is a widened shoulder here, but long term parking is not allowed. That is available at Wheeler Flats Trailhead approximately 1.0 mile north, near the interchange of Hwy-91 and I-70.

Mountain Bicycle Detour

Tenmile Range Detour: This optional detour sidesteps all of Segment 7 and the challenging high-altitude route over the Tenmile Range by using the very convenient Tenmile Bike Path. This detour is highly recommended, partly because it avoids a long trail-less, alpine route at the range crest and the difficult, steep approaches on either side. But also it would be a shame not to take advantage of this well-planned, paved path designed especially for bicycles.

Detour Description: This optional detour begins at the Goldhill Trailhead at the start of Segment 7. Pedal north and then west on the bike path which parallels Colorado Hwy-9 to Frisco. Head south as you enter Tenmile Canyon and pedal up the bike path, following the approximate route of the DSP&PRR Tenmile Canyon line. After approximately 12 miles of pleasant pedaling, you will arrive at Wheeler Flats Trailhead near Copper Mountain. Continue south on Hwy-9 for about 1 mile to where the trail crosses Hwy-9 at the start of Segment 8.

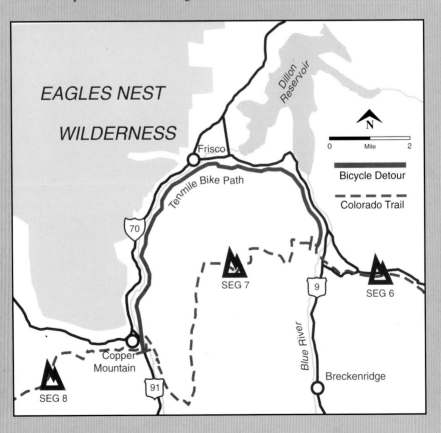

Tundra Plants

In portions of Segments 6 & 7, the CT passes into the open realm of the tundra for the first time. In Colorado, this alpine zone varies from above an altitude of 10,500 feet in the northern part of the state to more than 12,000 feet near the border with New Mexico. Above the treeline, a harsh environment exists — one where summer lasts a fleeting 30 to 40 frost-free days; and in winter, temperatures can fall to well below zero. In essence, the tundra is a cold desert offering precipitation levels of 20 inches per year or less, with moisture falling mainly as snow. How this snow is distributed by the wind dictates distribution of the hardy alpine plants.

The alpine tundra in Colorado, compared to other alpine regions in the lower 48 states, is particularly rich in numbers and species, putting on a spectacular display beginning with the first alpine forget-me-nots (*Eritrichium elongatum*) in June, until arctic gentians (*Gentiana algida*) in early September signal the rapid approach of fall. Most of these species are "cushion" plants or miniature versions of species common at

lower altitudes — a concession to a severe environment. The growth rate is slow, with some plants taking up to a century to produce a mat only a foot or so in diameter. All the more reason to stay on the trail, avoiding damage from lug soles.

As you progress westward on the CT, this summer display of wildflowers becomes even more striking with the deeper soils and more abundant moisture of the western ranges, reaching a climax in the high alpine basins of the San Juan Mountains.

Arctic gentian, September in the Tenmile Range.

Alpine forget-me-nots, June in the Tenmile Range.

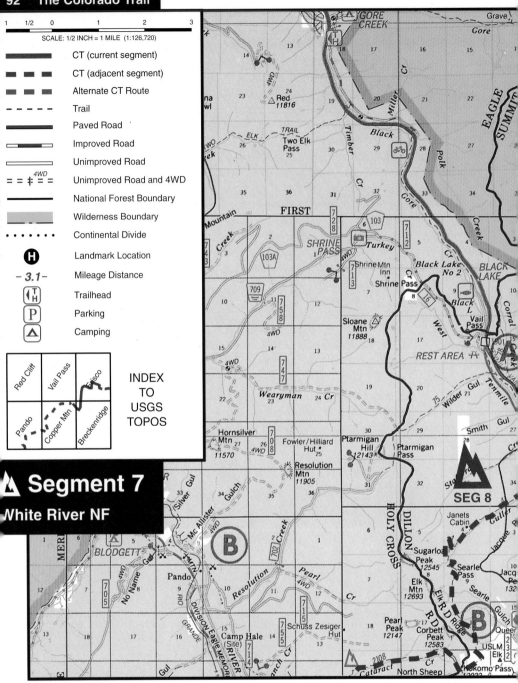

Segment 7
White River NF

Landmark Location	Mileage	From Denver	Elevation	Latitude	Longitude
Ⓐ Goldhill Trailhead	0.0	100.5	9200	39.541222	-106.041571
Ⓑ Rocky summit	2.3	102.8	10240	39.538115	-106.069527
Ⓒ Peaks Trail	3.2	103.7	9920	39.537494	-106.081088
Ⓓ Tenmile Range crest	7.8	108.3	12440	39.504586	-106.113416
Ⓔ Hwy-91	12.5	113.0	9800	39.492512	-106.135257

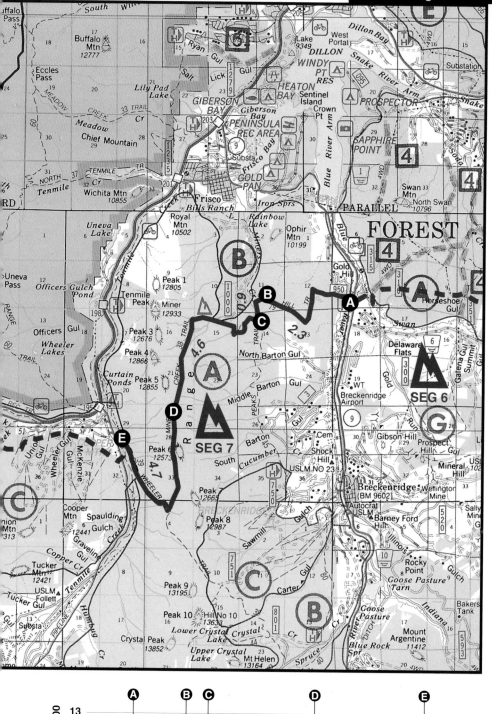

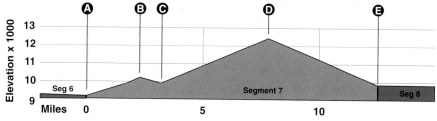

Segment 8
Copper Mountain to Tennessee Pass

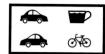

Distance: 24.4 miles
Elevation Gain: approx 4020 ft

CT sign near Tennessee Pass.

Gudy's Tip

"Be sure to stop for a quick shower under the falls along Cataract Creek near Camp Hale. There's even a resting bench. But take note of all the shell holes made during World War II training at Camp Hale in the Tennessee Pass area. They become "pitfalls" with night walking or with engrossing daytime conversation."

Trip Log

Date: _____ Notes: _____

_____

_____

_____

About This Segment

The DSP&PRR once had a whistle stop known as Solitude on its Tenmile Canyon line near present-day Copper Mountain Resort. Unfortunately, with the activity of the ski area and busy I-70, the isolation of the valley is a thing of the past. As recently as 1970, before the ski area was built and the highway widened, this valley was still known as Wheeler Flats, a throwback to the days when Judge John S. Wheeler would drive his stock over the Tenmile Range to graze in the valley's lush, boggy meadows. A little settlement developed here and served the Tenmile Mining District.

The glitzy ski resort in this valley today is typical of the shifting economic base in Colorado from mining to recreation, a transformation particularly noticeable throughout highly developed Summit County.

Copper Mountain is the only urban environment through which the CT passes, and it is indeed an imposing paradox for an otherwise wilderness trail. Some hikers might be persuaded to linger in the comfort of its civilization, while others would pass through attempting to ignore the metamorphosis from obscure mining community to chic ski resort. Whatever their inclination, the resort does provide weary backpackers the opportunity to recharge their batteries before submerging themselves again in the wilderness.

Hikers in this segment have a tremendous perch on Elk Ridge from which to view the Climax Molybdenum Mine and the immense tailing ponds which have completely inundated the historic Tenmile Mining District towns of Robinson and Kokomo. This mining district got its start when Leadville businessman George B. Robinson grubstaked two miners who subsequently discovered ten mines in the headwaters of Tenmile Creek. Robinson's namesake town had the distinction of being Colorado's highest incorporated town, and for a time threatened Leadville for dominance in the area. The little community of Kokomo, named by Indiana miners for their hometown, developed just downstream from Robinson.

Both the D&RG and the DSP&P felt confident enough about the upstart mining district to lay tracks into the valley. Merchant Robinson gained enough influence to emerge as Colorado's lieutenant governor in 1880, but unfortunately he enjoyed only one month of his term before being gunned down in a shoot-out involving a controversy over the ownership of the Smuggler Mine. Captain J. W. Jacque, for whom Jacque Ridge, Jacque Creek and Jacque Mountain apparently were named, was also involved in the fatal dispute.

As hikers descend into the headwaters of the Eagle River, they will pass through Camp Hale, one of Colorado's most fascinating ghost town sites. Construction of this Rocky Mountain outpost, named for Brigadier General Irving Hale, began in 1942 and was the wartime training base of the 10th Mountain Division. The troops were eventually attached to the 5th Army and sent to fight in Italy's Apennine Mountains. At its height in 1944, the camp held 15,000 men who trained during the summer and winter in the surrounding mountains. Cooper Hill Ski Area on Tennessee Pass was originally constructed as part of the camp. Here troops attached slats to their feet and learned techniques on the ski run that at the time had the world's longest T-bar. Camp Hale was largely abandoned after WWII, although sporadic use continued until 1963, after which the camp was completely dismantled. Trail crews working here in 1987 unearthed hundreds of spent ammo rounds while building trail in the vicinity of the shooting range.

Portions of the CT above Camp Hale follow the narrow gauge railroad grade that the D&RG abandoned in 1890, when the line was realigned and widened to standard gauge. This segment ends on Tennessee Pass, which was discovered in 1845 by Colonel John Fremont.

Additional Trail Information: Except along the first several miles of this segment through Copper Mountain Resort, backpackers will have an abundant selection of campsites from which to choose. The exposed, high altitude section from Searle Pass to Kokomo Pass, along which you are likely to find grazing domestic sheep, has only skimpy water supplies. Snowfields here may linger well into July. This same area has several abandoned vertical mine shafts, some of which are disturbingly close to the CT and partially camouflaged by low, bushy willows. Backpackers wandering on a somewhat independent course through here near dusk would be putting themselves at an obvious risk.

Please be aware that the trail route in the vicinity of the Copper Mountain base area and beyond to Guller Creek uses an assortment of maintenance roads and existing trails, where it is likely you will encounter novice horseback riders on day rides from the base. It is possible that you may get confused on this assortment of trails and roads and end up in the wrong place, especially so if trail markings are missing or vandalized. Take care to confirm your location from time to time in this area until you reach Guller Creek where the going is more obvious.

Trailhead/Access Points

Wheeler Flats Trailhead: The CT crosses Hwy-91 approximately 1.0 mile south from the I-70 interchange, but long term parking is not permitted on the widened highway shoulder. Instead you should leave you car at this trailhead. Go west from Denver approximately 79 miles on I-70 to the Copper Mountain/Leadville/Colorado Hwy-91 exit. Take the exit and cross over the freeway on an overpass, then drive just a few hundred feet and turn left onto the side road just opposite the entrance to Copper Mountain Resort. Continue down the side road 0.4 mile to where it deadends at the Wheeler Flats Trailhead parking area. To get to the trail, hike down the powerline access road which goes south from the trailhead on the east side of Tenmile Creek. Additional day-use parking is possible near the entrance to the large ski area parking lot just northeast of the CT bridge crossing of Ten Mile Creek. This eliminates the approximate 1.0 mile hike between the Wheeler Flats Trailhead and the CT. The lot itself is closed during the summer, but don't block the entrance to the lot.

Camp Hale (Eagle Park) Trailhead: From the top of Tennessee Pass, descend north on US-24 for 2.5 miles to the point where the CT crosses the highway. Then continue another 0.5 mile and go right on FS-726. Gradually descend on FS-726 for 3 miles to where it joins up with FS-714. The CT follows FS-714 for a short distance here as it skirts around a deep road cut, but don't park here to catch the trail. There is a primitive trailhead parking area about 1 mile west of this point on FS-714. Another route to this trailhead starts at the intersection of FS-702 and US-24 on the

Bus	Summit Stage	(970) 668-0999
Dining	Several in the resort	
Groceries	McCoy's Mountain Market	
	Village Square Bldg	(970) 968-2182
Info	Copper Mountain Chamber of Commerce	
	Snow Bridge Square Bldg	(970) 968-6477
Lodging	Copper Lodging Services	(800) 458-8386
Medical	closest in Vail	(970) 476-2451
Post Office	West Lake Lodge Bldg	(970) 968-2882

Copper Mountain Services

Distance From CT:	
	0 miles
Elevation:	9,600
Zip Code:	80443
Area Code:	970

Supplies, Services and Accommodations

The CT passes close to **Copper Mountain** resort at the start of this segment. Copper Mountain is not a town, but rather, a large ski resort developed since the 1970s. Overnight accommodations and restaurants may be pricey. There is a convenience store/gas station near Wheeler Flats Trailhead.

north end of Eagle Park near the railroad overpass. Follow FS-702 (Resolution Road) 1.0 mile, then go right onto FS-714 and continue at the eastern edge of the park 2.2 miles to the trailhead.

Tennessee Pass Trailhead: See Segment 9.

Maps and Jurisdiction

USFS map: White River National Forest, see pages 102-103.
USGS Quad. maps: Vail Pass, Copper Mountain, Pando, Leadville North.
Trails Illustrated map: # 109

Jurisdiction: Holy Cross and Dillon Ranger Districts, White River NF.

Trail Description

The CT in this segment begins at a widened shoulder on Hwy-91 approximately 1.0 mile south from the I-70 interchange. Long term parking is not allowed here, but is available at Wheeler Flats Trailhead. The trail begins an immediate ascent out of the valley, with intermittent views of the Copper Mountain golf course to the north. At **mile 0.2** (9880) you will pass under a power line, and then pass into and out of the forest while crossing several ski slopes.

At **mile 1.1** (9800) the trail seems to end at a base area maintenance building. However, continue ahead (west then west-northwest) to the rear of the building and keep going to the unloading area of a beginner chair lift. The trail begins again just beyond the chair lift unloading platform, and descends steadily. But it will only continue 0.2 mile before ending again on a wide gravel walk at the base area just opposite a complex of condominiums. Go left (west) on the gravel walk which will take you in 0.1 mile to a stream crossing overlooking the main Copper Mountain ski base area at **mile 1.4** (9760). From here, angle a little to the left (west-southwest) a

Hikers ascending on the CT near Searle Pass.

short distance across the ski slope on an obscure connecting "ditch" trail and then intersect a wide gravel maintenance road which also ascends from the base. (Be careful to avoid the more prominent "frisbee golf course" trail and mountain bike trail which also ascend from the base in this area.) Continue the ascent (west) on the gravel maintenance road for approximately 0.3 mile to a switchback and intersection with another road, where the trail leaves the road and continues heading west. In 0.2 mile go left (west) at a trail intersection, in another 0.5 mile fork right (west) at another trail intersection, and in another 0.4 mile take a sharp right (west) at another intersection to continue on the CT. (**ALERT: there are several confusing false side trails in this stretch that have been recently closed and re-vegetated, be alert to stay on the CT.**) After this bothersome maze from the base, the trail continues rather placidly across the western-most ski runs, bearing slowly from west to a more southerly direction, until it connects with a horse pack trail a short distance before entering the valley of Guller Creek. Cross Jacque Creek just upstream from an inviting meadow, where you will intersect an exising trail. Go left (southwest) on the trail and then cross to the west side of Guller Creek at **mile 4.3** (10,400). If you made it to this point successfully from the base area on the first try without backtracking, you are to be congratulated!

At **mile 5.0** (10,600), enter a linear meadow which extends along Guller Creek almost to timberline. The CT stays near the edge of the spruce forest, though at times it breaks into the elongated meadow, where there are more good campsites. Guller Creek, always nearby, is usually hidden in a mass of thick willows. The trail makes several switchbacks as it nears timberline and exits the trees at **mile 7.7** (11,600). Near timberline, you may notice a faint side trail which leads to Janet's Cabin, a shelter hut on the 10th Mountain ski system. No summer use of this hut is allowed.

Above timberline, the route is delineated mainly by posts and cairns, although due to heavy use the trail does mostly exist between here and Searle Pass. Cross the small upper headwaters of Guller Creek and continue past two switchbacks marked with cairns. The final approach to the pass is rocky and rough but again well marked with numerous cairns. Searle Pass, at **mile 8.9** (12,040), is a notch that tends to channel and increase the wind to bothersome levels, but try to take time to admire the fine vistas it gives of the Tenmile and Gore Ranges. From Searle Pass, the trail continues as a well-marked and mostly-recognizable foot path. For the first mile from Searle, it makes a traverse, bearing generally south at approximately 12,000 feet wandering in and out of many little side drainages. After that, it begins to undulate more as it approaches the base of Elk Ridge. Exposed campsites abound in the soft alpine grasses.

Approximately 2.4 miles beyond Searle Pass, a better trail becomes obvious as the CT ascends through several switchbacks to the rocky southern end of Elk Ridge. At **mile 11.5** (12,280) the trail levels out on the ridge, which offers commanding views of the unsightly remains of Bartlett Mountain, once 13,555 feet high but now largely reduced to the huge pile of tailings visible below.

Descend 0.5 mile along the trail, which is cut deeply into the side hill in places, to 12,000-foot Kokomo Pass. Follow a short but steep ravine as it descends northnorthwest from the pass down into a rolling alpine meadow on the headwaters of Cataract Creek. There is an established, well-used and very popular campsite with a view perfectly framed by the valley of Mount of the Holy Cross in the meadow at timberline just before you cross a small tributary stream. Just beyond, the trail enters the trees and descends through three long switchbacks, then assumes a westerly heading parallel to and slightly above the level of Cataract Creek. Continue descending in a spruce forest to an abandoned sawmill site near the creek at **mile 13.8** (11,000). For the next 2.4 miles, the CT follows an old logging road as it descends the steepening gorge of Cataract Creek. (**ALERT: As of 2/02, due to munitions found in the Camp Hale area, trail users are required to stay on the trail, with no camping or leaving the corridor between Cataract Creek and the South Fork of the Eagle River. White arrows sign the restricted corridor. If munitions are discovered, note the location and contact the Eagle County Sheriff at 970-479-2200. Check with the Forest Service for any lifting of these restrictions.**)

Follow the road through a switchback to the left at **mile 15.4** (10,200), avoid the faint continuation of another road which climbs ahead here. There is a challenging ford of Cataract Creek 400 feet beyond, but a log bridge just upstream has kept hiker's feet dry in the past. Avoid the ascending fork which branches left 600 feet beyond the creek, and continue straight ahead on the logging road. The final pitch of the road descends steeply to the upper end of a long meadow on the East Fork Eagle River. From here, a jeep track descends south 0.1 mile to FS-714, but don't take it. From this point, leave the old logging road and ascend at right (north) on a trail a few hundred feet to **mile 16.2** (9680), where a cute little arched bridge spans Cataract Creek just a few feet downstream from the falls that name it.

Continue along the trail in a meadow of fragrant sage and cinquefoil with views west towards the upper end of Eagle Park, which bustled with the wartime activities of Camp Hale. The trail joins up temporarily with FS-714 at **mile 17.0** (9400). FS-726 peels off to the south here and continues on to US-24. Continue 800 feet west on FS-714 and look for the obscure trail route which veers off into the meadow north of the road. The CT heads west here, paralleling FS-714 for 0.6 mile, after which it again joins the road at the Camp Hale (Eagle Park) Trailhead. Continue approximately 600 feet

Crossing a log bridge
near US-24.

west on FS-714 and then go left (south) on an intersecting road which takes you past a series of earthen mounds that were part of the old Camp Hale shooting range.

Cross the East Fork River on a bridge at **mile 18.2** (9320), just beyond the shooting range and near a line of dilapidated concrete bunkers. For the next 400 feet, the trail nearly disappears into thick, marshy meadow grasses, but it is visible on the hillside ahead. The route bears southwest through here and is marked by periodic cairns of crumbling concrete piers taken from some long forgotten military building. Shortly, the trail enters a lodgepole forest and begins an ascent. Turn through two short switchbacks and continue west to southwest for 0.5 mile, then exit briefly onto the upper end of the old "B" slope ski run, which is slowly being reclaimed by the forest. This vantage point gives one of the nicest views possible of the site of Camp Hale.

The CT now re-enters the lodgepole forest, heading in a more southerly direction and crosses FS-726 at **mile 19.1** (9680). The trail resumes on the opposite side of the road and continues in a southerly direction, at times closely paralleling the Forest Service road below. Jim Miller, Julie Mesdag and their maintenance folk annually rework this trail. They thoughtfully provided a view point and bench at a rock outcrop about 0.4 mile up from the road crossing. Follow the trail to US-24 at **mile 21.0** (10,000) and carefully cross the busy highway. Pass through a gate and proceed 200 feet on a railroad maintenance driveway which drops slightly to the railroad tracks. Cross the tracks and continue ahead (west) 400 feet on the faint, elevated grade of an abandoned railroad siding which is now thick with grass and partially flooded by a beaver pond. Continue along the grade, which fades away in the pond as the trail bears to the right (north-northwest).

Mount of the Holy Cross

From vantage points on Segment 8 of the CT, hikers have excellent views to the west of the photogenic 14er, Mount of the Holy Cross. Nearly a century ago, this was perhaps the most famous and revered mountain in America.

For decades in the early 1800s, explorers had brought back rumors of a great mountain in the west that displayed a giant cross on its side, yet the exact location was shrouded in mystery. The search for the peak became one of the most intriguing in the history of the west. F.V. Hayden set this as a top priority in the 1873 field session of his topographic survey. Hayden's team determined that the peak lay somewhere north and west of Tennessee Pass. After several arduous days of trail-less travel, Hayden reached the summit on August 22nd. Across the valley, on nearby Notch Mountain, famed western photographer W. H. Jackson captured an image of the immense snowy cross.

It's hard to imagine in today's age the impact, but in another generation, steeped in religious symbolism, Jackson's photo created a sensation in the country. Longfellow was moved to write a poem after viewing the image and well-known artists, such as Thomas Moran, made the arduous journey to Colorado to paint the peak. Hundreds of people made pilgrimages up Notch

In just a few hundred feet, at **mile 21.3** (9920), the CT turns south-southwest up the wide, expansive meadow encompassing Mitchell Creek. In about 0.3 mile, the trail enters an inviting lodgepole forest at the edge of the spacious linear meadow on your right. Before the trail begins a slow ascent away from the creek in another 0.5 mile, you might want to observe the water fowl that may be nesting in the many beaver ponds of the marshy meadow. At **mile 22.5** (10,200), the trail joins a jeep road deep in the forest. This road is the abandoned narrow gauge route of the D&RGRR. Head east-northeast on the road a short distance, then assume a more southerly bearing for a mile. Follow the road as it slowly bends to the east and passes the remains of several large coking ovens. Continue on the jeep road to Tennessee Pass at **mile 24.4** (10,424), where this segment ends on the west side of US-24 at the trailhead parking area.

Jackson's famous image.

Mountain to view the cross, faith healings were reported, and Congress established a national monument in 1929.

The mountain was used for mountaineering training by nearby Camp Hale troops during WWII, including a first-ever winter ascent of the 1,200-foot-high cross in December of 1943. But as time passed, religious interest faded and the monument status was rescinded shortly after the war.

A USGS survey determined that the 14,005-foot peak just barely qualified as a 14er (Hayden had listed it at 13,999 feet) and today, Mount of the Holy Cross is a favorite with peakbaggers.

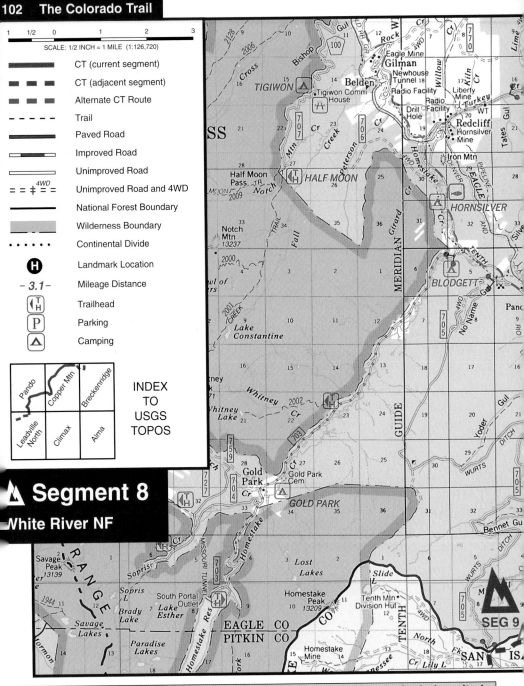

Scale: 1/2 inch = 1 mile (1:126,720)

CT (current segment)				
CT (adjacent segment)				
Alternate CT Route				
Trail				
Paved Road				
Improved Road				
Unimproved Road				
Unimproved Road and 4WD				
National Forest Boundary				
Wilderness Boundary				
Continental Divide				
H Landmark Location				
– 3.1 – Mileage Distance				
Trailhead				
P Parking				
Camping				

INDEX TO USGS TOPOS

Pando	Copper Mtn	Breckenridge
Leadville North	Climax	Alma

▲ Segment 8
White River NF

Landmark Location	Mileage	From Denver	Elevation	Latitude	Longitude
Ⓐ Hwy-91	0.0	113.0	9800	39.492512	-106.135257
Ⓑ Copper Mountain Base Area	1.4	114.4	9760	39.499407	-106.154177
Ⓒ Guller Creek	4.3	117.3	10400	39.488019	-106.189807
Ⓓ Searle Pass	8.9	121.9	12040	39.458247	-106.227683
Ⓔ Elk Ridge	11.5	124.5	12280	39.432149	-106.218106
Ⓕ Camp Hale	18.2	131.2	9320	39.424142	-106.297979
Ⓖ Tennessee Pass	24.4	137.4	10424	39.363309	-106.311332

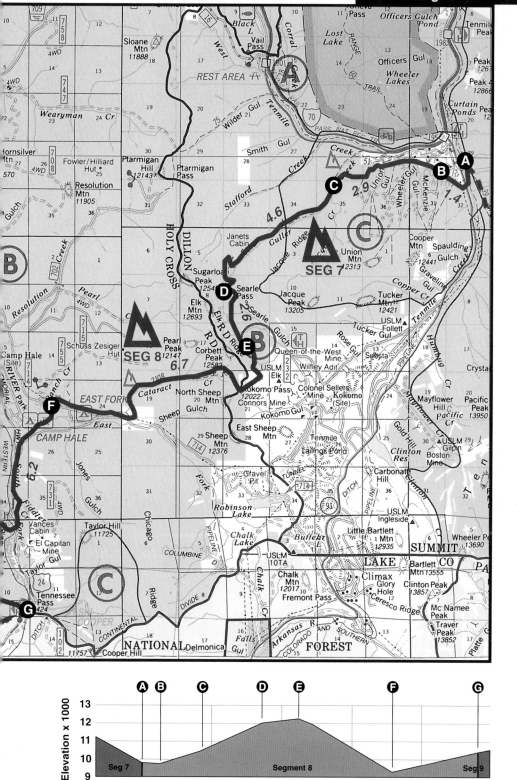

Segment 9
Tennessee Pass to
Hagerman Pass Road

Distance: 14.9 miles
Elevation Gain: approx 2120 ft

Sunrise, Porcupine Lakes.

Gudy's Tip

"In the Holy Cross Wilderness, there is a fascinating tundra walk between Longs Gulch and St. Kevins Lake Trailhead."

Trip Log

Date: _____ Notes: _____

_____

_____

_____

_____

About This Segment

At Tennessee Pass, the CT enters the skyscraping Sawatch Range and begins a trek southward along the eastern flank of these noble mountains. The Sawatch includes some of the highest elevations in Colorado, including the highest, Mount Elbert. There are many grand, glacier-scoured valleys leading into the range, and lovely, lake-filled basins as well. Much of the CT route follows the old Main Range Trail, which began as a Civilian Conservation Corps project in the 1930s.

Toward the end of this segment, the trail rounds the west edge of Turquoise Reservoir, a water storage basin for the immense Fryingpan-Arkansas Project. The original Turquoise Lake, which received its name from the precious stone mined in the area by early Indians and later collectors, was greatly enlarged when impounded by Sugarloaf Dam. This reservoir is one of six in the system, whose purpose is to divert water from the west slope's Fryingpan River and pipe it under the Continental Divide to east slope users via the Arkansas River. The trail parallels the project and passes Clear Creek and Twin Lakes Reservoirs further south, as well as the Mount Elbert hydro-station, all links in the long chain of the Pan-Ark Project.

This segment ends on the road where John J. Hagerman's Colorado Midland Railway once struggled to cross the Continental Divide at the lofty Hagerman Tunnel. Tennessee Pass, a somewhat inconspicuous but no less important crossing, was discovered by Colonel John C. Fremont in the summer of 1845, when he was on his way to California. The D&RG built a narrow gauge railroad over the pass in 1881, then standardized the line and built the tunnel under the pass in 1890. It is still in use today.

Additional Trail Information: This segment passes through a corner of Holy Cross Wilderness, where backpackers will find many campsites with backdrops of the Continental Divide's glaciated walls. Mountain cyclists must detour around the wilderness areas in Segments 9 and 10 (see the Mountain Bicycle Detour detailed in Segment 10). A series of blue diamond markers, beginning at Tennessee Pass, identify cross-country ski routes, many of which are part of the Tenth Mountain Trail Association ski system.

Trailhead/Access Points

Tennessee Pass Trailhead: Travel north from Leadville on US-24 approximately 9 miles to the top of Tennessee Pass. A parking area on the west side of the road provides adequate parking here. A trailhead bulletin board marks the CT. Don't be mislead by other trails, mostly cross-country ski routes, which also start here.

Wurtz Ditch Road (FS-100) Trail Access: Travel north from Leadville on US-24 approximately 7.5 miles to Wurtz Ditch Road (FS-100), which leaves the highway on the left (west). Go 1 mile on the dirt road and bear to the right as the road forks. Proceed 0.3 mile further, to a point where the CT crosses the road. There is room for only a few small cars here.

St. Kevins Gulch Trailhead (FS-107): This isolated portal into the Holy Cross Wilderness is ideal for those wanting to escape the crowds along most sections of the CT in the Sawatch Range. A high-clearance or 4WD vehicle is required on FS-107, once you leave the paved reservoir road. Although there are quicker and more direct routes to Turquoise Reservoir from Leadville, the most straightforward starts approximately 3.5 miles south of town on US-24. Turn right (west) onto Colorado Hwy-300 and proceed 0.5 mile on the paved road. Turn right (north) onto a road which is marked as the way to Turquoise Reservoir. Drive 1.8 miles north to a skewed three-way intersection. Go left onto the intersecting paved road which ascends 0.8 mile west to the reservoir, and go right onto the intersecting road. Follow this winding, paved road 5.0 miles until you come to the somewhat obscure FS-107, which takes off to the right (north). Avoid the side roads and respect the nearby private property as FS-107 passes through the old St. Kevins mining district. Continue ahead a total of 2.4 miles on the rough, steep road until it ends at a small parking area at the edge of the Holy Cross Wilderness. Pick up the trail as it passes through this parking area.

Hagerman Pass Road (FS-105) Trail Access, Lake Fork Trailhead, Boustead Tunnel parking area: See Segment 10.

Supplies, Services and Accommodations

Available in Leadville (see Segment 10).

Maps and Jurisdiction

USFS map: San Isabel National Forest, see pages 110-111.
USGS Quadrangle maps: Leadville North, Homestake Reservoir.
Trails Illustrated maps: # 126 and 127.

Jurisdiction: Leadville Ranger District, San Isabel NF.

Trail Description

From the parking area on the west side of Tennessee Pass, traverse just below the Continental Divide bearing generally west to southwest. Note the blue diamonds high up in the lodgepoles, for use by skiers in deep snow. In a few places the thick forest allows views to the south of the upper Arkansas Valley. Cross the sturdy Wurtz Ditch footbridge at **mile 2.5** (10,400). This artificial creek bed, which might be either gushing with water or completely dry, is a conduit that diverts water from the west side of the divide to the Arkansas River via Tennessee Creek.

Ascend 0.2 mile further to Wurtz Ditch road, where the somewhat obscure trail continues on the opposite side trending generally to the southwest. Pass through a clear-cut to Lily Lake Road at **mile 3.0** (10,350). Cross the road on an east-west diagonal, then continue a few steps on a side road that leads to a better road that goes south toward a meadow. Just before the road opens up in the meadow, the trail temporarily leaves the road at right to avoid some private property and bears south-southwest to southwest in the lodgepole forest. When you intersect the road again on the west edge of the meadow, go right (west-southwest) and continue a few steps to the crossing of the North Fork West Tennessee Creek at **mile 3.4** (10,320). A double log bridge is provided a few steps downstream of the road crossing. Proceed 200 feet to the deep ford of West Tennessee Creek. In the past, a couple of downed trees several hundred feet upstream provided a drier, but precarious, crossing. Just beyond West Tennessee Creek, as the road makes a bend to the left, the trail very obscurely leaves the road and continues ahead (south-southwest) at a "Closed To All Vehicles" boilerplate sign. The trail curves around to a westerly heading and joins an old road at **mile 3.7** (10360). The road becomes more trail-like as it ascends steadily in a westerly, then

Forest near Wurtz Ditch.

southwesterly, direction, paralleling West Tennessee Creek through a lodgepole forest. At **mile 4.7** (10,760) you will join up with another old road, whose unused portion has been well barricaded to prevent confusion. Proceed bearing generally southwest to west. Cross over a broad ridge at **mile 5.1** (10,840), then descend slowly through a lodgepole-spruce forest. Enter the elongated meadow of Longs Gulch 1 mile beyond, where you will be ascending west to west-southwest toward the very impressive head of this alpine cirque, passing the ruins of an old cabin.

A sign announces your entrance into Holy Cross Wilderness at **mile 6.5** (10,920). Cross to the south side of the creek 400 feet beyond and begin a steep ascent to the southwest. Top a broad saddle at **mile 7.4** (11,480), where the ponds of upper Porcupine Creek are nestled into spectacular alpine scenery. Descend 0.3 mile on the sometimes faint trail and cross Porcupine Creek. Follow the trail through a spruce-fir forest, then switchback up to tundra at 11,600 feet and enjoy views east and north of the Tenmile and Mosquito Ranges. Re-enter the trees at **mile 8.5** (11,680) and then descend to an old road. Continue the descent southward 0.6 mile, following an unnamed drainage that opens up into a meadow.

Briefly leave the wilderness at **mile 9.4** (11,240) where FS-107 ends at the primitive St. Kevin trailhead parking area. A sign here marks the wilderness boundary. Cross the small stream behind the sign, re-enter the wilderness, and proceed northwest on an abandoned road at the edge of the meadow. In 800 feet, the old road becomes a rocky trail as it bears left (west), enters the forest and rises slightly for a descent into the Bear Creek drainage. The terrain is so rocky around here that the trail seems to vanish at times into the surroundings. The CT passes above Bear Lake at **mile 10.1** (11,120) in rugged country which might make a usable but uncomfortable campsite. A side trail here going left (south) to the lake has caused some confusion in the past. Continue beyond the shores of the last picturesque lake and ascend to a timberline ridge at **mile 11.0** (11,280), where an impressive panorama of Mount Massive and Hagerman Pass come into view.

Descend steadily through a lodgepole forest to **mile 12.4** (10,440), where the trail passes under a powerline at the southern boundary of the Holy Cross Wilderness.

Crossing a bridge near Bear Lake,
Holy Cross Wilderness.

Pass under the powerline again 0.5 mile beyond and continue 600 feet to a convenient bridge at Mill Creek. Descend a few steps west-southwest from Mill Creek to the lower part of a meadow near the Lake Fork at **mile 13.1** (10,040), where a bulletin board at the Lake Fork trailhead has been erected for hikers. This trailhead is 300 feet west of a switchback on the paved reservoir road, just up from May Queen Campground.

Back at the bulletin board in the meadow, re-enter the trees, pick up an old jeep road ascending west, and continue to the crossing of the swiftly flowing Lake Fork on a long footbridge. Then continue a few steps uphill on the old jeep road, until the trail resumes at left (south to south-southwest). Pass under the powerline at **mile 13.4** (10,120) and continue to Glacier Creek, which is crossed on a corduroy bridge. Traverse southeast beyond the creek in a cool spruce-fir forest. The Charles H. Boustead Tunnel, which channels water from the head of the Fryingpan River, is 150 feet below your feet as you approach Busk Creek. After Busk Creek, the trail ascends to the Hagerman Pass Road at **mile 14.9** (10,360), where this segment ends. This is a trail access only; parking is not available at this point.

Skiing on the CT.

10th Mountain Division Hut System

For backcountry skiing, snowshoeing, and snowboarding enthusiasts, there are a number of winter accesses for the CT, usually where the trail crosses a major pass at a regularly plowed highway. Undoubtedly the best of these is the Tennessee Pass access, at the start of Segment 9; not only for a reputation for excellent snow conditions, but also, this access sits smack in the middle of an extensive network of mountain huts run by the 10th Mountain Division Hut Association.

The 10th is a non-profit organization founded in 1980 by a group of backcountry recreationalists, including several veterans of the famed US Army's 10th Mountain Division which trained at nearby Camp Hale in the 1940s.

The hut system occupies a large triangle between Vail, Leadville, and Aspen. Styled after the European tradition of hut-to-hut travel, 24 huts within the system provide overnight shelter for backcountry skiers, snow boarders, snowshoers, mountain bikers, and backpackers. Five of the huts were built with donations from family and friends to honor individuals who died serving the 10th Mountain Division during World War II.

The huts are situated between 9,700 and 11,700 feet and are designed for experienced backcountry travelers. Most of them operate in the winter between late November and late April, and then again for three months in the summer. Accommodations are best described as comfortably rustic, with bunks to sleep about 15 people in a communal setting. Huts are equipped with wood stoves for heating, propane for cooking, photovoltaic lighting, mattresses and utensils. You bring your own sleeping bag, food and clothing. Users melt snow in winter and collect water from streams in summer.

Over 300 miles of trails link the huts together and several sit close to the CT, including Janets Cabin, Vances Cabin, and Uncle Buds. Reservations are required. Contact The 10th at (970) 925-5775 or visit their website at www.huts.org. Please note that this site administers a system of huts, including those of the 10th as well as Alfred A. Braun Huts and Friends Huts.

Janets Cabin near Searle Pass, Seg. 8.

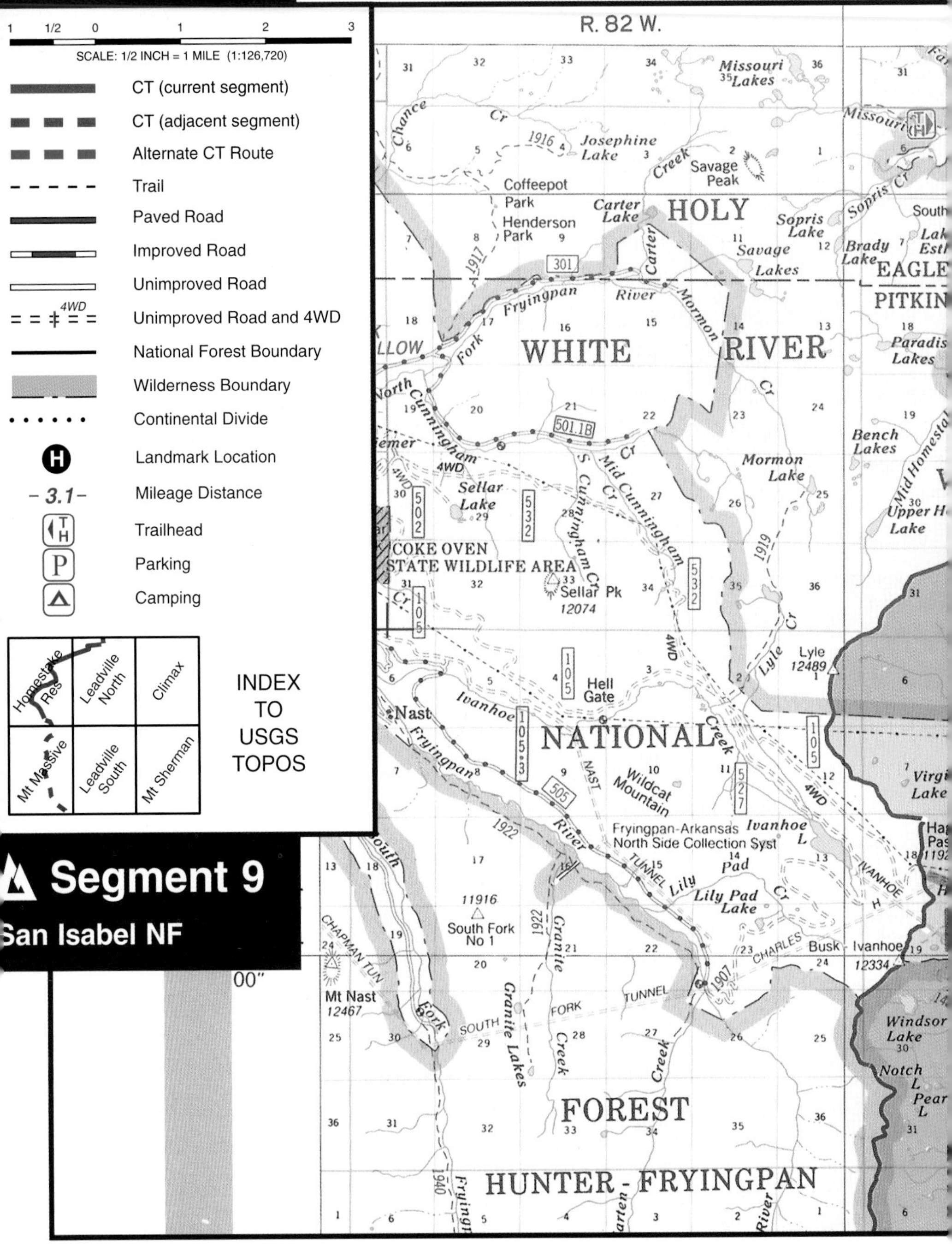

1 1/2 0 1 2 3		

SCALE: 1/2 INCH = 1 MILE (1:126,720)

▬▬▬▬	CT (current segment)
▬ ▬ ▬	CT (adjacent segment)
▬ ▬ ▬	Alternate CT Route
– – – – –	Trail
▬▬▬▬	Paved Road
▭▭▭	Improved Road
▭▭	Unimproved Road
= = ‡ = =	Unimproved Road and 4WD
▬▬▬▬	National Forest Boundary
▨▨▨	Wilderness Boundary
• • • • • •	Continental Divide
Ⓗ	Landmark Location
– 3.1 –	Mileage Distance
⊤H	Trailhead
P	Parking
△	Camping

INDEX
TO
USGS
TOPOS

Index grid: Homestake Res, Leadville North, Climax / Mt Massive, Leadville South, Mt Sherman

▲ Segment 9
San Isabel NF

Landmark Location	Mileage	From Denver	Elevation	Latitude	Longitude
Ⓐ Tennessee Pass	0.0	137.4	10424	39.363309	-106.311332
Ⓑ North Fork West Tennessee Crk.	3.4	140.8	10320	39.344732	-106.356920
Ⓒ Porcupine Lakes	7.4	144.8	11480	39.321255	-106.412924
Ⓓ Lake Fork	13.1	150.5	10040	39.284893	-106.446557
Ⓔ Hagerman Road	14.9	152.3	10360	39.269621	-106.432435

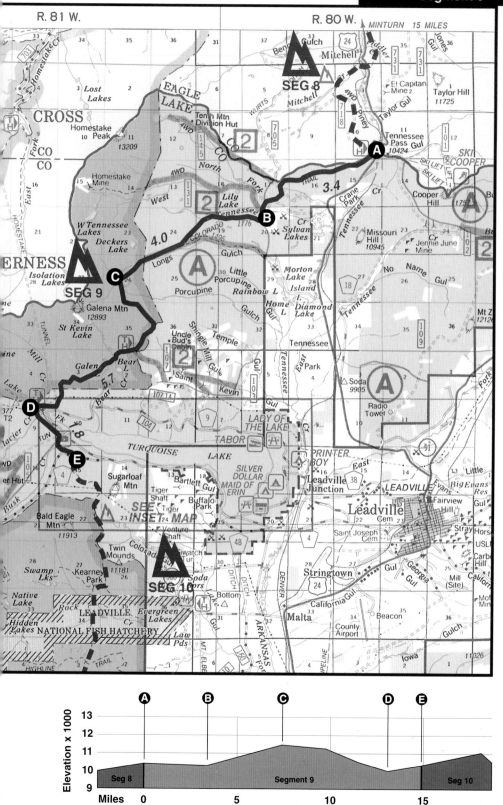

Segment 10
Hagerman Pass Road to Halfmoon Creek

Distance: 11.4 miles
Elevation Gain: approx 1760 ft

Snowflurries on the CT, Mt. Massive Wilderness.

Gudy's Tip

"*If your goal is to climb Mount Elbert, get a very early start. Thunderstorms and lightening can roll in by noon during the summer. And by starting early, you'll avoid the crowd of peakbaggers.*"

Trip Log

Date: _____ Notes: _____

_____

_____

_____

_____

About This Segment

The Hagerman Pass Road is named for John J. Hagerman, builder of the Colorado Midland Railway. His railroad followed the grade here to its Continental Divide crossing several miles up the road at 11,528-foot Hagerman Tunnel. The Midland then continued down the Fryingpan River to tap the Roaring Fork's profitable coalfields and silver mines. The right-of-way was abandoned by the railroad in 1920 and has been a dirt road ever since. It even served as an official state auto route in the 1920s, before more adequate highways were built over the Continental Divide.

In the early 1860s, placers flourished in the upper Arkansas country, and Abe Lee is credited with the original discovery of gold in California Gulch, today's Leadville. The gold soon played out, but then silver was discovered in the surrounding hills and by 1879 Leadville was a rip-roaring boomtown which lasted until the demonetization of silver in 1893. In later years, and today as well, the Climax Molybdenum Mine contributed to the local economy. At several points along this trail segment, hikers can view the Cloud City, its surrounding mine tailings, and Mosquito Pass to the east, over which many of the hopeful filtered into the valley.

This trail segment passes through the upper end of the Leadville National Fish Hatchery property. The buildings of the hatchery, located approximately 2 miles down the road east from the Rock Creek crossing, were built in 1889 and listed on the National Register of Historic Places in the 1970s. The hatchery is the oldest federal hatchery west of the Mississippi and second oldest in the federal hatchery system. The location was chosen because of the abundant supply of water from Rock Creek and nearby lakes teeming with native cutthroat trout. On July 1, 1889, Congress appropriated $15,000 to build the hatchery. The main building was greeted with glowing articles describing it as "the most magnificent building in western Colorado." It still exists today serving the same function it has for more than 100 years. For through-hikers, a visit to the hatchery buildings can be combined with a trip to Leadville, although it is not as direct as a route starting at the upper end of Turquoise Reservoir.

Additional Trail Information: This segment travels almost entirely within the boundaries of Mount Massive Wilderness. The wilderness gets its name from the 14,421-foot mountain, second highest in the state, which is easily climbable from the CT. Mountain bicyclists must detour this segment (see the Mountain Bicycle Detour).

Trailhead/Access Points

Hagerman Pass Road (FS-105) Trail Access: Although there are quicker and more direct routes to the start of this segment from Leadville, the most straightforward starts approximately 3.5 miles south of town on US-24. Turn right (west) onto Colorado Hwy-300 and proceed 0.5 mile on the paved road. Turn right (north) onto a road which is marked as the way to Turquoise Reservoir. Drive 1.8 miles north to a skewed three-way intersection. Go left onto the intersecting paved road which ascends 1.2 miles west to Sugarloaf Dam. Continue on the reservoir road 3.1 miles beyond the dam and go left onto a dirt road, the Hagerman Pass Road (FS-

105). Continue 0.9 mile up the road to the point where the CT crosses it. This is a trail access only with no parking area; parking is not allowed at this point. If you need off-road parking, there are two options. The most convenient is a primitive new trailhead area near the Lake Fork just above the reservoir. To find it, continue approximately 2 miles past the intersection with the Hagerman Pass Road on the paved reservoir road to a sharp switchback to the right, just beyond May Queen Campground. Leave the road and continue several hundred feet up the rough side road, which crosses over Mill Creek. There is a small, informal parking area (Lake Fork trailhead) here in the meadow; the CT is marked by a bulletin board. This point is mile 13.1 on the CT in Segment 9. For paved parking, continue 1.4 miles past the intersection with the Hagerman Pass Road on the reservoir road to the fisherman's parking area at the Boustead Tunnel outlet. To find the CT from this parking area, continue on the reservoir road 0.5 mile to the Lake Fork trailhead mentioned above.

Halfmoon Creek Trailhead: See Segment 11.

Maps and Jurisdiction

USFS map: San Isabel National Forest, see pages 118-119.
USGS Quadrangle maps: Homestake Reservoir, Mount Massive.
Trails Illustrated map: # 127.

Jurisdiction: Leadville Ranger District, San Isabel NF.

Trail Description

If it weren't for the sign pointing out the CT intersection on the Hagerman Pass Road, this inconspicuous crossing might be missed altogether. Early in the season, lingering snowbanks also make this point difficult to spot. From the road, the CT climbs steadily through a lodgepole forest. Several open areas along the way afford great views to the north of Galena Mountain and the Continental Divide. Reach the saddle just west and below Sugarloaf Mountain at **mile 1.2** (11,080), where the trail crosses a logging road. Continue south of the road and pass underneath a powerline into a clear-cut. The area around Leadville was heavily logged during the boom days to provide structural material for the town, mines and railroads. Perhaps this forest succumbed to that fate. You may encounter several areas where the trail has suffered severe erosion because of the timbering activity here, although the clear-cut does provide unparalleled views east and south across the upper Arkansas Valley.

Enter Mount Massive Wilderness 700 feet south of the road crossing, then descend slightly and re-enter the forest at **mile 1.6** (11,040), where the trail crosses a small stream. The trail traverses across several small gullies populated by spruce and fir in the cool, damp recesses, and lodgepole on the exposed, drier ridges. Top the saddle west of Twin Mounds at **mile 3.0** (11,000), then begin a descent south into Rock Creek drainage. Toward the end of the descent, the trail becomes wider, characteristic of an old, abandoned road. Bear to the right (west-southwest) on the trail at **mile 3.6** (10,600), as the old road appears to continue ahead. The CT crosses another old road 250 feet beyond. Continue ahead (west) as the trail bends around the

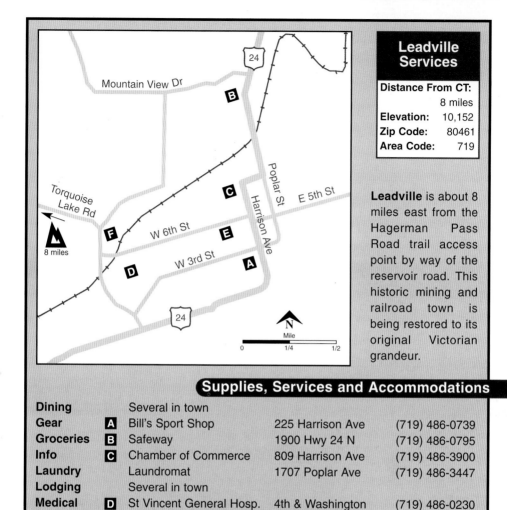

Leadville Services

Distance From CT:	
	8 miles
Elevation:	10,152
Zip Code:	80461
Area Code:	719

Leadville is about 8 miles east from the Hagerman Pass Road trail access point by way of the reservoir road. This historic mining and railroad town is being restored to its original Victorian grandeur.

Supplies, Services and Accommodations

Dining		Several in town		
Gear	A	Bill's Sport Shop	225 Harrison Ave	(719) 486-0739
Groceries	B	Safeway	1900 Hwy 24 N	(719) 486-0795
Info	C	Chamber of Commerce	809 Harrison Ave	(719) 486-3900
Laundry		Laundromat	1707 Poplar Ave	(719) 486-3447
Lodging		Several in town		
Medical	D	St Vincent General Hosp.	4th & Washington	(719) 486-0230
Post Office	E	Leadville Post Office	130 W 5th	(719) 486-9397
Showers	F	Lake Cty Rec Ctr	1000 W 6th	(719) 486-2564
		Also at the laundry (see above)		
Shuttle		Sagauche Guides (719) 486-1856 or Dee Hive (719) 486-2339		

southern edge of Kearney Park. After briefly leveling out here, the trail continues its southerly descent and enters Leadville National Fish Hatchery property.

The trail descends to the north bank of Rock Creek at **mile 4.4** (10,280), where you intersect an old road. This road leads approximately 2 miles east to the old historic hatchery buildings which have been in service since their completion in 1889 — this is an interesting side trip if you have the time. Continue on the trail 200 feet beyond the road crossing and cross the creek on a sturdy bridge. The trail ascends 0.3 mile from Rock Creek to South Rock Creek, which is spanned by a corduroy bridge. Leave the hatchery property in a somewhat spooky lodgepole forest, where the ground is pitted with large potholes that are likely to be filled with water early in the season.

At **mile 6.2** (10,960), the CT intersects the Highline Trail, which continues three steep miles northwest to Native Lake, a popular angler's refuge. The CT proceeds south and crosses North Willow Creek at **mile 7.2** (11,040). Ascend to a level spot south of North Willow Creek, beyond which you traverse into a sunny, open area with views east to the Mosquito Range.

Pass the side trail to Mount Massive's summit at **mile 8.1** (11,240). On this side trail, it is approximately 3.5 miles and 3,180 vertical feet to the summit of the 14,421-foot mountain, the second highest in Colorado. The CT traverses south from the Mount Massive Trail, then suddenly descends to cross Willow Creek at **mile 8.4** (11,00). Cross South Willow Creek 0.6 mile beyond and continue to **mile 10.4** (10,600), where a steep cross-country ski trail descends abruptly to the left. Continue ahead on the CT, which gradually descends to the wilderness boundary at the trailhead parking area on Halfmoon Creek Road at **mile 11.4** (10,080). The trail continues on the opposite side of the road, south of Halfmoon Creek.

Climbing Mt. Elbert and Mt. Massive

The two highest peaks in the state are tempting side trips for many hikers on this stretch of the CT. No technical skills are required for either climb. Still, one must regard these as serious undertakings due to potentially exposed weather conditions and strenuous high altitude hiking. Be prepared — start early, bring warm clothing and rain gear, and turn back if you encounter bad weather or experience symptoms of altitude sickness.

The Hayden Survey named Mt Massive (14,421') in the 1870s, and despite several attempts since to substitute names of various individuals, the superior descriptive appellation has stuck. Mt. Elbert (14,433') was not so lucky. Like so many other mountains in Colorado, it was named for a politician, Samuel H. Elbert, who was initially appointed by President Lincoln in 1862 as secretary of the new Colorado Territory. After a succession of posts, Elbert became a Supreme Court justice when Colorado achieved statehood. Elbert the mountain is the second highest peak in the contiguous United States — Mt Whitney in California tops it by only 60 feet.

Both summits can be reached by trail from the CT trailhead parking area on Halfmoon Creek Road. For Massive, reverse Segment 10 of the CT for 3 miles and pick up the Mt. Massive Trail, which you follow west, then north to the summit. For Elbert, go south on Segment 11 of the CT for 1.3 miles, then take the Mt. Elbert Trail another 2.5 miles west to the top.

Sunrise from on top of Mt. Elbert.

Mountain Bicycle Detour

Holy Cross/Mount Massive Wilderness Detour —

Segments 9 and 10 (San Isabel NF): In order to detour around the Holy Cross Wilderness and Mount Massive Wilderness, it is necessary to use a section of US-24. This highway is busy, without adequate shoulders, and care must be taken when riding this portion.

Detour Description: Pedal to **mile 2.7** (10,480) in Segment 9 where this detour begins on Wurtz Ditch Road. Leave the CT and descend 0.3 mile on the road, then go left on FS-100. Continue to US-24 at **mile 1.3** (10,120) and go right (south) on the highway. Carefully follow US-24 for 7.5 miles to Leadville, and continue south beyond the town to **mile 14.0** (9540), where you will turn right (west) onto Colorado Hwy-300. Proceed 0.8 mile on Hwy-300 and then turn left (south) onto Halfmoon Creek Road. Take a right (west) 1.2 miles beyond and follow the signs to Halfmoon Creek Campground. Continue beyond Halfmoon Creek and Elbert Creek Campgrounds to **mile 21.5** (10,080), where you pick up the CT again, heading south from the Halfmoon Creek Trailhead. This is the starting point of Segment 11.

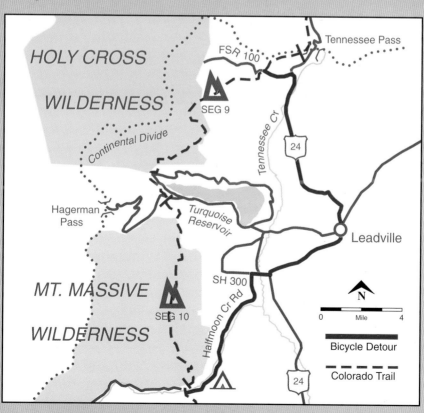

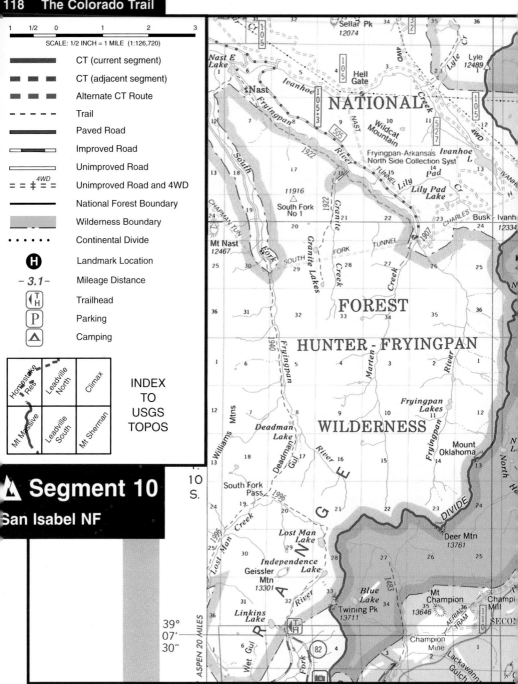

SCALE: 1/2 INCH = 1 MILE (1:126,720)

▬▬▬	CT (current segment)
▬ ▬ ▬	CT (adjacent segment)
▬ ▬ ▬	Alternate CT Route
- - - -	Trail
▬▬▬	Paved Road
▭▭	Improved Road
▭▭	Unimproved Road
= = ‡ = =	Unimproved Road and 4WD
▬▬	National Forest Boundary
▓▓	Wilderness Boundary
• • • • •	Continental Divide
H	Landmark Location
- *3.1* -	Mileage Distance
🚏	Trailhead
P	Parking
⛺	Camping

INDEX TO USGS TOPOS

Homestake Res	Leadville North	Climax
Mt Massive	Leadville South	Mt Sherman

▲ Segment 10
San Isabel NF

Landmark Location	Mileage	From Denver	Elevation	Latitude	Longitude
A Hagerman Pass Road	0.0	152.3	10360	39.269621	-106.432435
B Sugarloaf saddle	1.2	153.5	11080	39.260065	-106.421831
C Rock Creek	4.4	156.7	10280	39.225503	-106.423314
D Mount Massive Trail	8.1	160.4	11240	39.184466	-106.426767
E Halfmoon Creek	11.4	163.7	10080	39.151332	-106.418407

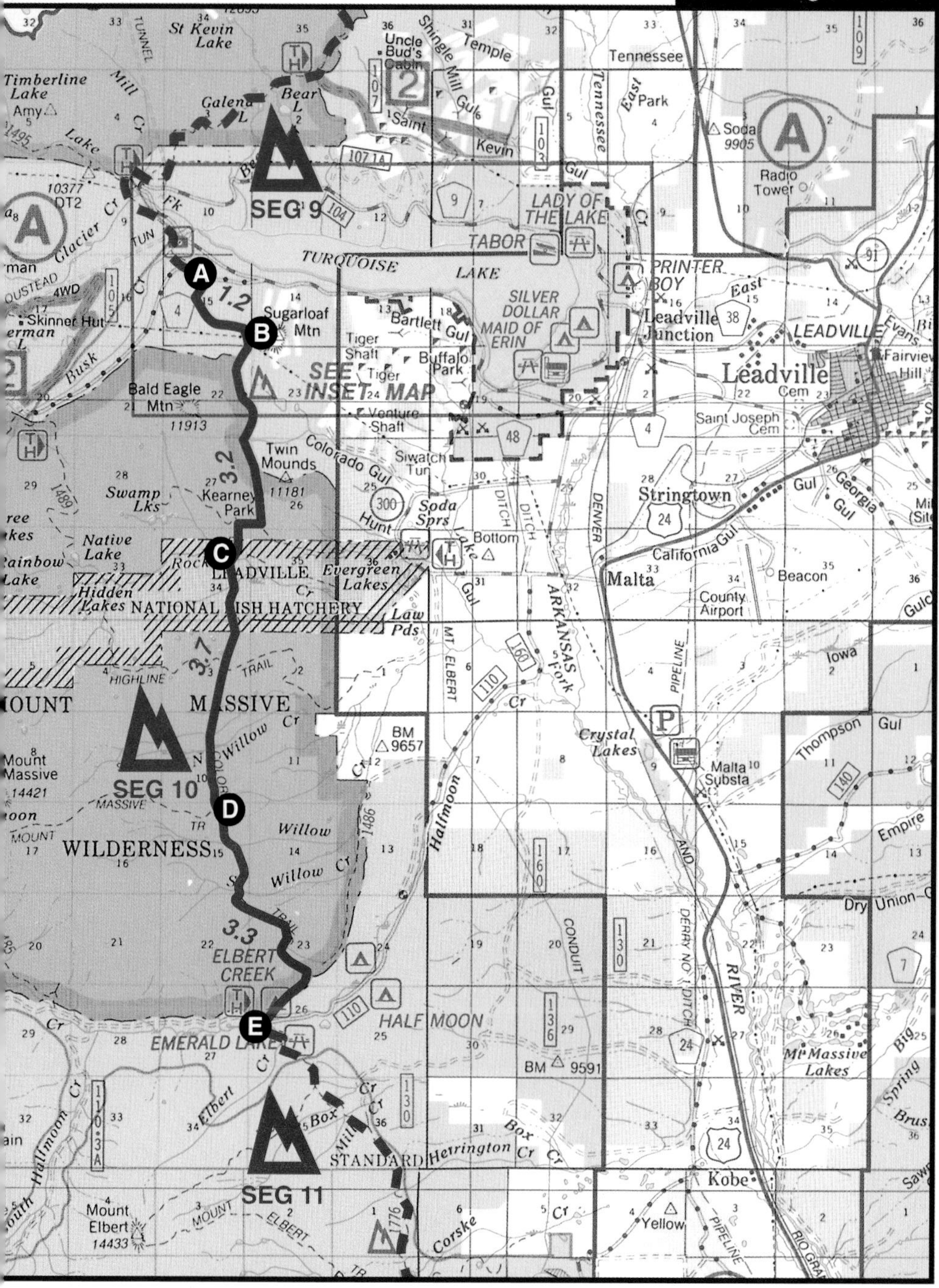

St Kevin Lake
Timberline Lake
Amy
Galena L
Bear L
SEG 9
Uncle Bud's Cabin
Shingle Mill Gul
Temple
Saint Kevin
Tennessee
East Park
Soda 9905
Radio Tower
LADY OF THE LAKE
TABOR
TURQUOISE LAKE
SILVER DOLLAR
MAID OF ERIN
PRINTER BOY
Leadville Junction
LEADVILLE
Leadville
Fairview Hill
Cem
Saint Joseph Cem
Glacier Cr
Skinner Hut
Busk
Sugarloaf Mtn
Bartlett Gul
Tiger Shaft
Buffalo Park
Tiger
SEE INSET MAP
Bald Eagle Mtn 11913
Venture Shaft
Sivatch Tun
Twin Mounds
Colorado Gul
Swamp Lks
Kearney Park 11181
Soda Sprs
Hunt
Bottom
Stringtown
California Gul
Malta
Beacon
County Airport
Native Lake
Rainbow Lake
Hidden Lakes
LEADVILLE NATIONAL FISH HATCHERY
Evergreen Lakes
Law Pds
HIGHLINE TRAIL
MOUNT MASSIVE WILDERNESS
SEG 10
Mount Massive 14421
Willow Cr
BM 9657
Halfmoon
Crystal Lakes
Malta Substa
Thompson Gul
Empire
Iowa
ARKANSAS Fork
DENVER AND RIO GRANDE
PIPELINE
ARKANSAS RIVER
DERRY NO 1 DITCH
CONDUIT
Dry Union
Mt Massive Lakes
ELBERT CREEK
HALF MOON
EMERALD LAKE
BM 9591
SEG 11
Box Cr
STANDARD
Herrington
Mount Elbert 14433
MOUNT ELBERT
Kobe
Yellow
Corske
Spring
1.2
3.2
3.7
3.3
A
B
C
D
E

A
B
C
D
E
13
12
11
10
9
Elevation x 1000
Seg 9
Segment 10
Seg 11
Miles
0
5
10

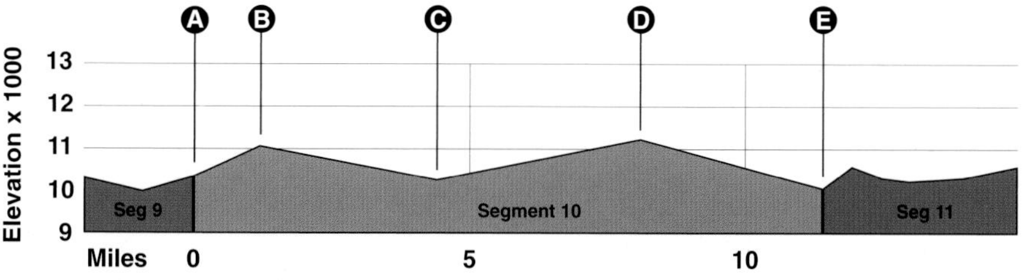

Segment 11
Halfmoon Creek to Clear Creek Road

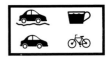

Distance: 19.9 miles
Elevation Gain: approx 1520 ft

The old Interlaken resort hotel, near Twin Lakes.

Gudy's Tip

"The previous route over Hope Pass has been replaced by a more direct one. Those still choosing to climb Hope Pass know why it is so named: 'Hope I never have to go over that pass again with a full pack.'"

Trip Log

Date: _____ Notes: _____

_____

_____

_____

_____

On your way to the trailhead on Halfmoon Creek, take notice of the water diversion structures which are a part of the Pan-Ark Project. Twin Lakes Reservoir is also a part of this immense project which diverts water from the west slope under the Continental Divide to the east slope via the Arkansas River. Twin Lakes was enlarged in 1972 to serve the Mount Elbert powerplant. This pumped storage station generates electric power in high demand periods by using water stored in a forebay above the plant.

At the head of the reservoir is the village of Twin Lakes. Twin Lakes was first established as Dayton and got its start, as did most of the towns in the upper Arkansas, in the brief but energetic gold placer boom of the 1860s. After the boom, the people of Dayton recognized their town was unique because of the incredible mountain scenery and the two lakes at their doorsteps. As early as 1866, Bayard Taylor was informing the world of the beauty of the area.

By the late 1870s, Dayton and the Twin Lakes had become a popular resort area. One hotel, run by John Stanley and Charles Thomas, was established on the south shore of the lower lake and was known as Lakeside House. James Dexter acquired the property in 1883 and transformed it into an impressive resort. After improvements, the complex consisted of a dance pavilion, stables, the main hotel and an annex, storage buildings, laundry and a complete water system. Dexter was so enchanted with the location that he built himself a private, two-story log cabin with Victorian trim. To fit the mood of the expansion, the isolated retreat was renamed Interlaken. The resort was very popular with anglers, tourists and nature lovers of the late 1800s, and it is a pity that the picturesque refuge went into a decline after the turn of the century. The main culprit in that decline seems to have been the transformation of the lakes into a reservoir which backed up water over the stage road serving the complex.

When Twin Lakes was further enlarged in the 1970s, the Department of Reclamation decided to save the dilapidated buildings from inundation. The buildings were moved slightly uphill from their original locations, stabilized and given a fresh coat of paint. Thus the isolated remains of Interlaken still exist for us to ponder today.

Probably no other section of the CT gives such an obvious view of glacially deposited debris as the stretch from Twin Lakes to Clear Creek. The parallel ridges bordering the lower valley are lateral moraines, debris deposited by advancing glaciers. The original configuration of Twin Lakes, slightly altered because of its enlargement into a reservoir, was the result of damming by terminal, or end, moraines, deposited at the glaciers' snouts. These unconsolidated deposits, which include gold gouged out of the Sawatch Range and transported into the valley by water and ice, made possible the placer boom of the 1860s. The Arkansas River was pushed against the east side of the valley by the ancient ice flows, so that it now runs in a tight channel between the glacial debris and the hard, ancient core of the Mosquito Range. Those wishing to inspect the 1.7-billion-year-old Precambrian crest of the Sawatch Range can do so here by following a side trail to the top of 14,433-foot Mount Elbert, the highest point in Colorado.

Hikers in this segment during the first weekend of August will be sharing a portion of the route with hardy runners participating in a torturous annual mountain marathon called the Leadville 100.

Additional Trail Information: Years ago when the idea of a Colorado Trail was first conceived, a lower-elevation route south of Twin Lakes reservoir between the Lake Creek and Clear Creek drainages was planned, and several miles of trail were actually built in the vicinity of Lost Canyon and Cache Creek. But work on this route was halted in the 1970s due to problems with access across private property and switched to the much longer, pre-existing, high trail further west over Hope Pass, which served as the official CT route from 1987 to 1999. However, during the summer of 2000, these access problems were resolved, and the route via Cache Creek was opened. Look for this new low-elevation route to leave the trail south of the reservoir between the dam and the old Interlaken site. Mountain bikers will be particularly appreciative of this new alternative, much preferable to both Hope Pass and the dangerous alternate route down US-24.

The area of the new CT route in Cache Creek was one of the earliest areas of placer mining in the state. The first placers appeared in the spring of 1860, and the famous Silver King of Leadville, HAW Tabor, got his start here. Unfortunately, today the maze of old trails and mine roads, eroded stream banks, piles of worked-over soil, and rusting mine equipment takes most of the luster off its significant history. Keep in mind that the high trail over Hope Pass will continue to be open for those wanting to stretch their lungs, but it will not be the official route. Some hikers may want to do the Hope Pass route, which offers a stunning alpine experience not possible at the played-out placers in Cache Creek, but they will have to contend with the extra elevation and distance, including the long trek down County Rd-390 back to trailhead at the end of this segment.

Trailhead/Access Points

Halfmoon Creek Trailhead: Travel south of Leadville on US-24 approximately 3.5 miles and turn right (west) onto Colorado Hwy-300. Drive 0.8 mile and turn left (south) on a dirt road showing the way to Halfmoon Campground. Continue another 1.2 miles and turn right. It is an additional 5.5 miles on the bumpy road to the trailhead parking area, which is on the north side of the road just beyond an earth fill bridge creek crossing.

Lakeview Campground Trailhead/Twin Lakes Reservoir Trail Access: Travel south of Leadville and go west on Colorado Hwy-82 for approximately 4.0 miles. Turn right (north) on Lake Co Rd-24 and ascend 1.0 mile to Lakeview Campground. A trailhead parking area is provided within the campground. You can also park at the Mount Elbert powerplant visitor parking area, whose entrance is on the highway 0.5 mile beyond Lake Co Rd-24. The CT runs right next to the parking area adjacent to the powerplant building. Finally, several fisherman parking areas convenient to the CT are provided on the north side of Twin Lakes Reservoir.

Clear Creek Road Trailhead: See Segment 12.

Twin Lakes, an old mining town and perhaps Colorado's oldest resort town, is approximately 1.0 mile west of the CT crossing on Hwy-82. The Twin Lakes Store is a delighful old general store, and now convenience/gas store, which provides the basics and has a very small post office within to serve the locals.

Twin Lakes Services

Distance From CT:	
	1 miles
Elevation:	9,210
Zip Code:	81251
Area Code:	719

Supplies, Services and Accommodations

Dining	Twin Lakes Nordic Inn	6435 Hwy 82	(719) 486-1830
Gear	Twin Lakes Store	6451 Hwy 82	(719) 486-2196
Groceries	See Twin Lakes Store above		
Laundry	Win Mar	Hwy 82 & Hwy 24	(719) 486-0785
Lodging	Twin Peaks Cabins	889 Hwy 82	(719) 486-2667
	Win Mar	Hwy 82 & Hwy 24	(719) 486-0785
	Twin Lakes Roadhouse/Lodge		(888) 486-4744
Medical	Nearest in Leadville		
Post Office	See Twin Lakes Store above		
Showers	Win Mar	Hwy 82 & Hwy 24	(719) 486-0785

Maps and Jurisdiction

USFS map: San Isabel National Forest, see pages 126-127.
USGS Quad maps: Mount Massive, Mount Elbert, Granite, Winfield, Mount Harvard.
Trails Illustrated map: # 127.

Jurisdiction: Leadville Ranger District, San Isabel NF.

Trail Description

From the trailhead parking area, cross the road to the north side of Halfmoon Creek and immediately intercept the CT as it heads south through a lodgepole forest. This trail is popular because it is one of the most direct routes up Mount Elbert, which was named for territorial governor Samuel Elbert. Ford Elbert Creek at **mile 0.4** (10,160) and notice how the creek has been diverted from its original streambed as shown on the topographical map. Terminate your ascent at **mile 1.0** (10,600) and begin a gradual descent. In 0.3 mile, you will pass a side trail at right which leads to the summit of Mount Elbert. Continue downhill 0.5 mile to Box Creek, then proceed beyond an old intersecting road which crosses the CT on a diagonal. Cross Mill Creek in a marshy area at **mile 2.0** (10,280). The trail joins an old road 0.3 mile beyond and begins an ascent to the south-southeast. This old road splits at **mile 2.8** (10,400); the right fork is barricaded, so follow the left fork. The CT becomes more trail-like as it descends quickly into the Herrington Creek drainage. Ford the creek at **mile 3.1** (10,320), ascend steeply to the old road continuation at left (east-southeast), then continue a southerly ascent. At the upper end of the road, enter the west edge of an elongated meadow and continue to a broad saddle at **mile 3.8** (10,600), where, if you look closely, Turquoise Reservoir is visible to the north.

Descend from the saddle through an aspen forest to a meadow at **mile 4.1** (10,440), where the CT becomes more trail-like and veers to the right (southwest). The trail stays to the right (west) and above several small beaver ponds on Corske Creek. Continue to **mile 4.5** (10,520), where there are two consecutive and potentially confusing trail junctions. At the first junction go right (west), and continue a few steps to the second junction, where you will find a trail register. The trail which climbs steeply ahead here is another route to the summit of Mount Elbert. The CT leaves the ascending path at the second junction squarely to the left (south). Continue south on the CT and cross a fast flowing stream at **mile 4.8** (10,520) on a sturdy bridge. Pick up a jeep road at this point, and descend on it heading generally south, then southeast, and finally east, through an aspen forest. Keep descending on the road to **mile 6.5** (9640), where the trail resumes on your right (southeast). Just ahead is Lake Co Rd-24, which leads from Colorado Hwy-82 to the Mount Elbert forebay and Lakeview Campground.

The trail drops through an aromatic sagebrush field which allows views south into the huge glacial basin containing Twin Lakes. Pass the trailhead parking area within Lakeview Campground at **mile 6.7** (9560) and continue descending beyond the campground to **mile 7.1** (9320), where a pedestrian underpass at Hwy-82 ensures safe passage. South of Hwy-82, the trail leads east and dips briefly into a cheerful ponderosa grove that blooms with an understory of pasque flowers in June. The trail here was constructed with the help of Governor Richard Lamm in September of 1985. When the trail breaks out of the scattered ponderosa, the Mosquito Range and a huge lateral moraine that extends east are visible. The more-than-century-old buildings of Interlaken are barely visible on the south shore.

Some CT trekkers have complained bitterly about the long trudge around the bare north side of Twin Lakes Reservoir through the fields of sagebrush. Admittedly, this section can seem unbearably long to weighted-down backpackers on warm, sunny afternoons. Better, perhaps, to plan this stretch in the early morning when the fragrant smell of sage is still hanging in the cool air. Also, be aware that this stretch is difficult to follow in places from the powerplant to the dam, mostly owing to the fact that it is hard to maintain a trail in the gravelly glacial soils. To make matters worse, many of the trail markers and cairns are continuously vandalized. Still, this section of trail can be enjoyable and educational under the right conditions and state of mind given its uncommon geologic and aesthetic characteristics. Trail maintainer Craig Nelson is particularly enthusiastic about this section of trail from the lake to Hope Pass because of the great variety it offers in its 3500 feet of elevation change.

Pass the Mount Elbert powerplant at **mile 7.7** (9280) and continue east along the treeless north shore, where the reflection of Mount Hope sparkles on the water's surface. Cross the earthen dam at **mile 10.9** (9200) and continue south on the gravel road until you can skirt the southeast edge of the reservoir using a dirt road which goes southwest then west. **(ALERT: As of 9/17/02, for the time being, hikers are no longer permitted to cross the dam due to national security concerns. Users may continue east along Hwy-82 for 1/4 mile until it crosses the river, then west along the first dirt road, leading back to the trail at the south end of the dam.)**

Follow the winding dirt road 0.4 mile west along the fluctuating shoreline until the trail leaves the road in a field of sage near the forest's edge. The trail on the south shore is in stark contrast to the trail on the north shore. The cool forest, which sharply slopes down to the nearby lapping shoreline, generates a laziness and repose to be remembered. There are a few level campsites along here for those who want the moment to linger. From the south shore, the recessional moraine across the lake is very obvious. The huge undulations created by the receding glaciers are more fully revealed in the setting sun.

Continue west along the south shoreline to **mile 12.8** (9240). Look for a trail junction where the CT takes a hard left (east-southeast), ascending the steep, wooded hillside. Those wanting to use the old CT route up and over Hope Pass should continue ahead west along the reservoir for approximately another 3.5 miles then go south ascending Little Willis Gulch. Even if you don't use the old Hope Pass route, it is recommended that you drop your packs here and take the short side trip to visit the old Interlaken site, approximately 1 mile west.

The CT ascends about 0.5 mile to a ridge then drops a few steps southwest to a junction with an old road that ascends west up a shallow gully. Follow this old road to the right (west) for another 0.5 mile, then look for the CT to fork to the left (south). The CT bears generally southeast to south in an aspen/lodgepole forest for 1.5 miles to the crossing of a Forest Service road. At **mile 16.3** (9800) the trail seems to end at a second Forest Service road. Be aware that the route of the CT from here to the end of this segment uses a confusing combination of old trails and roads through the historic old Cache Creek placer area. Trail markers are usually present at critical junctions; however, if the markers were vandalized, these junctions would be very difficult to spot. Until this route becomes established, it will be difficult to follow. If you sense you've lost the route, take time to retrace your steps until you regain your orientation.

From mile 16.3 above, descend on the Forest Service road at left (east-southeast) for approximately 0.1 mile, to the edge of a pleasant meadow surrounded by aspens where an informal car camping area has been established. As the Forest Service road bends to the left (north), the CT forks to the right (east) and after a short distance, ties into an older existing trail. This old trail descends generally south to east 0.7 mile to an old mine road within the placer district. Go right (south) on this old mine road following it generally southeast to south through intermittent sage meadows and forests of lodgepole and aspen, and avoiding the many side trails and roads. At **mile 17.8** (9360) go right (south) on another intersecting mine road which parallels a powerline up a worked-over wash. Just a few feet down this road you'll cross over historic Cache Creek. Continue south on this road as it ascends beyond the powerline; the further you go the more the road deteriorates into an old mine trail. At **mile 18.6** (9760) look for the CT to fork left (south) as the old mine trail begins to orient more in a westerly direction. The CT ascends in a southerly direction a few hundred feet to the top of the moraine, then descends steeply on its rocky, exposed south slope. The moraine can be seen extending several miles east to the narrow gorge containing the Arkansas River. Join up with an old mine road in 0.5 mile and continue the descent to **mile 19.9** (8960) to the trailhead on Clear Creek Road, Chaffee County Road-390.

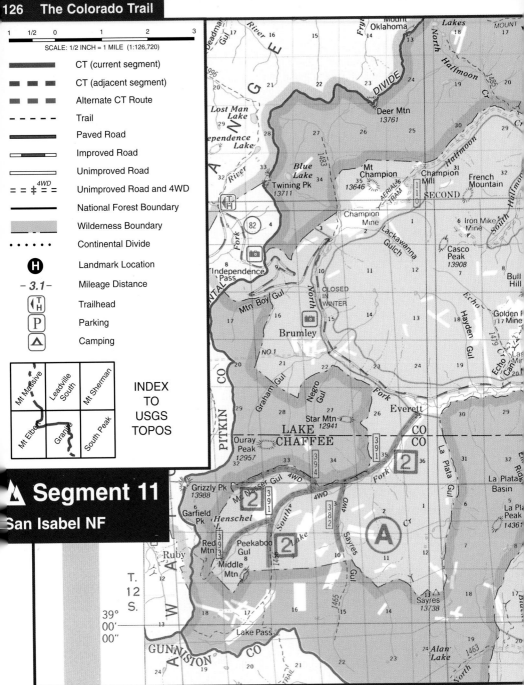

Landmark Location	Mileage	From Denver	Elevation	Latitude	Longitude
A Halfmoon Creek Trailhead	0.0	163.7	10080	39.151332	-106.418407
B Mount Elbert Trail	1.3	165.0	10560	39.144085	-106.407564
C Lakeview Campground	6.7	170.4	9560	39.098035	-106.366638
D Twin Lakes Dam	10.9	174.6	9200	39.080426	-106.303012
E Clear Creek Road Trailhead	19.9	183.6	8960	39.017812	-106.297793

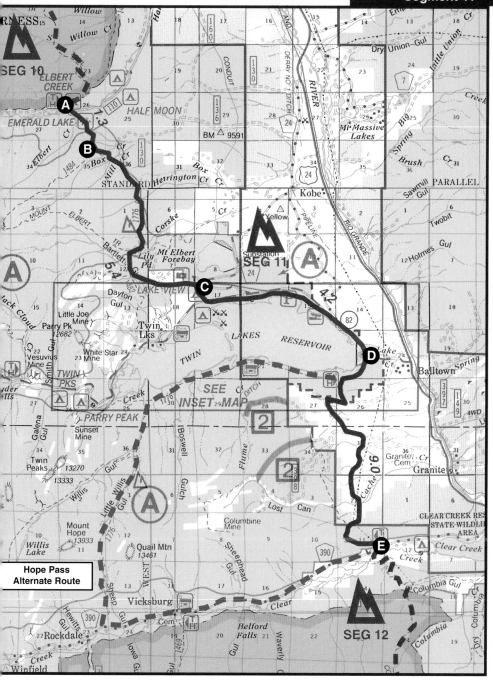

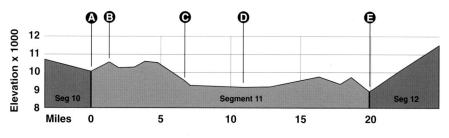

Segment 12
Clear Creek Road to North Cottonwood Creek

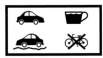

Distance: 18.2 miles
Elevation Gain: approx 4520 ft

Collegiate Peaks Wilderness boundary, near Pine Creek.

Gudy's Tip

"*If you have the time, a hike up Pine Creek into Missouri Basin is a rewarding side-trip. In this emerald-clad basin, you are seemingly in the very heart of the sky-touching Collegiates, surrounded by four 14ers — Harvard, Missouri, Belford and Oxford.*"

Trip Log

Date: _____   Notes: _____

_____

_____

_____

Perhaps the most stately section of the Sawatch Range is the portion known as the Collegiate Peaks, a collection of 14,000-foot mountains rising above high extended ridges and deep valleys. The CT continues southward in this segment along the eastern slopes of the Collegiates, ascending and descending the magnificent terrain. The backpacker will find exceptional campsites all along the way, as well as side trails leading to alpine lakes and isolated niches. The mountain climber will be challenged by several high peaks that rise near the trail, including 14,420-foot Mount Harvard, 14,153-foot Mount Oxford and 14,073-foot Mount Columbia.

This portion of the CT begins in private property on the Clear Creek road but soon rises out of the valley and enters the Collegiate Peaks Wilderness, where it remains for most of the segment. Mountain bicyclists are reminded that they will need to detour this segment, as well as the north portion of Segment 13 (see Mountain Bicycle Detour).

The stunning Collegiate Range was first surveyed in 1869 by a university team, thus accounting for the range's unique name. It was Professor Josiah Dwight Whitney, the head of the Harvard School of Mining and Geology, who led a group of science students into Colorado Territory to give them experience and also to compare the heights of the Colorado Rockies with those of California's Sierra Nevada. The group climbed and named Mount Harvard to honor their institution. Mount Yale was named after Whitney's alma mater. Mount Columbia didn't join the roster of the distinctive group of Ivy League fourteeners until 1916, when it was named by Roger Toll, an official of the Colorado Mountain Club.

Additional Trail Information: The private property in the first mile of this segment has been problematic in years past. For a short time in the mid-1990s, access was denied primarily due to the actions of a few rude and thoughtless hikers. However, by 1999 the route across the old barnyard and pastures was open. In any event, do not tarry in crossing the private property, and be considerate.

Clear Creek Road Trailhead: Travel north from Buena Vista on US-24 and turn left (west) on Chaffee Co Rd-390. Drive 3.0 miles to the informal trailhead parking area on the north side of the dirt road. To find the old CT route (now an optional choice) over Hope Pass, proceed west up Rd-390 an additional 6.3 miles to where the road makes a wide bend just beyond the restored town of Vicksburg. A side road goes right (north) here for several hundred feet, to where the trail begins its steep ascent to Hope Pass.

North Cottonwood Creek Road Trail Access: See Segment 13.

Available in Buena Vista (see Segment 13).

Maps and Jurisdiction

USFS maps: San Isabel National Forest, see pages 134-135.
USGS Quad maps: Granite, Mount Harvard, Harvard Lakes, Buena Vista West.
Trails Illustrated map: # 129.

Jurisdiction: Leadville Ranger District, San Isabel NF.

Trail Description

The CT immediately enters private property at the trailhead on the south side of Chaffee Co Rd-390. Latch the gate behind you and continue ahead on the road, avoiding the right fork to the private residence. Cross to the south side of Clear Creek on a wide bridge and pass through a gate. Just beyond the bridge at **mile 0.1** (8960), go left (east) off the road and follow a faint trail across a boggy area. In a few hundred feet the trail rises out of the low area onto a sagebrush meadow above the creek. Continue east following a very faint path that can be difficult to spot, but that is confirmed in a few places with broken down cairns. As you approach the powerline ahead, the faint path will connect into an old jeep track.

Just before you would pass under the powerline on the jeep track at **mile 0.5** (8960), turn onto another, fainter jeep track which heads to the right (south). Six hundred feet beyond, top a small, bald rise which until now has concealed from view a gateway through a fence. From this point, continue a few more steps south then south-southeast to the edge of the trees. Here, you should see to your left (east) a sturdy boilerplate "Closed To All Vehicles" sign concealed in the trees at **mile 0.7** (8960). This marks where the trail begins its ascent out of the valley. Just up the trail is an interesting and historic area of rare "Ute Trees," where large patches of inner and outer bark were scraped from the ancient Ponderosa by the Utes for medicinal purposes and other functional uses. There are other places near the CT where these incredibly significant historic and ancient Ponderosa exist, but you will have to search them out for yourself.

Pass through a burned-out lodgepole forest which is slowly coming back to life and switchback uphill in the vicinity of the powerline. Enter damp, but usually waterless, upper Columbia Gulch at **mile 1.9** (9640), where the CT crosses an old road in a sagebrush meadow encircled by aspen and lodgepole. As the trail re-enters the trees, it crosses the boundary into Collegiate Peaks Wilderness and resumes its ascent southward in an aspen forest. Lodgepole begin to outnumber aspen as the trail rises onto the rocky mountainside above the gulch. The trail switchbacks to the right at **mile 2.9** (10,040) and moves onto a sunnier exposure. Continue the ascent, crossing several small streamlets which form the headwaters of Columbia Creek. Mount the ridge extending east of Waverly Mountain at **mile 4.8** (11,640). From here, Mount Harvard's impressive crest is dominant on the southern skyline.

The CT drops quickly through a lodgepole forest to its intersection with the Pine Creek Trail in the spacious, grassy valley at **mile 6.4** (10,400). Here, there are several well-established campsites with the meandering creek nearby. Follow the Pine Creek Trail 500 feet downstream to a bridge which crosses to the south side of the creek.

At this point, a fork to the left goes downstream, parallel to Pine Creek, to end at a trailhead on US-24. Be attentive here; we've heard of several parties that mistakenly continued down this trail instead of staying on the CT. After the bridge crossing, continue straight ahead on the CT and begin a long ascent out of the Pine Creek Valley.

At **mile 8.1** (11,520), pass an unmarked and indistinct side trail to the right, which leads in 0.3 mile to Rainbow Lake, a delightful camping spot in the trees just below timberline. Continue climbing through a ghost forest and proceed to a windy, exposed point with a line of sight up the Arkansas Valley. Duck back into the trees and climb to a ridge extending northeast from Mount Harvard at **mile 8.8** (11,800). For the next mile, the CT traverses through alpine flowers and grasses with stands of spruce and bristlecone growing at the upper limits of their life zones. The open tundra areas provide views across the valley to the Buffalo Peaks, which are the southernmost mountains in the Mosquito Range.

Descend to the crossing of Morrison Creek at **mile 9.8** (11,560). Approximately 0.7 mile beyond, pass the Wapaca Trail, which descends to the left. Continue through a spruce forest to Frenchman Creek at **mile 11.8** (10,960) and cross the Harvard Trail

Gunnison Spur

The Colorado Trail Foundation has been working for a number of years on the completion of the Gunnison Spur to the Colorado Trail. It is planned that it will begin on the south side of Twin Lakes and proceed over Hope Pass, then up the South Fork of Clear Creek and over the Continental Divide near Lake Ann, down the high ground between Illinois Creek and Texas Creek, and up the Taylor River to a foot bridge across the Taylor just south of Dinner Station Campground. From there it will generally follow the high ground between the Taylor River and Brook Trail Creek/Clear Creek to where they join near One Mile Campground. From there it will proceed south via various jeep tracks and trails in the Beaver Creek drainage before turning southwest to Signal Peak and on to the trailhead at Western State College in Gunnison. The

estimated distance for the Spur when completed is about 50 miles.

The Gunnison Spur has been signed but vandalism has taken a toll. Motorized traffic has also presented some problems, so that the CTF has not yet produced an official map or guide for the Spur, nor begun maintenance of it. It is still a work in progress with an uncertain completion date.

The Three Apostles, landmarks along the Gunnison Spur, in the South Fork of Clear Creek.

500 feet beyond. Some people head west up this side trail to the head of Frenchman Creek for a climb up Harvard and Columbia from their east extending ridges. The CT continues southeast from this trail junction and rises slightly to cross a ridge at **mile 12.6** (11,160). At **mile 14.1** (10,640) pass above a neglected mine whose operator left in such a hurry that he forgot his ore cart.

Just beyond the mine, pass an old road which is more steeply inclined than the CT. Descend to Three Elk Creek at **mile 15.1** (10,280) and, 300 feet further along, pass at a right angle the trail which ascends to a cirque formed by Mount Columbia's southeast face. Here the trail leaves the wilderness area and continues south to upper Harvard Lake, which is more like a pond, and the lower lake at **mile 15.4** (10,280). Descend 0.2 mile from the lakes and ford a stream, then begin a traverse at about 10,000 feet through a lodgepole forest which has, in places, a lush understory of purple lupine.

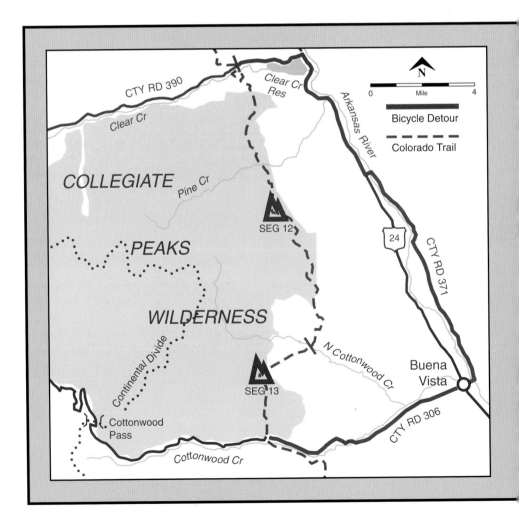

Pass over a ridge at **mile 17.5** (9880) and switchback down into an area of mountain mahogany that allows views west up the Horn Fork Basin to the Continental Divide and east into the Arkansas Valley. End this segment on the North Cottonwood Creek Road in a lodgepole-fir forest at **mile 18.2** (9400). If you are continuing on the CT, hike approximately 0.1 mile west down the road and look for the trail where it resumes at left.

Mountain Bicycle Detour

Collegiate Peaks Wilderness Detour — *Segment 12 and 13 (San Isabel NF):* It is necessary to use a section of US-24 for this detour, but the distance spent on the busy highway can be reduced by using Chaffee County Rd-371 for the last 10 miles into Buena Vista. This detour gives unobstructed views of the Collegiate Range, especially so if you choose to follow Rd-371, which parallels the east bank of the Arkansas River through sagebrush and piñon meadows. This county road follows the abandoned route of the Colorado Midland Railway south to Buena Vista using a series of tunnels hewn out of the granite basement rocks of the Mosquito Range. The railroad was built through here in 1886 and had a whistle stop known as Wild Horse near the tunnels. Can you identify the rock formation known as Elephant Rock, which was so popular with passengers that they often pleaded with the conductor to stop the train so they could take photographs?

Detour Description: Begin this detour at the start of Segment 12 on Chaffee Co Rd-390. Pedal east 3 miles on Rd-390 and turn right (south) onto US-24. Carefully continue south on US-24 for 5.9 miles, then turn left onto Chaffee Co Rd-371. You can continue on US-24 to Buena Vista if you wish, or you can cross the Arkansas River on Rd-371 and then resume a southerly course on the abandoned Colorado Midland grade to Buena Vista at **mile 18.8** (7690). Once in town, turn right (west) onto Main Street and continue a few blocks to the stoplight at US-24. Proceed west across US-24 on Main Street, which becomes Chaffee Co Rd-306 (Cottonwood Pass Road) beyond the city limits. Continue to the Avalanche Trailhead parking area at **mile 28.4** (9360), where you will rejoin the CT. This point is mile 6.6 (9360) of Segment 13.

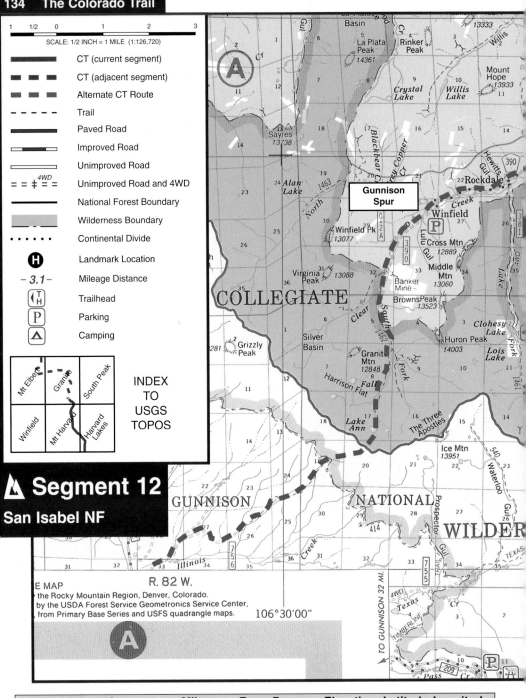

SCALE: 1/2 INCH = 1 MILE (1:126,720)

————	CT (current segment)
– – – –	CT (adjacent segment)
▬ ▬ ▬	Alternate CT Route
- - - - -	Trail
————	Paved Road
▭▭▭	Improved Road
▭▭▭	Unimproved Road
= = ‡ = =	Unimproved Road and 4WD
————	National Forest Boundary
	Wilderness Boundary
• • • • • •	Continental Divide
H	Landmark Location
– 3.1 –	Mileage Distance
[T/H]	Trailhead
[P]	Parking
[△]	Camping

INDEX
TO
USGS
TOPOS

Mt Elbert | Granite | South Peak
Winfield | Mt Harvard | Harvard Lakes

▲ Segment 12
San Isabel NF

E MAP
the Rocky Mountain Region, Denver, Colorado.
by the USDA Forest Service Geometronics Service Center,
from Primary Base Series and USFS quadrangle maps.

R. 82 W.

106°30'00"

Landmark Location	Mileage	From Denver	Elevation	Latitude	Longitude
Ⓐ Clear Creek Road Trailhead	0.0	183.6	8960	39.017812	-106.297793
Ⓑ Waverly Ridge	4.8	188.4	11640	38.975227	-106.285366
Ⓒ Pine Creek	6.4	190.0	10400	38.964860	-106.276168
Ⓓ Harvard ridge	8.8	192.4	11800	38.946233	-106.270335
Ⓔ North Cottonwood Creek Road	18.2	201.8	9400	38.865650	-106.240372

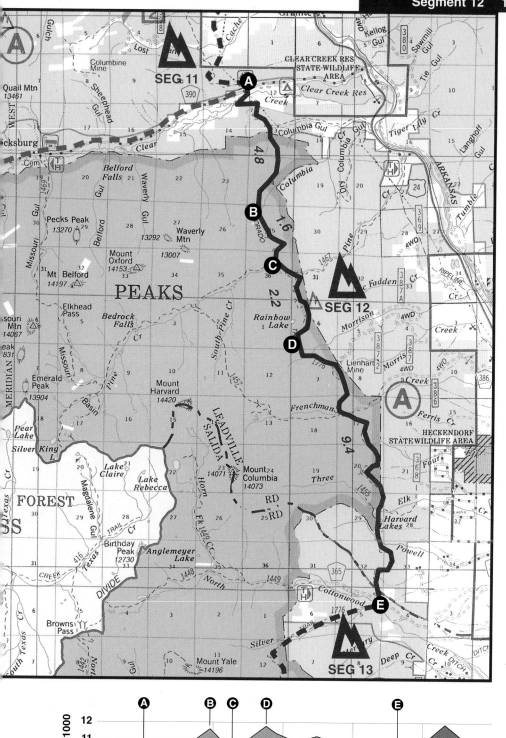

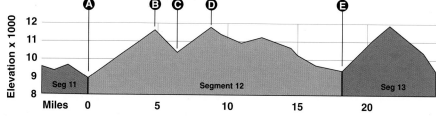

Segment 13

North Cottonwood Creek Road to Chalk Creek Trailhead

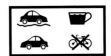

Mt. Princeton from Mt. Yale.

Distance: 22.2 miles
Elevation Gain: approx 3720 ft

Gudy's Tip

"Watch out for the missed signs at the Chalk Cliffs. The route along the road is a temporary solution to skirt private property."

Trip Log

Date: _____ Notes: _____

_____

_____

_____

_____

About This Segment

Near the end of this segment, the CT traverses Mount Princeton's lower eastern flank and descends into Chalk Creek, which was named for the white, crumbly pillars that support the mountain's southeast ridge. This unusual formation is the result of granitic rock which was kaolinized (altered) by hydrothermal solutions rising from cooling magma along fault and fracture zones in the area. Chalk Creek has always been popular for its hot springs and remains well known today. Trail crews working in this location always had plenty of volunteers, who were often released by their team leaders early in the afternoon—only to reconvene a few minutes later at the hot springs.

Mount Princeton, which is known for the magnificent symmetrical profile it displays to motorists descending Trout Creek Pass, is a large body of relatively young 30-million-year-old quartz monzonite porphyry intruding into ancient Precambrian metamorphic rocks. It was originally called Chalk Mountain by the Wheeler Survey. Henry Gannett of the Hayden Survey gave the mountain its present name.

Additional Trail Information: Completion of the last 5 miles of this segment is still awaiting the acquisition of rights-of-way. Until that happens, the trail route uses an assortment of county roads to reach the trailhead at Chalk Creek. The trail between North and Middle Cottonwood Creeks crosses the southeast corner of the Collegiate Peaks Wilderness and passes within 2 miles and 2,300 vertical feet of 14,196-foot Mount Yale. Mountain bicyclists are reminded that they must detour around the wilderness area within this segment, rejoining the trail at the Avalanche Trailhead (see Mountain Bicycle Detour in Segment 12.) However, some cyclists may want to bypass a difficult section of the trail at the start of Segment 14 by taking a second detour that begins where Segment 13 crosses Chaffee Co Rd-162 (see Mountain Bicycle Detour in this segment.)

Trailhead/Access Points

North Cottonwood Creek Trail Access: This approach begins with a left turn (west) onto Crossman Street (Chaffee Co Rd-350) from US-24 at the north end of Buena Vista. Proceed 2 miles and turn right (north) onto Chaffee Co Rd-361. After 0.9 mile, make a sharp left turn (south) onto Chaffee Co Rd-365, which is rough and may not be suitable for conventional cars. The road shortly turns west and continues approximately 3.5 miles to a small parking area at an obscure trail access point. From here, the CT heads north to Harvard Lakes and, eventually, Clear Creek; 0.1 mile beyond is the trail access point for the southbound CT. Parking at both places is limited.

Avalanche Trailhead (Cottonwood Pass Road): From US-24 in Buena Vista, turn west at the stop light onto Main Street, which becomes Chaffee Co Rd-306 as it leaves the city limits. Travel approximately 9.5 miles west from Buena Vista on Rd-306 to Avalanche Trailhead. The CT is marked where it crosses the trailhead parking area.

Chalk Creek Trailhead: See Segment 14.

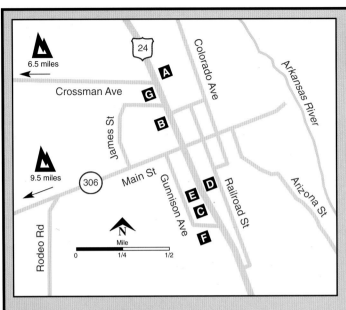

Buena Vista Services

Distance From CT:	
	9.5 miles
Elevation:	7,954
Zip Code:	81211
Area Code:	719

Dining		Several in town.		
Gear	**A**	Trailhead Ventures	707 Hwy 24 North	(719) 395-8001
Groceries	**B**	Leevers Super Market	400 Hwy 24 North	(719) 395-2714
	C	City Market	428 Hwy 24 South	(719) 395-2431
Info	**D**	Chamber of Commerce	343 Hwy 24 South	(719) 395-6612
Laundry	**E**	Morrison's Laundromat	410 Hwy 24	no phone
Lodging		Several in town.		
Medical	**F**	Mountain Medical Centre	36 Oak	(719) 395-8632
Post Office	**G**	Buena Vista Post Office	110 Brookdale Ave	(719) 395-2446

Supplies, Services and Accommodations

Buena Vista, as might be gathered by its Spanish name, is a beautiful place to visit because of its mild year-round climate and striking location in the Arkansas Valley, between the mineralized Mosquito Range and the towering Sawatch. The town is an ideal resupply point for long-distance trekkers because the CT through here is approximately halfway between Denver and Durango. The most direct way to reach Buena Vista from the CT is to follow Chaffee Co Rd-306 approximately 9.5 miles east from Avalanche Trailhead.

Maps and Jurisdiction

USFS map: San Isabel National Forest, see pages 142-143.
USGS Quadrangle maps: Buena Vista West, Mount Yale, Mount Antero.
Trails Illustrated map: # 129.

Jurisdiction: Salida Ranger District, San Isabel NF.

This segment of the CT begins approximately 0.1 mile west of the trail access point at the end of Segment 12. Parking here is limited and usually crowded with the vehicles of those climbing Mount Yale.

Proceed south from the road, cross North Cottonwood Creek and sign in at the register. Ascend in a lodgepole forest on the north side of Silver Creek, passing outcrops of banded Precambrian metamorphic rock. Continue to a valley meadow, where a large beaver pond backs up Silver Creek at **mile 2.2** (11,040). Campers here will be bedding down in the shadow of Mount Yale, which is visible to the southwest. Continue 0.2 mile up the valley and cross to the creek's south side. Ascend the north slope of Mount Yale's east extending ridge, passing through a spruce-fir forest, and enter the Collegiate Peaks Wilderness. Top the saddle between Silver Creek and Middle Cottonwood Creek at **mile 3.3** (11,880). Mount Yale is a steep ridge climb west from this point, with some rock scrambling along the way. The spruce trees at the saddle are sparse enough to allow a striking and rarely seen view of Mount Princeton and its long, elevated western ridge.

Descend south from the pass through a stately bristlecone forest. Pass a good campsite on flat ground, situated in a lodgepole forest, at **mile 4.8** (10,640). Hughes Creek is just a short walk down into the gully west of here. Curve to the left into a dry ravine at **mile 5.3** (10,560) and continue descending through a sparse limber pine and Douglas fir forest that allows a view up the valley of Middle Cottonwood Creek. In another 0.4 mile you will drop to an area too exposed and dry for these trees to survive. Here, mountain mahogany clings to a tenuous existence on the rocky hillside. Notice also the obvious avalanche chutes across the valley on the side of Sheep Mountain.

Exit the wilderness area at **mile 6.3** (9400). Pass the trail register in 700 feet and go right (west) a short distance beyond on an intersecting old road. Bear left (southwest) off the old road to the Avalanche Trailhead parking area at **mile 6.6** (9360). Continue south-southwest across the large parking area and pick up the trail on the opposite side. In a few steps, you'll cross to the south side of Chaffee Co Rd-306 and continue down a short side road. This leads to an informal car-camping area on the north shore of Middle Cottonwood Creek. Bend to the left here, toward the east end of the car-camping area and pick up the CT, which parallels the creek before crossing it on a bridge at **mile 6.8** (9320). The trail is carved deeply into the side of the steep south bank of Middle Cottonwood Creek, and fireweed grows profusely in the disturbed soil. Continue east 200 feet beyond the bridge crossing and enter the bottom of an avalanche chute thick with young, wispy aspen. Most of the older trees here have been fallen in the direction of the avalanche flow. This chute was seen during the descent on the opposite side of the valley, and can be seen to extend nearly to the top of Sheep Mountain.

The trail ascends and then traverses the north slope of Sheep Mountain, providing views of Rainbow Lake through a cool forest. Descend gradually to the eastern foot of Sheep Mountain, just west of the confluence of South and Middle Cottonwood Creeks, where the trail opens up into a sunnier and less dense forest. Fork to the left (north-northeast) where the trail splits near the entrance to some private property at **mile 8.9** (9000). Continue 400 feet downhill and cross to the east

Aaron Locander crossing the bridge at Chalk Creek.

side of South Cottonwood Creek Road (Chaffee Co Rd-344). Follow a side road east which leads first to an informal car-camping site and then to a bridge across South Cottonwood Creek. Turn left (north-northeast) immediately after the bridge and parallel the creek downstream. In a short distance, the trail orients generally east-northeast to east and slowly pulls away from the creek. It crosses a dirt road at **mile 9.6** (8880), then maneuvers through a series of switchbacks which take you out of the valley. After the crossing of South Cottonwood Creek, there are several side trails which peel off the CT and lead to private property. Be alert to stay on the official route.

At **mile 10.8** (9440), turn right (south) onto an old road. Go uphill through an aspen forest another 350 feet, then fork to the left (east) where the road splits. Proceed another 350 feet past the fork and then leave the old road where the trail resumes to the left (north-northeast) at **mile 11.0** (9560). The trail continues its ascent to a point slightly above the saddle west of Bald Mountain at **mile 11.6** (9880) and then begins a long traverse bearing generally southeast, dipping in and out of several drainages. Cross the meager flow of upper Silver Prince Creek at **mile 13.3** (9840) and continue a half-mile further to the trickle in Maxwell Creek.

The trail descends gradually through a varied forest of fir, pine and aspen to a jeep road crossing and, 0.1 mile beyond, a comfortable log bridge across Dry Creek at **mile 15.5** (9600). This creek, contrary to its name, usually has a good, swift flow. Continue on the CT to a switchback on FS-322 at **mile 16.7** (9480). An information board here explains the route the CT will follow on county roads for the next 5.5 miles.

Descend at left for 0.9 mile on the rough dirt road. Where FS-322 splits, continue straight ahead (east), avoiding the right fork which leads to private property. The Forest Service road joins up with Chaffee Co Rd-322 approximately 0.2 mile beyond. Follow the graveled county road 0.6 mile east to where it makes a bend to the left (north). Continue in a north-northeast direction on the road approximately 0.2 mile to the black-topped Chaffee Co Rd-321. Follow this road south, east, west then south again approximately 1.3 miles as it makes a winding descent to the intersection with Chaffee Co Rd-162 at **mile 19.7** (8160). For those requiring a pause to soak their bones before continuing, Mount Princeton Hot Springs is immediately south across the road.

Proceed 1.4 miles west and southwest on paved Rd-162, then veer to the left (west-southwest) onto Chaffee Co Rd-291. Continue 1.1 miles down this quiet, tree-lined road to the trailhead parking area on Chalk Creek. This segment ends here at **mile 22.2** (8360), where the trail resumes its southerly course at the footbridge over the creek.

Raspberry Gulch Detour — *Segments 13 and 14 (San Isabel NF):* This optional detour was once advised to avoid a steep and poorly maintained section of the trail in the northern part of Segment 14. However, the trail was rerouted in 1989 around this problem section and therefore the detour is not as critical as before. It remains in because some mountain cyclists may prefer the smooth, graded county roads to the trail, and because the steep, gravelly switchbacks at the beginning of Segment 14 continue to be a difficulty for cyclists.

Detour Description: Follow the official CT to **mile 19.7** (8160) in Segment 13. Turn left (east) onto Chaffee Co Rd-162 and pedal 0.7 mile to Chaffee Co Rd-270. Proceed southeast, then east, on Rd-270, which soon takes on a southerly heading. Continue to **mile 4.6** (8200) and go right (west) on Rd-272. Turn left (south) at an intersection 2 miles beyond and continue on Rd-272 to **mile 8.2** (8920), which is the Browns Creek Trailhead. Continue up the Browns Creek Trail to **mile 9.6** (9600), where you will rejoin the CT again. This point is mile 6.4 (9600) in Segment 14.

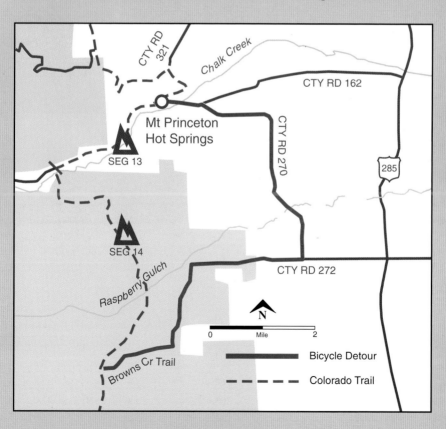

Map Legend

Symbol	Description
1 1/2 0 1 2 3	SCALE: 1/2 INCH = 1 MILE (1:126,720)
━━━━━	CT (current segment)
▬ ▬ ▬	CT (adjacent segment)
▬▬ ▬▬	Alternate CT Route
- - - - -	Trail
━━━━━	Paved Road
▭▬▬▭	Improved Road
▭▭▭	Unimproved Road
= = ‡ = =	Unimproved Road and 4WD
━━━━━	National Forest Boundary
▓▓▓	Wilderness Boundary
• • • • •	Continental Divide
Ⓗ	Landmark Location
– 3.1 –	Mileage Distance
(T/H)	Trailhead
Ⓟ	Parking
⌂	Camping

INDEX TO USGS TOPOS

Tincup | Mt Yal | Buena Vista West
Cumberland Pass | St Elmo | Mt Antero

▲ Segment 13
San Isabel NF

Landmark Location	Mileage	From Denver	Elevation	Latitude	Longitude
Ⓐ North Cottonwood Creek Road	0.0	201.8	9400	38.865650	-106.240372
Ⓑ Silver Creek saddle	3.3	205.1	11880	38.847557	-106.281345
Ⓒ Avalanche Trailhead	6.6	208.4	9360	38.813596	-106.280375
Ⓓ Bald Mountain saddle	11.6	213.4	9880	38.793986	-106.226610
Ⓔ Chaffee Co Rd-162	19.7	221.5	8160	38.732923	-106.163436
Ⓕ Chalk Creek Trailhead	22.2	224.0	8360	38.716701	-106.199539

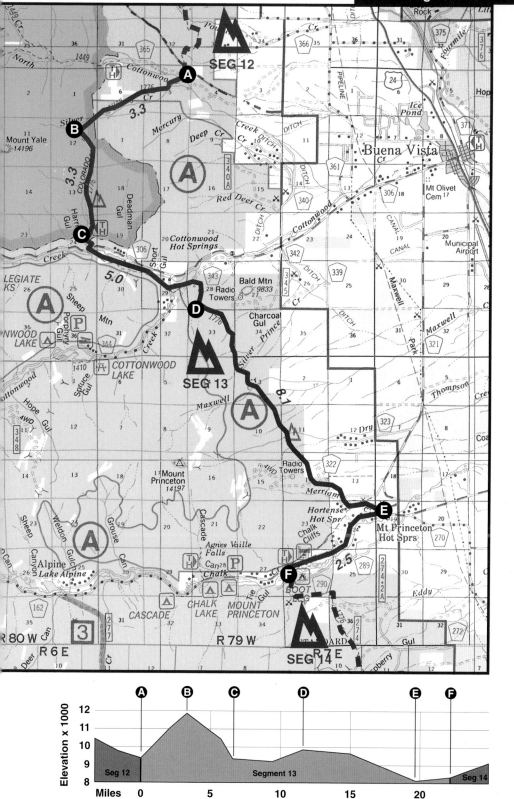

Segment 14
Chalk Creek to US-50

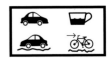

Distance: 20.0 miles
Elevation Gain: approx 3320 ft

Trail crew at work on the CT near Mt. Shavano.

Gudy's Tip

"The short but often overlooked five-mile stretch between Shavano Campground and US-50 wanders through lovely aspen and lodgepole pine forests."

Trip Log

Date: _____ Notes: _____

_____

_____

_____

_____

About This Segment

The southernmost peaks of the Sawatch Range honor the memory of the once mighty Ute Indian nation. Starting at Chalk Creek, the trail rounds the eastern flank of 14,269-foot Mount Antero, which is named after a Ute chief of the Utah-based Unitah band. The trail then continues south to 14,229-foot Mount Shavano, who was a medicine man and chief of the Ute Tabeguache band. On the southern horizon rises the broad Mount Ouray and Chipeta Mountain. These landmarks are named for the last great Ute chief, the diplomatic spokesman for the Ute nation, and his wife.

Mount Antero and its neighbor to the south, 13,667-foot Mount White, are popular with the rockhounding crowd. Gemologists have been flocking to the peaks ever since Nathaniel Wannemaker discovered aquamarine near the 14,000-foot level on Mount Antero in the 1880s. The crest of the mountain was designated as Mount Antero Mineral Park in 1949. The bronze plaque set on that date still greets its peak-baggers just below the summit.

Additional Trail Information: As with previous segments in the Sawatch, this section subjects trail users to a fair amount of elevation gain, but also has long stretches of mostly level walking. Your efforts are rewarded with grand panoramas of the lower Arkansas Valley and the northern Sangre de Cristo Range. Backpackers will find many potential campsites, as well as occasional gushing streams to satisfy thirsts produced by the warmer temperatures of the lower elevations.

Trailhead/Access Points

Chalk Creek Trailhead: Travel south from Buena Vista on US-285 to Nathrop. Go right (west) onto Chaffee Co Rd-162. Proceed approximately 6 miles and bear to the left on Chaffee Co Rd-291. Continue up the tree-lined dirt road 1.1 miles to the trailhead parking area near the footbridge over Chalk Creek.

Browns Creek Trailhead: Travel south from Nathrop on US-285. Go right (west) on Chaffee Co Rd-270 and proceed 1.5 miles up this road. Continue straight ahead on Chaffee Co Rd-272 as Rd-270 bears to the right. Drive ahead on Rd-272 approximately 2 miles and bear to the left (south) at an intersection. From this intersection it is 1.6 miles further south on Rd-272 to Browns Creek Trailhead. From here, follow the trail west 1.4 miles to where it joins up with the CT.

Angel of Shavano Trailhead: From the intersection of US-285 and US-50 at Poncha Springs, go west approximately 6 miles on US-50 to Chaffee Co Rd-240 (North Fork South Arkansas River Road). Go right (north) on Rd-240 and proceed along the dirt road 3.8 miles to the trailhead parking area opposite Angel of Shavano Campground.

US-50 Trail Access: See Segment 15.

Maps and Jurisdiction

USFS map: San Isabel National Forest, see pages 150-151.
USGS Quadrangle maps: Mount Antero, Maysville.
Trails Illustrated map: # 130.

Jurisdiction: Salida Ranger District, San Isabel NF.

Salida Services

Distance From CT:	
	13 miles
Elevation:	7,036
Zip Code:	81201
Area Code:	719

Salida, the old railroad town, and now, main commercial center for the lower Arkansas valley, is about 13 miles east of the CT crossing on US-50. **Poncha Springs**, 8 miles east of the crossing, has a restaurant and a small convenience store. Monarch Spur RV Park, about 1 mile east of the CT on Hwy 50, has camping and showers. The Monarch Mountain Lodge, about 4.5 miles west of the CT on Hwy-50, has lodging and a mail drop.

Supplies, Services and Accommodations

Bus	**A**	TNM & O (Greyhound)	731 Blake St	(719) 539-7474
Dining		Several in town		
Gear	**B**	Headwaters Outdoor	228 North F St	(719) 539-4506
Groceries	**C**	Safeway	232 G St	(719) 539-3513
	D	Salida Food Town	248 W Hwy 50	(719) 539-7500
Info	**E**	Chamber of Commerce	406 W Rainbow Blvd	(719) 539-2068
Laundry	**F**	Lazrine's Coin-op	E St and 14th St	(719) 539-3659
Lodging		Several in town		
Medical	**G**	Heart of Rockies Med. Ctr.	448 East 1st St	(719) 539-6661
Post Office	**H**	Salida Post Office	310 D St	(719) 539-2548
Showers	**J**	Salida Hot Springs	410 W Hwy 50	(719) 539-6738

Trail Description

From the bridge over Chalk Creek at the trailhead parking area, the trail begins a gradual ascent out of the broad valley. Just up from the stream, a side trail branches left to Bootleg Campsite. This little public oasis surrounded by private property is thoughtfully provided by the Forest Service for backpackers who might otherwise have difficulty finding a place to camp.

The CT continues 0.4 mile southeast beyond the creek and joins up with Chaffee Co Rd-290, which is the abandoned grade of the DSP&PRR. Go right (west) on Rd-290 for just a few steps and notice that the trail resumes again to the left on the south side of the road. Follow the trail to a fork at **mile 0.7** (8680). Go left to stay on the CT; the right fork continues to an old quarry. The delicate trickle of a small stream can be heard below as you ascend the trail, which clings to the steep side of the ravine. Curve to the left (east) at **mile 0.9** (8840) and enter a small, grassy side canyon which might make a good campsite if the little stream mentioned above is still flowing. Aspen, fir and spruce inhabit the cooler north facing slope of the canyon, while the sunny south facing slope can support only piñon pine and mountain mahogany.

Continue east to the head of the canyon and maneuver through a series of gravelly switchbacks. Top the sandy saddle above the canyon at **mile 1.3** (9200) and bear left (northeast) along the ridgeline, ascending the sandy trail. In 0.1 mile, you top out on a knoll. Take a few minutes to admire this seldom seen view of the Chalk Cliffs to the north. Descend from the knoll through two switchbacks, then assume an easterly heading and enter a small elevated meadow. As the trail enters a grouping of aspen, it appears to be funneling down a more defined gully. Just beyond the aspen grove, the trail bears to the right and almost imperceptibly pulls away from the drainage line of the small gully. Before you know it, you are well above the small gully and then descending to an arid bench of piñon and mountain mahogany well above the surrounding country to the east. At **mile 2.2** (9000), avoid the fork at left (east). The CT orients south here and drops steeply on a rocky trail to the broad and usually dry Eddy Creek drainage.

For the next several miles, the trail will traverse at or near 9000 feet and bear to the south to southeast. This section of trail was re-routed in 1989 to avoid an excessively steep and eroded section further west. It crosses a recently burned area between Eddy Creek and Raspberry Gulch, and has received complaints by hikers expecting a more "aesthetic" experience. Remember that this area is the lowest section of the CT in the Arkansas Valley and afternoon temperatures under skies with no shade can be extremely uncomfortable. Keep in mind also that there are no reliable water sources from Chalk Creek 7 miles to Browns Creek. Despite its unpleasantness, the burned-out forest does provide unparalleled vistas north to Chalk Cliffs and east to the lower Arkansas Valley.

Continue in a southerly direction, crossing Eddy Creek road and passing through the most distressing section of the burn area. At **mile 4.0** (8960), the trail descends a side hill and crosses Raspberry Gulch Road (Chaffee Co Rd-273). Beyond Raspberry Gulch Road, there are few signs of the burn, and the trail stays in a sunny area of scattered ponderosa pine. At **mile 4.7** (9000), just after crossing an eroded jeep road, the trail drops into a deep and wide, but normally dry, gully. Rise to the opposite side of the gully into another meadow of scattered ponderosa pine, and continue 0.2 mile to the first in a series of three poorly built switchbacks. Here, the trail begins a long ascent bearing generally west to southwest. Where the trail descends slightly and then orients briefly south at **mile 5.6** (9400), it picks up the route of an old mine road, which is not apparent but for the fact that you now have a wider, and correspondingly more eroded, tread. Just 0.2 mile beyond, thoughtful trail builders have constructed a detour around a particularly rough and steep section in the old road.

The CT gets uncomfortably rocky and steep just before a confusing intersection at **mile 6.2** (9720). You want to continue on the CT here to the left (southeast then south) and avoid the forks to the right (north) and straight ahead (south-southwest). Just above the ponds on Little Browns Creek at **mile 6.4** (9600) you will join up with the Browns Creek Trail, up from the Browns Creek Trailhead. Ascend southwest past an old fork to the left, which descends to some beaver ponds, and continue to a trail junction at **mile 6.6** (9640), where the Browns Creek Trail continues ahead to Browns Lake. The CT goes left (east then south) at this junction and continues 400 feet to Little Browns Creek. In another 600 feet, you will cross Browns Creek.

Continue on the trail 700 feet past Browns Creek to another trail intersection. Go straight ahead here (south) and avoid the fork leading downhill to the left, which is the Wagon Loop Trail that takes you back to the Browns Creek Trailhead. Ascend slightly and then traverse through a lodgepole forest to Fourmile Creek at **mile 8.8** (9680). The trail grazes a jeep road 0.7 mile beyond here and continues to Sand Creek at **mile 10.0** (9600).

The trail ascends to a gravelly ridge at **mile 11.1** (10,160), then descends into a damp gully 0.4 mile beyond. The trail then ascends to another high point, where Mount Ouray and Chipeta Mountain can be seen to the south through the fir-lodgepole forest. Descend to Squaw Creek at **mile 12.2** (9760) and continue 0.2 mile further to where the CT joins a jeep road and continues south. The Mount Shavano Trail ascends to the right at **mile 12.7** (9880). This comfortable side trail ascends to within 800 vertical feet of 14,229-foot Mount Shavano. About 0.2 mile beyond the intersection with the Mount Shavano Trail, you will cross a cattle guard and leave the jeep road as it descends to the left. Notice that the rather obscure trail continues ahead (south-southwest) through a grassy meadow ringed with aspen. Pick up an obvious trail in 400 feet on the opposite side of the meadow and cross a jeep road at **mile 13.2** (9800). About 0.4 mile beyond, pass through a meadow which is often trampled by cattle. The trail might be a little hard to spot here but becomes easier to follow once it re-enters the aspen. Not long after re-entering the forest, the CT descends into a lodgepole forest.

Pass through a gate and ascend slightly to a ridge at mile 14.2 (9640), where the forest stops abruptly. Descend a sunny slope and re-enter the trees just before the Angel of Shavano Trailhead parking area on the north side of Chaffee Co Rd-240 at **mile 14.9** (9160). The trail continues on the opposite side of the road just beyond the Angel of Shavano Campground sign and in 800 feet crosses a footbridge over the fast flowing North Fork. Steer through several switchbacks and ascend to a lodgepole forested ridgetop at **mile 16.5** (9760). The trail then descends 0.3 mile in a pronounced ravine, after which it bends to the right (south-southwest) and begins a traverse. In approximately 0.5 mile, the trail skirts the northwest side of Dry Lake, an isolated, often scummy, pond with no inlet or outlet.

Continue west beyond the pond. At **mile 17.5** (9560), the original trail was obscured by logging activity, although young lodgepole pines promise a new forest. A reconstructed trail bears generally south along the east edge of the logged forest. Approach the southern edge of the logged area in 0.1 mile, where the three closed logging roads lead east, west and south. The trail cuts west-southwest across the revegetated roads.

Descend to Lost Creek at **mile 17.8** (9400) and cross a jeep road just west of the creek. Proceed south and west to a small open area at **mile 18.8** (9360). The sometimes faint trail proceeds 0.1 mile around the north and west perimeter of this open area and then crosses a dirt road. Descend to Cree Creek at **mile 19.3** (9200). Backpackers should note that this is the last decent camping opportunity north of US-50. The trail ascends south from Cree Creek to the edge of the lodgepole forest, where the South Arkansas Valley and US-50 come into view. Continue south underneath a powerline tower and descend an exposed south facing slope on a rocky old road. Cross the abandoned D&RG railroad grade at **mile 19.9** (8880), then enter a ponderosa forest and continue 450 feet to US-50. This trail segment ends here on the highway at **mile 20.0** (8840).

Angel of Shavano

A side trail leads to 14,269-foot Mount Shavano from the CT, Segment 14, for those so inclined. For the more adventurous (and properly equipped) hiker, you can descend the peak in unique and fun fashion by *glissading,* sliding on your butt, down the long snowfield known as the Angel of Shavano.

This unique formation is an 800-foot-tall, snow-filled gully on the east face of Mount Shavano, sprouting two branches at the top, which resembles an angel with outstretched arms. It is visible, early in the summer, from throughout the lower Arkansas Valley and has spawned a couple of colorful legends.

In one, the Angel is a Native American princess who magically turned into snow during a severe drought, so that her water might sustain life in the valley. In another, it is a warrior, perhaps Shavano himself, who sheds tears of meltwater in grief over the loss of his ancestral lands.

The Angel is in best condition in May and early June, with both arms usually gone by the 4th of July. The angle of the snow is less than 30 degrees and it is rarely icy. But to prevent going out-of-control and being injured, it is mandatory to have an ice axe and know how to use it.

Climb the peak by the Mount Shavano Trail, where it intersects the CT at mile 12.7. Hike west, then north, up the switchbacks to treeline, then follow the trail as it angles west, up to a saddle south of the top. Head north over easy slopes to the summit. On your way back, pick an arm (one starts near the summit, the other, from back at the saddle) and go for it. Hikers without an ice axe should simply retrace their steps.

At the bottom, bushwhack a short distance northeast to regain the trail.

SCALE: 1/2 INCH = 1 MILE (1:126,720)

Symbol	Description
CT (current segment)
CT (adjacent segment)
Alternate CT Route
Trail
Paved Road
Improved Road
Unimproved Road
Unimproved Road and 4WD
National Forest Boundary
Wilderness Boundary
Continental Divide
H	Landmark Location
- 3.1 -	Mileage Distance
TH	Trailhead
P	Parking
A	Camping

INDEX TO USGS TOPOS

Cumberland Pass · St Elmo · Mt Antero · Whitepine · Garfield · Maysville Mtn

⛰ Segment 14
San Isabel NF

Landmark Location	Mileage	From Denver	Elevation	Latitude	Longitude
Ⓐ Chalk Creek Trailhead	0.0	224.0	8360	38.716701	-106.199539
Ⓑ Eddy Creek	2.2	226.2	9000	38.708602	-106.181884
Ⓒ Browns Creek Trail	6.4	230.4	9600	38.666697	-106.180002
Ⓓ Mount Shavano Trail	12.7	236.7	9880	38.602091	-106.195237
Ⓔ Angel of Shavano Trailhead	14.9	238.9	9160	38.585094	-106.218898
Ⓕ Lost Creek	17.8	241.8	9400	38.565203	-106.228954
Ⓖ US-50	20.0	244.0	8840	38.543307	-106.241961

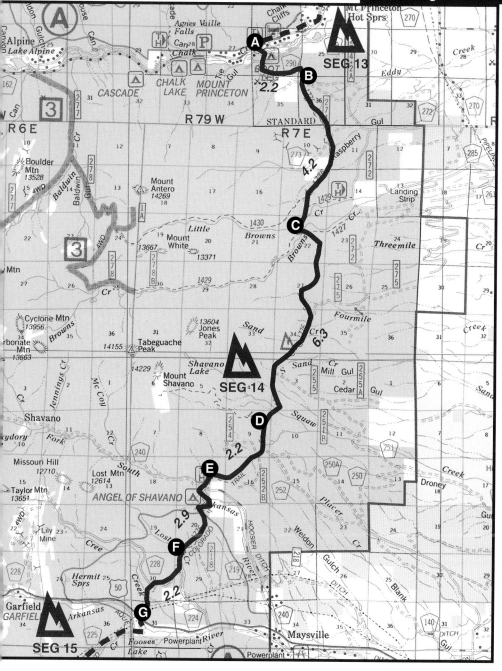

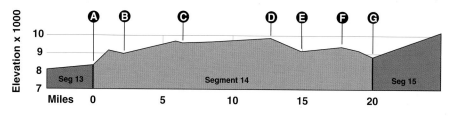

Segment 15
US-50 to
Marshall Pass

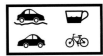

Distance: 14.0 miles
Elevation Gain: approx 3440 ft

Turning aspen along the CT near Marshall Pass.

Gudy's Tip

"Once up on the Divide, you'll have unobstructed views in every direction. Three of our mightiest mountain ranges — the Sawatch, the San Juan, and the Sangre de Cristo — reach for the sky."

Trip Log

Date: _____ Notes: _____

_____

_____

_____

_____

About This Segment

Just before the trail drops down to Marshall Pass at the end of this segment, it skirts the western ridge which connects 13,971-foot Mount Ouray and 12,850-foot Chipeta Mountain. These mountains are named for the Ute chief who represented the Ute nation during the disastrous treaty negotiations of the late 1880s, and for his wife. The area around Marshall Pass marks the southernmost point of the Sawatch Range, although it can also be thought of as the junction of three major mountain ranges: the Sawatch to the north, the Sangre de Cristo to the southeast and the Cochetopa Hills to the southwest.

The rocks in the Mount Ouray area are ancient sedimentary and metamorphic Precambrian, mostly derived from ancient volcanoes. Interestingly, these 1.7-billion-year-old rocks underlie adjacent and similar 30-million-year-old volcanic rocks in the next trail segment southwest of Marshall Pass.

Additional Trail Information: Long-distance trekkers will want to make sure they are well supplied before progressing south of US-50. The next supply point is Creede, nearly a hundred miles away.

The CT mounts the Continental Divide in this segment and wanders along one side or the other of its crest for the next 130 miles, coinciding in most places with the Continental Divide Trail. The trail from the head of South Fooses Creek to Marshall Pass traverses the first portion of this high altitude route, offering expansive and inspirational views of the Cochetopa Hills and the upper Gunnison Basin. Convenient sources of water will be less available once you rise out of the Fooses Creek drainage and mount the divide, but small springs usually cross the trail south of Fooses in normal years until mid to late summer, and the headwaters of Green and Agate creeks are a short distance below the trail.

Trailhead/Access Points

US-50 South Fooses Creek Trailhead: From the intersection of US-285 and US-50 at Poncha Springs, drive west approximately 9 miles on US-50 to Fooses Creek Road (Chaffee Co Rd-225). The CT crosses the highway here and follows Fooses Creek Road, which continues southwest from US-50. A widened shoulder here offers limited and short-term parking opportunities. If you choose to drive up the road, a high-clearance vehicle is recommended. It is 2.9 miles up the rough road to the trail access point on South Fooses Creek. Be aware that the first 0.7 miles is across private property. Take the left fork 0.1 mile in from the highway, and left again at junctions located at miles 1.7, 2.0 and 2.8. The last will take you to the obscure trail access point on South Fooses Creek. There are no facilities here.

Marshall Pass Trailhead: See Segment 16.

Maps and Jurisdiction

USFS maps: San Isabel NF, Gunnison NF, see pages 156-157.
USGS Quadrangle maps: Maysville, Garfield, Pahlone Peak, Mount Ouray.
Trails Illustrated maps: # 130 and 139.

Jurisdiction: Salida Ranger District, Gunnison Ranger District.

Supplies, Services and Accommodations

Available in Salida (see Segment 14).

Trail Description

Starting on US-50 just east of Garfield, follow Fooses Creek Road 2.9 miles to the trail access point. The road crosses private property for the first 0.7 mile. Fork left at 0.1 mile in from the highway, and left again at junctions located at miles 1.7, 2.0 and 2.8. The trail resumes at **mile 2.9** (9560), where it crosses Fooses Creek. Continue up South Fooses Creek 300 feet where a section of forest has been administered as explained by the interpretive sign. Blue diamonds here mark cross-country ski routes.

Cross over to the east side of South Fooses Creek at **mile 3.4** (9720) and ascend through a lodgepole forest. After fording the creek to the west side at **mile 4.3** (9840), continue 0.4 mile to a very labor-intensive section of turnpike tread constructed specifically to keep your feet dry in marshy terrain.

Cross to the east bank of South Fooses Creek at **mile 5.0** (10,160). Continue to a meadow in the shadow of Mount Peck and negotiate a quick double switchback, which helps ease the ascent, at **mile 6.2** (10,520). Enter another grassy area 0.4 mile beyond and begin to rise higher on the mountainside. The trail here is rough and rocky at times. As the CT gains elevation, it crosses several streamlets which form the headwaters of South Fooses Creek.

At **mile 8.3** (11,600) the trail enters the tundra, where a receding blanket of snow in early summer reveals a field of marsh marigolds. Top out on the Continental Divide at **mile 8.5** (11,920). Angle left (southeast), following the sign which points the way to Marshall Pass. Look closely for the tiny alpine forget-me-nots which carpet the gravelly ridge. The trail, although obscure for several hundred feet, soon resumes and traverses the southwest slope of minor summit Point 12,195, then continues due south on the divide ridge, passing cairns constructed from white quartz. Mount Ouray and Chipeta Mountain can be inspected closely from here, and further to the south rises 13,269-foot Antora Peak.

The trail descends through a spruce forest, then opens into a small meadow on the divide at the head of Green Creek at **mile 10.1** (11,480). The trail in this small opening is somewhat overgrown with grass. A small lean-to shelter at the edge of the trees here might provide some protection from afternoon showers. For those contemplating an overnight stay, the headwaters of Green Creek are not more than a 0.3-mile walk downstream from here.

The CT re-enters the trees on the east side of the meadow, and is pointed out by a sign showing the way to East Agate Creek. Continue south and re-enter the tundra at **mile 10.4** (11,480). The trail crosses a small spring here, then passes into a ghost forest, perhaps the site of a long-ago forest fire. The tundra foliage is lush and colorful and contrasts sharply with the gray, rocky slopes of Mount Ouray to the east. The Agate Creek Trail descends to the right at **mile 11.2** (11,720). Just beyond, the CT enters a spruce forest and begins a gradual descent. The trail crosses a rockslide in 0.3 mile, where thistles and columbine grow out of the jumbled, rocky terrain. Continue bearing generally south past a small stream and pick up a jeep road (FS-

243.2G) at **mile 12.6** (11,400). From the site of an old quarry, this road continues the descent south passing a spring in several hundred feet that muddies the road until mid-summer. Cross a cattle guard at **mile 13.4** (11,000) and continue 0.4 mile through two switchbacks down to the Marshall Pass Road. The Marshall Pass Trailhead is located at this point. Ascend 0.2 mile south on the pass road to the deep roadway cut, which is the summit of the pass and the end of this segment at **mile 14.0** (10,880). The CT leaves the main pass road just before the roadway cut, and continues south on a side road.

Continental Divide National Scenic Trail

The Continental Divide National Scenic Trail (CDNST) passes through five western states from Canada to Mexico, as it winds a path through the majestic Rocky Mountains and encounters some of America's most dramatic scenery.

The CT and the CDNST are contiguous for about 200 miles in Colorado, including a long section that begins in Seg. 15 near Marshall Pass and diverges, over 100 miles later, near Stony Pass in Seg. 23.

First envisioned in 1968 by Benton Mackaye, founder of the Appalachian Trail, the 3,100-mile CDNST is still only about 70% complete today. The Colorado portion has one of the highest completion rates at 90%. The trail achieves its highest point in Colorado, passing over 14,270-foot Grays Peak, and includes a network of trails 759 miles long, beginning in Mount Zirkel Wilderness at the Wyoming border and entering New Mexico through the spectacular San Juans.

The Continental Divide Trail Alliance (CDTA) estimates that only about a dozen people undertake the entire six-month journey from Canada to Mexico each year. As is the same for the CT, few individuals finish the entire Colorado portion of the CDNST but thousands enjoy day hikes or week-long backpacks on segments of it.

The first complete hike of the length of Colorado's Continental Divide was done by Carl Melzer, his son, Bob, and Julius Johnson in 1936. This was truly a pioneering trip, considering the incomplete maps and sketchy information available to them at that time. (The Melzers had a string of accomplishments. They were also the first to climb all of Colorado's 14ers in one summer (1937) and the first to climb all of the 14ers in the 48 states (1939) — all before Bob was 11 years old!)

For more information about the trail, contact CDTA at 303-838-3760 or visit their website at www.cdtrail.org.

Sign at the Continental Divide, above Fooses Creek.

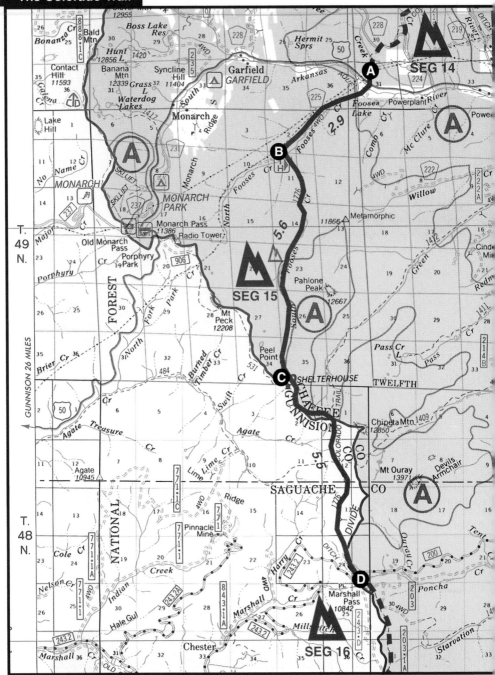

Landmark Location	Mileage	From Denver	Elevation	Latitude	Longitude
Ⓐ US-50	0.0	244.0	8840	38.543307	-106.241961
Ⓑ South Fooses Creek Trailhead	2.9	246.9	9560	38.522842	-106.275206
Ⓒ Continental Divide	8.5	252.5	11920	38.454526	-106.276496
Ⓓ Marshall Pass	14.0	258.0	10880	38.391695	-106.246137

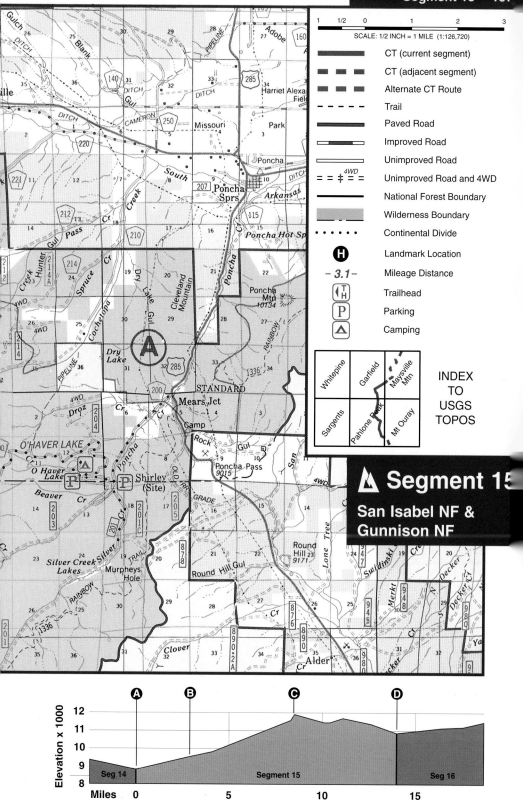

SCALE: 1/2 INCH = 1 MILE (1:126,720)

CT (current segment)
CT (adjacent segment)
Alternate CT Route
Trail
Paved Road
Improved Road
Unimproved Road
Unimproved Road and 4WD
National Forest Boundary
Wilderness Boundary
Continental Divide
Landmark Location
Mileage Distance
Trailhead
Parking
Camping

INDEX TO USGS TOPOS

| Whitepine | Garfield | Maysville Mtn |
| Sargents | Pahlone Peak | Mt Ouray |

Segment 15

San Isabel NF & Gunnison NF

Segment 16
Marshall Pass to Sargents Mesa

Distance: 14.5 miles
Elevation Gain: approx 3080 ft

Cabin above Tank Seven Creek.

Gudy's Tip

"Sargents Mesa teems with its hundreds of grazing elk and numerous trout-filled beaver ponds."

Trip Log

Date: _____ Notes: _____

_____

_____

_____

_____

About This Segment

This segment enters the Tertiary lava flows, volcanic tuffs and breccias of Colorado's southwestern mountains. Before making the transition to the dramatic scenery of the San Juans, the CT continues south and southwest from Marshall Pass through the more mellow Cochetopa Hills, providing glimpses of the La Garita Mountains ahead and the Sawatch Range behind.

The lands west of the divide here made up part of the huge Ute Indian Reservation of 1865, which was moved further west three years later. Marshall Pass was discovered in 1873 when a bad toothache persuaded Lieutenant William Marshall of the Wheeler Survey to take a shortcut from Silverton to the dentist in Denver. It was Otto Mears who built the toll road over the pass and who later sold it to the D&RG. Rails were laid over Marshall Pass in 1881 to connect the mineral-rich Gunnison country to the east slope.

Additional Trail Information: Because the trail remains near the crest of the Continental Divide, water may be a concern for backpackers looking for a campsite. The only place you will find running water along this segment of the trail is where you briefly parallel Tank Seven Creek, although it is feasible to detour into upper Silver Creek closer to Marshall Pass in order to resupply.

Confusion in the trail route caused by logging operations southwest of the pass and in the vicinity of Cameron Park have been largely eliminated by re-routes and better trail identification. However, you still may encounter some of this logging activity in the future, as well as portions of the trail that might be faint or otherwise difficult to follow. It would be wise to keep map and compass handy to confirm your location in these situations.

The Rainbow Trail ties into the CT on the Continental Divide at the head of Silver Creek. This continuous, 100-mile flank trail traverses the east side of the Sangre de Cristo Range from this point southeast to Music Pass, at the head of Sand Creek just north of Great Sand Dunes National Monument. Along the way, there are numerous side trails which lead to isolated lakes and mountaintops within the Sangres. Needless to say, a Rainbow Trail detour would offer a unique diversion to the standard Denver to Durango Colorado Trail trek. For details about the Rainbow Trail, contact the Salida Ranger District.

Trailhead/Access Points

Marshall Pass Trailhead: Travel approximately 5 miles south of Poncha Springs on US-285 and turn right (west) at the Marshall Pass and O'Haver Lake Campground turnoff. Proceed on Chaffee Co Rd-200 and 202 for 13.0 miles to the trailhead, just before the roadway cut at the top of the pass. To continue into Segment 16, follow south on the pass road then bend to the left on FS-203 off the main road at the roadway cut. The trail heading north to South Fooses Creek and Segment 15 leaves the pass road just opposite the trailhead, following FS-243.2G.

Sargents Mesa Trail Access (FS-855): See Segment 17.

Supplies, Services and Accommodations

No convenient supply points.

Maps and Jurisdiction

USFS maps: San Isabel NF, Gunnison NF, Rio Grande NF, see pages 162-163.
USGS Quadrangle maps: Mount Ouray, Bonanza, Chester, Sargents Mesa.
Trails Illustrated map: # 139.

Jurisdiction: Salida Ranger District, Gunnison Ranger District, and Saguache
   Ranger District.

Trail Description

From the east side of the roadway cut at the top of Marshall Pass, the CT bears
to the left (south-southeast) temporarily following a jeep road (FS-203). Avoid the
left fork 300 feet beyond (FS-203.2) which descends east into Poncha and Starvation
Creeks. Continue south-southwest on the jeep road another 200 feet then go left
(south-southeast) on an old jeep track that has been closed to vehicles and steeply
ascends a grassy hill. In 700 feet a recently built trail leaves the jeep track at right
(south) and continues a steep ascent to a pleasant ridgetop on the Continental Divide
with views east to the Sangre de Cristo Range and west to the Gunnison Basin. From
here the trail rambles along the divide, then briefly assumes the route of an old
logging road as it ascends a ridge jutting east of the divide. There is a switchback to
the right (west) at **mile 1.2** (11,200), which is notable because you do not want to
continue straight ahead here on the more obscure trail.

The CT follows mostly on or near the top of the broad divide ridge in and out
of the forest to **mile 2.5** (11,160), where it intersects an old logging road at a Forest
Service directional sign. Bear left (south) here ascending the log road for about 0.4
mile until it levels out and leaves the logging area behind. The contiguous Rainbow
and Silver Creek Trails descend to the left at **mile 3.6** (11,240). If you need water,
the head of the creek is only a short hike down the valley, which also makes a nice
camping spot at the foot of Antora Peak. The Silver Creek Trail ends in a few miles
where it meets the county road up from US-285. But the Rainbow Trail continues,
heading east and then southeast for its 100-mile journey along the east side of the
Sangre de Cristo Range.

From the Silver Creek-Rainbow Trail junction, the CT ascends an old jeep track
south-southwest then west through a meadow of blue flax. As you approach the trees
ahead, be on the lookout for the trail to leave the jeep track at right (west-northwest).
The CT then traverses west on the north side of Point 11,862 (which is about 0.8 mile
east-southeast of Windy Peak) at about the 11,600-foot level. This minor, otherwise
common, summit is notable in that it is the high point about which three major
Colorado water sources part—the Gunnison, the Rio Grande, and the Arkansas.
Curiously, it lacks a name. Years ago, James R. Wolf of the Continental Divide Trail
Society suggested the names "Arkarado Grande Peak" or "Triple Divide" in his
classic and pioneering guide to the CDT (Southern Colorado, Volume 5).

At **mile 4.6** (11,560), you pass through a gate west-northwest of Point 11,862.
This marks the Continental Divide and the boundary between the Gunnison and Rio
Grande National Forests. Continue southwest from the gate on the trail about 100

feet, and join another jeep track which descends to the saddle between Point 11,862 and Windy Peak. From the saddle, ascend west on the trail to the south slope of Windy, then level out at **mile 5.1** (11,680) just below the summit in an open area. From here you can survey your route west to Sargents Mesa and Long Branch Baldy. In approximately 0.2 mile, the trail joins the broad, forested divide ridge west of Windy Peak and begins a descent bearing generally west.

Hiking through a burn area on the Continental Divide in Segment 16.

Cross Jay Creek Road at **mile 6.6** (10,880) and continue descending generally west through a lodgepole forest. The trail ends its long descent at **mile 7.4** (10,560) and begins a series of ups and downs on the crest of the divide, still heading west. Join up with a swath cut through the forest for a natural gas pipeline at **mile 8.4** (10,640) and follow the swath 200 feet south to where the trail resumes at right. About 0.2 mile beyond, the CT follows the divide as it makes a rapid turn from west to south, and then continues along the broad ridge over occasional small knobs.

Make a sharp right at **mile 10.6** (10,560) and descend to the ford on Tank Seven Creek, which received its unusual name from a D&RG water stop downstream from this point. Backpackers should be aware that Tank Seven Creek is the last water until Baldy Lake, 11 miles to the west. Join up with the old road on the west side of the creek at **mile 11.1** (10,280). Proceed south and then west up the old road, which parallels Tank Seven Creek, to grassy Cameron Park at **mile 12.3** (10,800), where the trail levels out briefly and crosses FS-578. A couple of dilapidated cabins here might provide minimal protection in a downpour.

The area around the Cameron Park has been heavily logged, and it is necessary to remain as close as possible to upper Tank Seven Creek on the trail in the elongated meadow so as to not get lost in the maze of roads on either side. From FS-578, the trail heads west to west-southwest, ascending in the narrowing upper portion of the park. Cross a logging road at **mile 13.2** (11,080) and continue 0.2 mile west, where the trail levels out briefly again as it exits the extreme upper portion of Tank Seven Creek and opens into the lower end of expansive Sargents Mesa. At this point, the mesa is surrounded by a tight formation of spruce and spotted with occasional groves, a combination that conceals its true extent. The trail bears right here (north-northwest to north) for several hundred feet to detour a marshy spot. As you proceed, the trail becomes less identifiable until it ties into an old, obscure jeep track (FS-486) at **mile 13.5** (11,240), which bears west-southwest to southwest. As you ascend on FS-486, a large alpine meadow will open up and reveal views north to the southern Sawatch. Continue south then southwest ascending on the jeep track, until FS-855 ties into it at **mile 14.5** (11,600). Segment 16 comes to an end here, at this obscure Forest Service road intersection on Sargents Mesa.

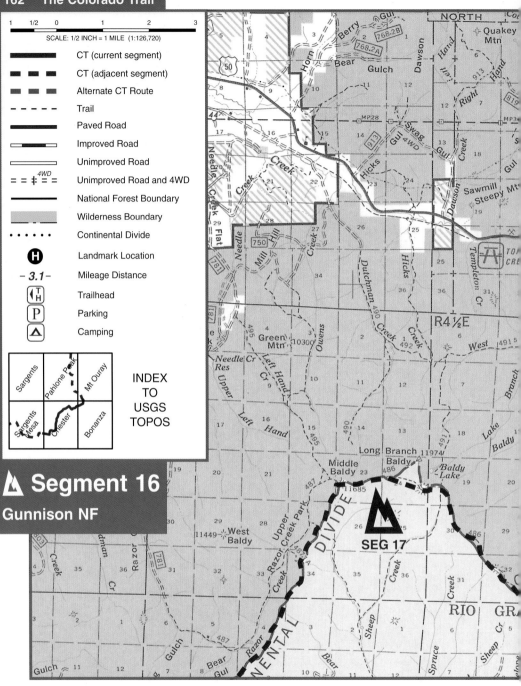

SCALE: 1/2 INCH = 1 MILE (1:126,720)

CT (current segment)	
CT (adjacent segment)	
Alternate CT Route	
Trail	
Paved Road	
Improved Road	
Unimproved Road	
Unimproved Road and 4WD	
National Forest Boundary	
Wilderness Boundary	
Continental Divide	
Landmark Location	
Mileage Distance	
Trailhead	
Parking	
Camping	

INDEX
TO
USGS
TOPOS

▲ Segment 16

Gunnison NF

Landmark Location	Mileage	From Denver	Elevation	Latitude	Longitude
Ⓐ Marshall Pass	0.0	258.0	10880	38.391695	-106.246137
Ⓑ Point 11,862	4.6	262.6	11560	38.349606	-106.257062
Ⓒ Tank Seven Creek	11.1	269.1	10280	38.313684	-106.332571
Ⓓ Sargents Mesa	14.5	272.5	11600	38.290800	-106.378033

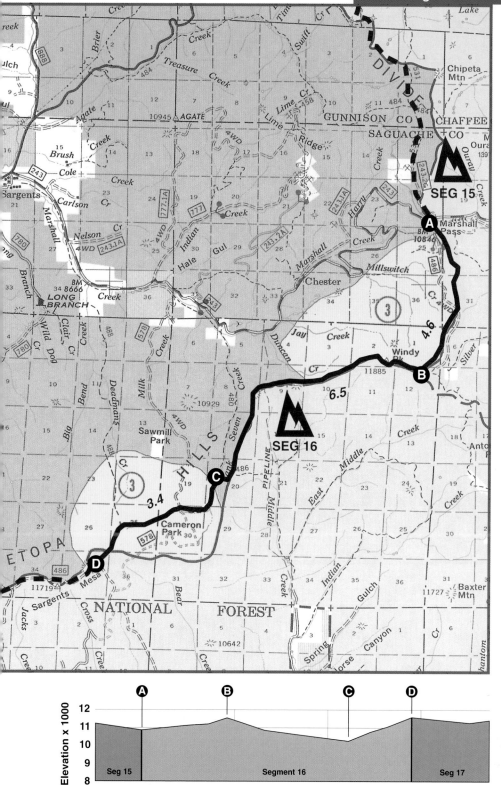

Segment 17
Sargents Mesa to
Colorado Hwy-114

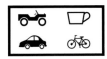

Distance: 20.3 miles
Elevation Gain: approx 2440 ft

Cairn along the Continental Divide.

Gudy's Tip

"Baldy Lake after Sargents Mesa is worth the quarter-mile detour; it's a watery haven along a dry segment of the trail."

Trip Log

Date: _____ Notes: _____

_____

_____

_____

_____

About This Segment

This segment continues through the Cochetopa Hills and, with the exception of a short bypass into upper Razor Creek, remains on the broad, forested crest of the Continental Divide until reaching Lujan Creek Road. Introspective backpackers will love the isolation of the Cochetopa Hills but should be aware that no drinking water is available along the first 7 miles of this segment. Not until reaching Baldy Lake, which is 0.5 mile off the trail, can one be assured of water. Backpackers bypassing Baldy Lake may be faced with a 20-mile dry run between viable water sources in late summer. Upper Razor Creek (and Park) is an ideal place to camp, although the stream may not be flowing here later in the summer. In the past, some parties have missed the CT junction back to the divide at Razor Creek, and have instead continued down the creek many miles before realizing their error. The trail is better identified here than before; nevertheless, be extra attentive in this area.

The trail in this segment is not as heavily used as other portions of the CT, and may be obscure or poorly marked in places. Map and compass readings may be necessary from time to time to confirm your location. The Cochetopa Hills are composed of the relatively recent (Tertiary age) lava flows, volcanic ash and breccias that form much of the San Juan Mountains.

Trailhead/Access Points

Sargents Mesa (FS-855) Trail Access: From Saguache on US-285 in the San Luis Valley, drive west on Colorado Hwy-114 for 10.5 miles and turn right (north) onto Saguache Co Rd-EE38 (also marked as Saguache Co Rd-38FF). Proceed 0.8 mile to a fork and bear to the left on Rd-EE38. Approximately 5 miles beyond, make a sharp right onto Rd-EE38 (also marked as FS-855 at the National Forest boundary). Continue approximately 10 miles, then go left at a fork (the right fork, FS-578, enters a confusing labyrinth of logging roads which eventually passes through Cameron Park). Proceed on the left fork 0.4 mile to the end of the improved road. FS-855 continues as a jeep road another 0.7 mile where it dead-ends into FS-486, which is the CT route in the upper park on Sargents Mesa and the start of this segment.

Lujan Creek Road Trail Access: From Saguache on US-285 in the San Luis Valley, drive west on Colorado Hwy-114 approximately 30 miles to the summit of North Pass (also sometimes called North Cochetopa Pass). Descend 1.1 miles from the pass to Lujan Creek Road (Saguache Co Rd-31CC, FS-785), which ascends to the right (northeast) and is the route of the CT. Follow this narrow, rough and steep dirt road, which is an impassable quagmire in rainy weather, 2 miles to a switchback to the right. Avoid the side road which forks to the left here. In another 0.1 mile you will top the divide at a cattle guard, and then immediately face a fork in the road. Go left and continue east 0.1 mile to where the CT leaves the road to the left (north).

Colorado Hwy-114 Trail Access: See Segment 18.

Supplies, Services and Accommodations

No convenient supply point.

Maps and Jurisdiction

USFS maps: Rio Grande NF, Gunnison NF, see pages 168-169.
USGS Quadrangle maps: Sargents Mesa, West Baldy, North Pass.
Trail Illustrated map: # 139.

Jurisdiction: Saguache Ranger District and Gunnison Ranger District.

Trail Description

From the upper end of Sargents Mesa, the CT follows FS-486 both to the left (southwest) and to the right (northeast) from the spot where FS-855 dead-ends into it. Bear to the left on FS-486 to start this segment and ascend slightly. Almost immediately you will enter a patchy spruce forest as the road trends southwest and levels out on the large, rolling summit of the mesa. The La Garita Mountains are visible ahead, just above the horizon. The road skirts around the north side of a burned-out knob on the west end of the mesa at **mile 1.0** (11,640) and descends 1.3 miles beyond to a saddle on the divide between Long Branch and Jacks Creek. Here, as the road descends ahead (south), the obscure CT leaves the road at right (west). Be attentive here; some hikers have missed this critical junction in the past. Continue 800 feet west on the faint trail, across the gravelly saddle, to **mile 2.4** (11,160), where you will cross another faint trail which leads north down into the Long Branch, and eventually to the Long Branch Ranger Station just off US-50 west of Sargents. Ascend to the south side of a minor divide summit, Point 11,547, then begin a stroll northwest along the broad, undulating Continental Divide ridge on a trail which is rocky and sometimes hard to spot, but usually well blazed.

Intersect the trail to Baldy Lake at **mile 6.9** (11,480). The lake, which is located in a cirque below Long Branch Baldy, is 0.5 mile down this side trail to the right (north). From this trail intersection, ascend 0.4 mile west to a high point south of Long Branch Baldy summit. Slowly descend 1.2 miles west to the saddle, then ascend to the large summit of Middle Baldy at **mile 9.2** (11,680), where you get a view of the huge Gunnison Basin from the summit's treeless west side. Descend from the summit, then pass a side trail which descends north into Dutchman Creek at **mile 9.8** (11,380).

Continue south-southwest on the CT and enter the upper part of Upper Razor Park 0.2 mile beyond the Dutchman Creek Trail junction. Descend on a well-beaten path southwest across the park, aiming for the funnel formed by the trees in the lower part of the meadow. As you re-enter the trees, double trails that

Alpine sunflowers.

parallel each other continue the descent to **mile 10.4** (10,920), where the dual trails converge and cross to the east side of Razor Creek. The creek will probably not be flowing here later in the summer. Parallel the creek south to **mile 10.7** (10,880) and then bear left (east-southeast) away from the creek. The CT continues about 200 feet across a meadow, then enters the trees, heading for the top of the divide.

In a short distance the CT aligns itself again on the wide crest of the Continental Divide, passing a side trail to Razor Creek at **mile 12.3** (10,960). Trail conditions improve as you

Wet crossing of one of the usually dry creekbeds along Segment 17.

progress south to south-southwest on the divide. Ascend to a minor summit, Point 11,017, at **mile 14.4**, then descend 0.7 mile to a forested saddle. Ascend steeply from the saddle on several reconstructed switchbacks to an old logging road at mile 16.1 (11,000). The original route of the CT followed the logging road downhill to the right, but in 1988 volunteers rebuilt a seriously neglected footpath, giving hikers the opportunity to remain on a trail for another 1.5 miles.

Bear left (south) on this old road and follow it a few steps to a broad, forested ridge, which is again the crest of the Continental Divide. The old logging road here changes into a trail and begins a descent to the south, still on the ridge of the Continental Divide. The trail swings through several long switchbacks on its way to Lujan Creek Road at **mile 17.8** (10,320), passing through an alternating forest of aspen, lodgepole and bristlecone.

Bear right (west) on the Lujan Creek Road and continue several hundred feet to a cattle guard, the boundary between the Rio Grande and Gunnison National Forests. Follow the road approximately 500 feet and bear downhill to the left (southwest) at the switchback. Avoid the logging road which continues north from this switchback. Follow the Lujan Creek Road downhill (southwest), at times immediately adjacent to the creek, and join up with Colorado Hwy-114 at **mile 20.0** (9680). Continue 0.3 mile southwest, carefully paralleling the highway, to a widened shoulder on the south side of the highway at **mile 20.3** (9600), where this segment comes to an end.

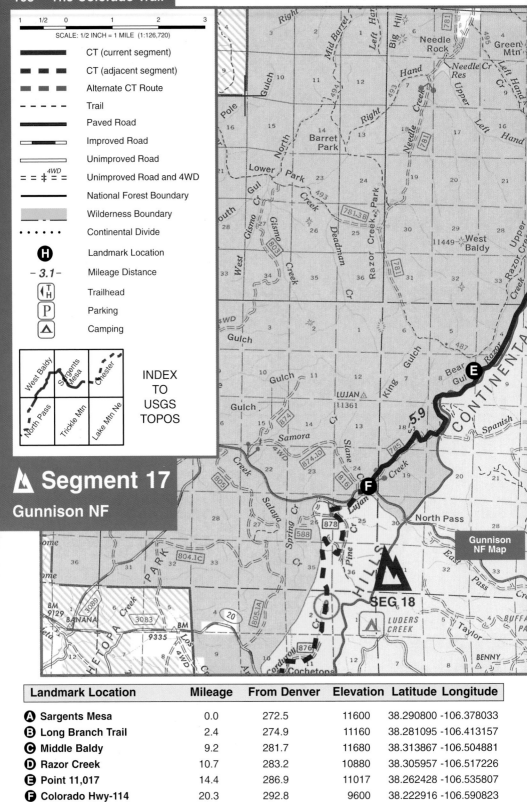

1	1/2	0	1	2	3

SCALE: 1/2 INCH = 1 MILE (1:126,720)

▬▬▬▬	CT (current segment)
▬ ▬ ▬	CT (adjacent segment)
▬ ▬ ▬	Alternate CT Route
– – – –	Trail
▬▬▬▬	Paved Road
▭▬▭	Improved Road
▭▭▭	Unimproved Road
= = ‡ = =	Unimproved Road and 4WD
▬▬▬▬	National Forest Boundary
▬▬▬	Wilderness Boundary
• • • • •	Continental Divide
H	Landmark Location
– *3.1* –	Mileage Distance
(T/H)	Trailhead
P	Parking
▲	Camping

INDEX TO USGS TOPOS

West Baldy | Sargents Mesa | Chester
North Pass | Trickle Mtn | Lake Mtn Ne

▲ **Segment 17**

Gunnison NF

SEG 18

Gunnison NF Map

Landmark Location	Mileage	From Denver	Elevation	Latitude	Longitude
A Sargents Mesa	0.0	272.5	11600	38.290800	-106.378033
B Long Branch Trail	2.4	274.9	11160	38.281095	-106.413157
C Middle Baldy	9.2	281.7	11680	38.313867	-106.504881
D Razor Creek	10.7	283.2	10880	38.305957	-106.517226
E Point 11,017	14.4	286.9	11017	38.262428	-106.535807
F Colorado Hwy-114	20.3	292.8	9600	38.222916	-106.590823

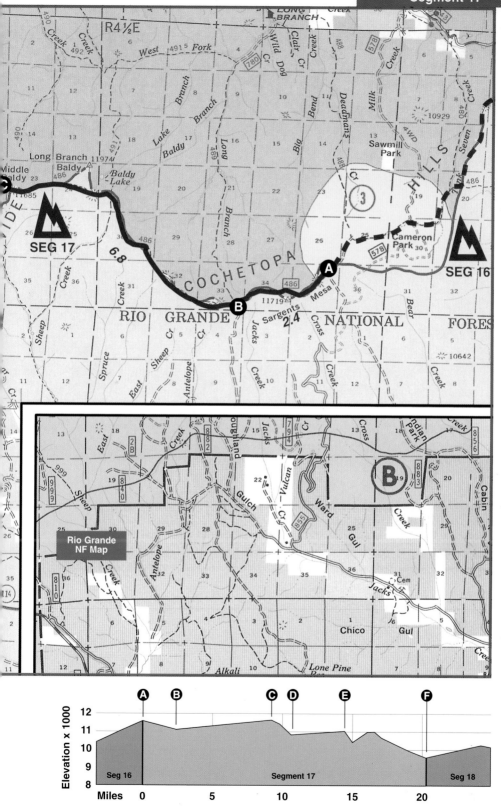

Segment 18
Colorado Hwy-114 to
Saguache Park Road

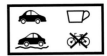

Distance: 12.9 miles
Elevation Gain: approx 1220 ft

Sunrise on Lujan Creek.

Gudy's Tip

"Water sources on these ranch roads are few and far between. And what can be found is often besmirched by cow pies. Emergency water can be found at Luders Campground, about 2 miles east on the Cochetopa Pass road."

Trip Log

Date: _____ Notes: _____

_____

_____

_____

_____

About This Segment

The Cochetopa Gap has been used for centuries by humans and animals shuttling between the San Luis Valley and the Gunnison Basin. Few other Continental Divide crossings in the state have such an impressive background, probably because the Cochetopa Gap extends for miles, providing several relatively easy passages rather than a single isolated notch as is characteristic of most other Colorado passes. To the Utes, their ancestral "Buffalo Gate" (as the word Cochetopa is roughly translated) had a significance that today is only hinted at by the three relatively minor Continental Divide auto routes over the gap: North Pass on Colorado Hwy-114, South Pass on Saguache Co Rd-17FF and Cochetopa Pass, the historic route of the Saguache-San Juan toll road, on Saguache Co Rd-NN14.

The gap was already well trampled by the Utes and buffalo when the Spanish governor of New Mexico, Juan Bautista de Anza, led his army into the San Luis Valley in 1779. De Anza's object was the Comanche Greenhorn, but during his pursuit he did not fail to notice the long, low point in the mountains to the west, which he correctly deduced was the divide between the Rio Grande and the western San Juan country. By 1825, Antoine Robidoux was directing pack trains over the gap, after first entering the San Luis Valley via Mosca Pass in the Sangre de Cristo Range.

Probably the area's most dramatic event took place just southwest of here in the winter of 1848-49 when Colonel John Charles Fremont led a party into the region to explore potential railroad routes. Unfortunately, guide Bill Williams aimed in the wrong direction and the expedition ended up somewhere on the high ridges of the La Garita Mountains. A fierce blizzard resulted in the deaths of 11 of the original 35 men. Some of the survivors were accused, but never formally charged, of cannibalism. A more infamous cannibal, Alferd Packer, made his way over the gap in April of 1874, after having survived the winter by murdering and devouring his five fellow travelers. Packer was later arrested in Saguache.

Otto Mears and Enos Hotchkiss built a toll road from Saguache to Lake City over Cochetopa Pass in 1874, after the gap was skirted by trans-Continental railroad builders. Today, the rarely used but historic North, South and Cochetopa Passes result in a quiet that generates an appropriate mystical feeling of antiquity.

Additional Trail Information: Backpackers will find meager water supplies along this segment. Lujan, Pine, Archuleta and Los Creeks all have small flows. Special measures may have to be taken during dry years or in late summer. A small spring at Luders Creek Campground could be detoured to in emergencies. The CT in this segment uses a curious assortment of logging, jeep, Forest Service and county roads, relying on its own built trail only for a few stretches. A map and compass might come in handy to help decipher the maze.

Mountain cyclists should refer to the Mountain Bicycle Detour for a description of the long detour, starting on the Cochetopa Pass Road, that will take them around the La Garita Wilderness.

Trailhead/Access Points

Colorado Hwy-114 Trail Access: From Saguache on US-285 in the San Luis Valley, go west on Colorado Hwy-114 approximately 30 miles to the summit of North Pass. Descend 1.1 miles on the west side of the pass to Lujan Creek Road (Saguache Co Rd-31CC), which ascends to the right (northeast) and is the route of the CT in Segment 17. Continue on Hwy-114 for 0.3 mile to a widened shoulder of the highway, which is not graded for parking. The CT continues south from here across the meadow of Lujan Creek. Another trail access point, away from the activity of the highway, is up Lujan Creek Road (Rd-31CC). Refer to Lujan Creek Road Trail Access as described in Segment 17.

Cochetopa Pass Road (Saguache Co Rd-NN14) Trail Access: From Saguache on US-285 in the San Luis Valley, go west on Colorado Hwy-114 approximately 21 miles and bear to the left on Rd-NN14 (FS-750), which is the historic route of the original Cochetopa Pass Road. Follow the road to Luders Creek Campground, then continue approximately 1.8 miles further to the summit of Cochetopa Pass. Descend 1.2 miles west of the pass to FS-876 (Corduroy Road), which leaves the Cochetopa Pass Road to the right (north) and is the route of the CT. From this point, the CT follows the pass road for the next 0.5 mile as it descends through two switchbacks. No parking is provided at this trail access point.

Saguache Park Road Trail Access: See Segment 19.

Supplies, Services and Accommodations

No convenient supply point.

Maps and Jurisdiction

USFS map: Gunnison National Forest, see pages 176-177.
USGS Quadrangle maps: North Pass, Cochetopa Park.
Trails Illustrated map: # 139.

Jurisdiction: Gunnison Ranger District, Gunnison NF.

Trail Description

At the widened shoulder 1.4 miles west of North Pass on Hwy-114, proceed southwest through the gate and drop down slightly into the lush meadow of Lujan Creek. Ford the creek at **mile 0.2** (9560) and rise above the marshy lowlands surrounding it. Follow the trail-less route, which is marked with flimsy carsonite posts that wave pitifully in the breeze, in a more westerly direction. Shortly, you will curve to the left (south) and follow the posts into Pine Creek drainage. Join up with an old logging road at **mile 0.8** (9560). Continue south up the valley and avoid the fork to the left 0.1 mile beyond. Cross over to the west side of the creek at **mile 1.6** (9680) and take time to admire the cinquefoil and sego lily which adorn the area. Go right at the fork 0.1 mile beyond, where the logging road begins an ascent out of Pine

Cochetopa Dome.

Creek Valley. Continue along the road as it bends around and assumes a northerly direction. Switchback to the left at **mile 2.4** (9920) and resume a southerly bearing.

The logging road ends in a cul-de-sac at **mile 3.4** (10,000). Begin a much steeper ascent, still in a southerly direction, from the end of the road following a route that has been cleared and bulldozed but without a built tread. Reach the saddle between Lujan and Archuleta Creeks at **mile 3.7** (10,240) and pass through a gate. Descend 0.1 mile on a cleared route to another old logging road (FS-876). Go left on this logging road which descends south in the upper drainage of Corduroy Creek. Reach the Cochetopa Pass Road at **mile 6.4** (9760).

Follow the pass road downhill to the right 0.5 mile, through two switchbacks, to where a jeep road (FS-864.2A) leaves the graded road to the left (south). Cross over to the south side of Archuleta Creek on a dirt fill bridge and continue on the jeep road which parallels the pass road and the tiny flow of the creek upstream for several

Pocket Gophers

The long, sinuous casts, packed with dirt, and scattered over the grasslands and meadows of the Cochetopa Gap are evidence of pocket gophers at work.

This small, thickset, and mostly nocturnal animal is a regular biological excavation service, with burrow systems that may be over 500 feet long, representing removal of nearly three tons of soil. Excess soil is thrown out in characteristic loose mounds. But it is the conspicuous winter casts that attract the attention of curious hikers. These are actually tunnels made during the winter, through the snow and along the surface of the ground, and packed with dirt brought up from below.

Sometimes their endless burrowing activities can undermine an area to such an extent that a passing hiker can be surprised when the ground suddenly gives way under foot.

Here in Colorado, pocket gophers are found well up into the meager soils of the alpine zone and are a major factor in the soil-building process in mountain areas.

hundred feet. Bend slowly to the right as the jeep road angles south up a shallow intersecting valley. At times the road seems to disappear into the lush grasses of the broad meadow. Avoid the fork to the right, which cuts up into the hillside, and continue a slow bend to the southwest at the edge of the meadow. Pass through a gate at the indistinct divide between Archuleta and Los Creeks at **mile 7.7** (9800) and descend west into the wide, grassy valley. About 0.1 mile beyond the gate, continue west on FS-864.2A and avoid the fork to the left. Begin paralleling the main flow of Los Creek in 0.5 mile. Continue west on the north side of the creek, which is almost hidden by willows and cinquefoil.

Cross Los Creek as it turns north at **mile 8.9** (9560), just upstream from a stock pond. Just after the creek crossing, follow FS-787.2A as it ascends west out of Los

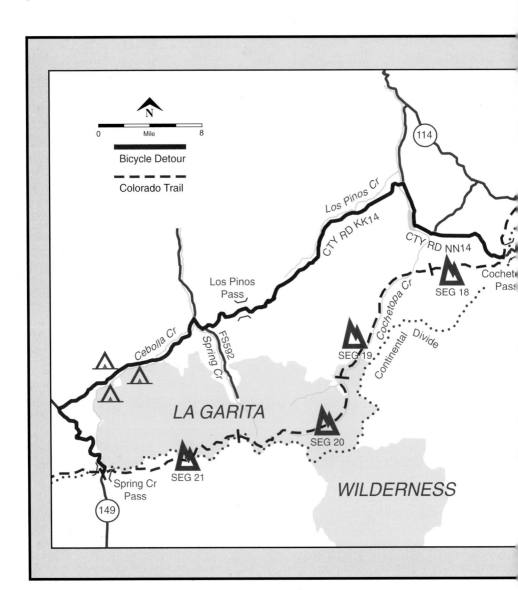

Creek drainage. Top a grassy saddle 0.5 mile beyond and descend bearing generally west on the rocky Forest Service jeep track which parallels a fence. A full view of broad Cochetopa Dome dominates the scenery to the north. Level out as the jeep track enters the edge of immense Cochetopa Park at **mile 10.4** (9400). In 0.8 mile, fork to the right just beyond a gate and continue on FS-787.2A to Saguache Park Road (Saguache Co Rd-17FF) at **mile 11.4** (9340). Turn left (south) onto the graded county road and continue to a cattle guard at a wooded saddle. Descend west along the road, then bend back to the south and ascend slightly to **mile 12.9** (9520). This segment terminates here as the CT route joins a jeep track (FS-787.2D) to the right and leaves the Saguache Park Road in a meadow at the edge of the forest.

Mountain Bicycle Detour

La Garita Wilderness Detour — *Segments 18, 19, 20 and 21 (Gunnison NF):* This mandatory detour is necessary to avoid the La Garita Wilderness and an extended high-altitude, mostly trail-less route across Snow Mesa and the Continental Divide.

The La Garita Wilderness detour and the following optional detour around Coney Summit are designed to be used together by cyclists wishing to continue the detour. Bicyclists will be pedaling along backcountry Forest Service roads that follow parts of the historic Saguache-San Juan Toll Road built by Otto Mears in 1874. They will also pass by the site of the original Ute Agency on Los Piños Creek. The detour passes several National Forest campgrounds on Cebolla Creek. The final miles are spent ascending Colorado Hwy-149 to Spring Creek Pass, where you can join the high-altitude route of Segment 22. Or you can descend Hwy-149 to Lake San Cristobal and continue the detour with the Coney Summit Detour.

Detour Description: This detour begins on the Cochetopa Pass Road (Saguache Co Rd-NN14) at **mile 6.4** (9760) of Segment 18. Descend on the dirt road past two switchbacks and continue pedaling ahead (northwest) on the road as the CT bears to the left up Archuleta Creek. Continue past Dome Reservoir to **mile 10.8** (8979) and turn left onto Saguache Co Rd-KK14 (Los Piños-Cebolla Road). Pass beyond the old Ute Agency to **mile 19.6** and continue ahead on Los Piños-Cebolla Road, avoiding Big Meadows Road which forks to the left. Continue 10 miles to Los Piños Pass. Descend from the pass to **mile 33.9** and continue ahead (northwest) on the Los Piños-Cebolla Road for 1 mile then go left (west) at the intersection. Gradually ascend along Cebolla Creek to **mile 50.0** (11,320) where the Forest Service road joins up with Colorado Hwy-149. If you insist on pedaling the route over Coney Summit (not recommended), go left here and ascend 7.6 miles further to Spring Creek Pass where you will rejoin the CT at the beginning of Segment 22. If, however, you decide to continue the detour, refer to the Coney Summit Detour (see Segment 22), which will direct you to descend at right here on Hwy-149.

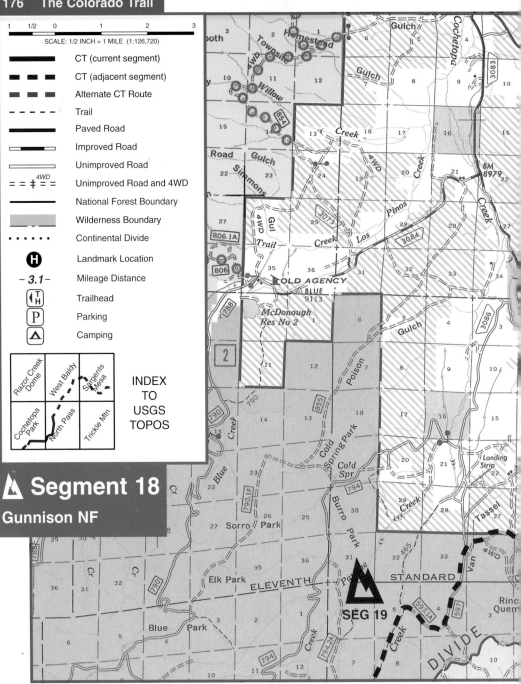

Legend

▬▬▬	CT (current segment)
▬ ▬ ▬	CT (adjacent segment)
▬ ▬ ▬	Alternate CT Route
– – – –	Trail
▬▬▬	Paved Road
▭▭	Improved Road
▭▭	Unimproved Road
= = ‡ = =	Unimproved Road and 4WD
+ +	National Forest Boundary
▓▓	Wilderness Boundary
• • • • •	Continental Divide
Ⓗ	Landmark Location
– 3.1 –	Mileage Distance
🄣🄷	Trailhead
🄟	Parking
🄰	Camping

SCALE: 1/2 INCH = 1 MILE (1:126,720)

INDEX TO USGS TOPOS

Razor Creek Dome	West Baldy	Sergents Mesa
Cochetopa Park	North Pass	Trickle Mtn

▲ Segment 18
Gunnison NF

Landmark Location	Mileage	From Denver	Elevation	Latitude	Longitude
Ⓐ Colorado Hwy-114	0.0	292.8	9600	38.222916	-106.590823
Ⓑ Lujan-Archuleta Creeks saddle	3.7	296.5	10240	38.192028	-106.604559
Ⓒ Los Creek	8.9	301.7	9560	38.149512	-106.644190
Ⓓ Saguache Park Road	12.9	305.7	9520	38.131511	-106.696445

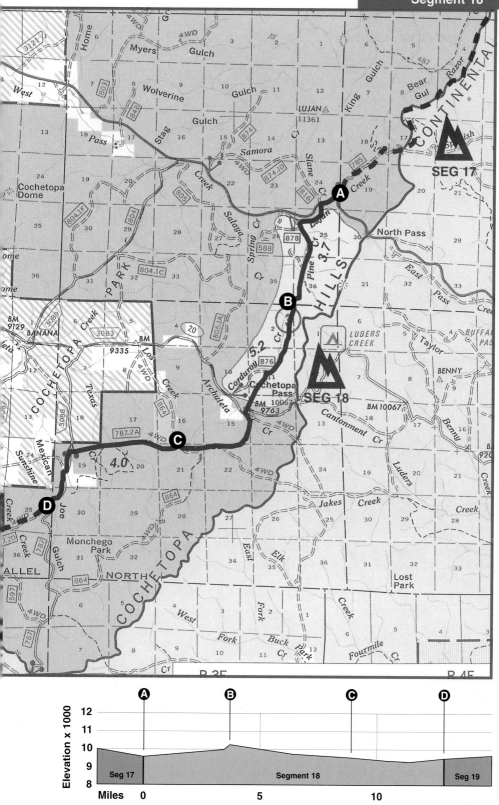

Segment 19
Saguache Park Road to Eddiesville Trailhead

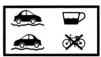

Welcome to Eddiesville.

Distance: 13.5 miles
Elevation Gain: approx 1660 ft

Gudy's Tip

"The La Garita Wilderness is so remote that few travel here and you are unlikely to meet other hikers. The loneliness is offset by the complete solitude that you find."

Trip Log

Date: _____ Notes: _____

_____

_____

_____

_____

About This Segment

The CT in this segment crosses several small, and usually dry, drainages while skirting the southern boundary of Cochetopa Park on existing jeep roads. Expect meager water supplies until you reach Cochetopa Creek. Backpackers will find many grassy campsites once in the broad, isolated valley of the creek, but may experience some aggravating moments if they unintentionally stray off the sometimes obscure trail which parallels the creek to Eddiesville Trailhead. The crossing of Cochetopa Creek has always been problematic and is more so lately because of the enterprising nature of the local beaver population. Expect a confusing, difficult and mushy ford.

The last several miles of this segment take you into La Garita Wilderness, where mountain bicycles are not allowed (refer to the Mountain Bicycle Detour in Segment 18).

Trailhead/Access Points

Saguache Park Road Trail Access: From Saguache on US-285 in the San Luis Valley, go west on Colorado Hwy-114 approximately 30 miles to the summit of North Pass. Continue on Hwy-114 west of the pass approximately 5.2 miles and go left (south) on Saguache Co Rd-17GG. Continue on the dirt road approximately 5.2 miles around the southeast side of Cochetopa Dome. Go left (east) onto Rd-NN14, the Cochetopa Pass Road. Drive 1.1 miles east on the pass road and go right (south) on Rd-17FF (FS-787), the Saguache Park Road. Continue approximately 2 miles up Rd-17FF to a cattle guard, which signals your entry into Gunnison National Forest. The CT takes off immediately to the left (east) at this point, following a jeep track (FS-787.2A). From this point, the CT follows the Saguache Park Road (FS-787) as it continues ahead (south) 1.5 miles until it veers to the right (southwest) off FS-787 at another jeep track (FS-787.2D). No parking area is provided at either of these trail access points on the Saguache Park Road.

Eddiesville Trailhead: See Segment 20.

Supplies, Services and Accommodations

No convenient supply point.

Maps and Jurisdiction

USFS map: Gunnison National Forest, see pages 182-183.
USGS Quadrangle maps: Cochetopa Park, Saguache Park, Elk Park.
Trails Illustrated map: # 139.

Jurisdiction: Gunnison Ranger District, Gunnison NF.

Trail Description

At the beginning of this segment, the CT leaves the Saguache Park Road and joins up with a rocky jeep track (FS-787.2D) at right, which proceeds southwest through the meadow. At **mile 0.1** (9520), continue straight ahead (southwest) and avoid the right fork. Ascend in a small gully of scattered spruce, pine and aspen to a small rise, then descend slightly into the dry gully of Sunshine Creek where fields of sego lily bloom in early summer. Ascend to a low, open ridge dividing Ant and Sunshine Creeks, then descend to the usually dry Ant Creek at **mile 1.2** (9720). Pass through a gate on each side of the creek. Just beyond the gate on the west side of the creek, the CT joins another jeep track that comes in from the right. Continue ahead (south-southwest) approximately 300 feet, then avoid the left fork which goes south, and continue west at the edge of the forest along the southern boundary of Cochetopa Park. The rounded, smooth profile of Cochetopa Dome dominates the foreground, while the Elk Mountains provide a snowy backdrop far to the north.

Descend slowly, entering the Quemado Creek drainage to a confusing junction at **mile 2.2** (9760), where several jeep tracks come together. Continue 0.2 mile northwest from this junction on an obscure jeep track, then bear to the left (west) on another set of tracks which take you over a dirt fill creek crossing in 150 feet. Climb west out of the drainage to a high point, where you pass through a gate at **mile 3.2** (9960). Descend west and then south into Van Tassel Gulch. Bottom out in the dry gulch at **mile 3.7** (9840) and ascend slightly 500 feet to a jeep road (FS-597). Turn left (south) onto the road and ascend on the west side of the wide gulch through a sparse aspen forest.

Top the saddle at **mile 5.4** (10,400) in a small clearing ringed with aspen, where the jeep road forks. Bear right here onto another jeep road (FS-597.1A) which descends and slowly bends to the west. As the road continues to drop, it slowly assumes a more northerly direction and eventually breaks out of the trees and switchbacks to the left (southwest) at **mile 6.5** (9960). Continue 0.2 mile southwest to a pond at a confusing junction of jeep tracks. Follow a sketchy trail as it proceeds between the west shore of the pond and a small knoll. Trail maintainer Stew Brown suggests that you climb the knoll to check out your route up the creek to the south. Pick up the jeep track again southwest of the pond and descend steeply to **mile 7.0** (9720) at the level of the broad valley bottom of Cochetopa Creek. Look for an obscure trail at left, just above the marshy valley bottom, which begins a long, gradual ascent south and southwest parallel to the creek.

Cross a small stream just as the trail leaves the jeep track and continue south on the east side of the broad valley. Cochetopa Creek meanders through the grassy valley bottom, which offers many spacious campsites for backpackers. The sometimes obscure trail bears generally south-southwest and begins to take on the character of a jeep track in 0.7 mile. Ascend to a high point above the creek in the surrounding forest at **mile 9.5** (9960), then descend steeply 0.1 mile to a small side stream. Fight your way through some overgrown willows here and 100 feet beyond, look for the trail to bear right (southwest). In a few steps you'll be continuing southwest on a grassy, elevated bench above and parallel to Cochetopa Creek.

Toward the southern end of the grassy bench at **mile 10.2** (9960), the trail descends quickly to the level of the creek and disappears in a willowy sand bar and area of ponds. This is the infamous Cochetopta crossing. Before you descend to the level of the ponds, look across the creek to the southwest and notice the large rock cairn on the opposite bank and the trail rising out of the drainage—this is where you want to end up. Unfortunately, entrepreneurial beaver teams in this location have made the previous trail crossing unrecognizable and infinitely more difficult, and a better ford may be found upstream or downstream of this point. Most descend on the trail to the willows and continue on a sketchy path near the floodplain several hundred feet upstream to a possible ford between two large ponds. More recently, some people have continued through the forest at the level of the grassy bench to an area upstream of the ponds and make a crossing at a point approximately opposite of the large rock cairn. However, keep in mind that all crossings are subject to change from year to year based on the persuasions of the beaver. In any event, expect a deep and precarious crossing. Once across the creek, head south-southwest to the large rock cairn on the west bank just above the level of the willows. The trail is indistinct in the floodplain until you rise above the creek. Ascend southwest from the cairn to the grassy bench on the west side of the creek at **mile 10.5** (10,000). From here, another trail continues downstream (northeast). Because this junction is obscure, it could be a problem for CT hikers headed eastbound for Saguache Park Road.

Cochetopa Creek in the La Garita Wilderness.

Continue along the trail south-southwest up the west side of Cochetopa Creek and ford the rushing side drainage of Nutras Creek at **mile 10.8** (10,000). Several logs to the left of the normal trail ford provide a drier crossing during times of high water. This may be a weak consolation considering the drenching you just received at the Cochetopa crossing. You will enter La Garita Wilderness here. Approximately 0.5 mile beyond, the trail ascends near the banks of Cochetopa Creek on a mostly treeless slope with a southern exposure, which can be uncomfortably warm on summer afternoons. The trail levels out on a rolling, grassy bench well above the creek beyond **mile 12.0** (10,240). This area is heavily grazed, and numerous parallel and side trails have been one result. Be alert to stay on the main trail which stays on the grassy bench between the creek below and the forest on the hillside above, and continues generally southwest to south-southwest.   Continue to the isolated Eddiesville Trailhead parking area at **mile 13.5** (10,320), where the CT briefly leaves the La Garita Wilderness.

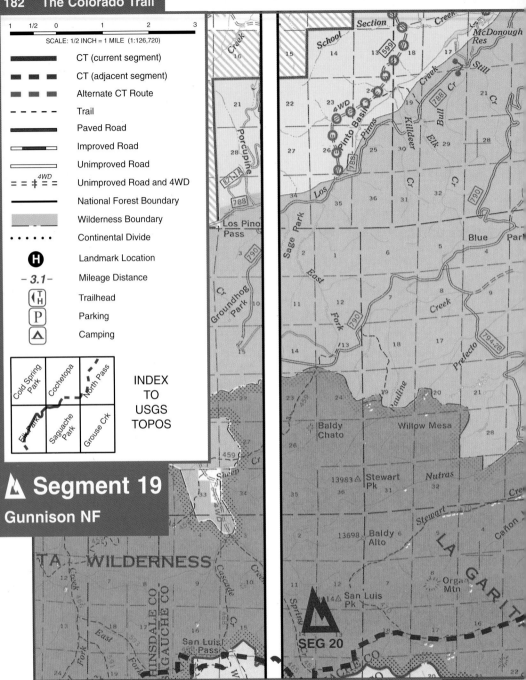

SCALE: 1/2 INCH = 1 MILE (1:126,720)

CT (current segment)	
CT (adjacent segment)	
Alternate CT Route	
Trail	
Paved Road	
Improved Road	
Unimproved Road	
Unimproved Road and 4WD	
National Forest Boundary	
Wilderness Boundary	
Continental Divide	
H	Landmark Location
– 3.1 –	Mileage Distance
T H	Trailhead
P	Parking
△	Camping

INDEX TO USGS TOPOS

Cold Spring Park | Cochetopa | North Pass
Elk Park | Saguache Park | Grouse Crk

⛰ Segment 19
Gunnison NF

Landmark Location	Mileage	From Denver	Elevation	Latitude	Longitude
Ⓐ **Saguache Park Road**	0.0	305.7	9520	38.131511	-106.696445
Ⓑ **Van Tassel saddle**	5.4	311.1	10400	38.096305	-106.762332
Ⓒ **Cochetopa Creek**	7.0	312.7	9720	38.101555	-106.777390
Ⓓ **Eddiesville Trailhead**	13.5	319.2	10320	38.026639	-106.833799

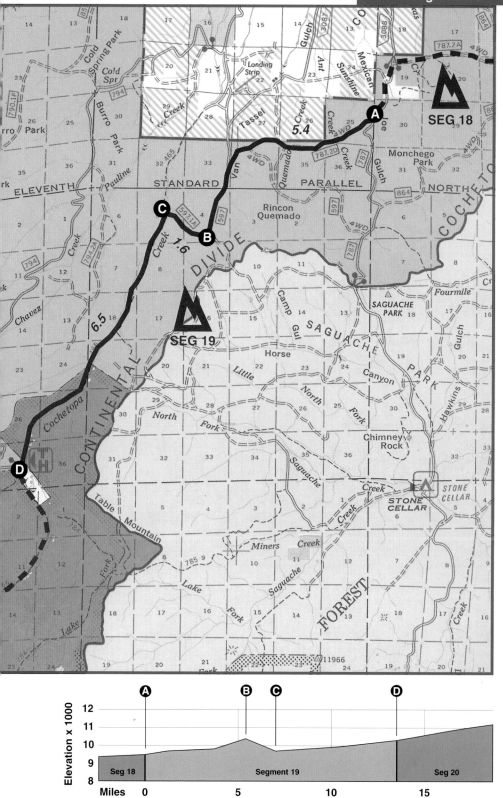

Segment 20
Eddiesville Trailhead to San Luis Pass

Distance: 12.2 miles
Elevation Gain: approx 2960 ft

An outfitter passing on the Skyline Trail by Cochetopa Creek.

Gudy's Tip

"It is a temptation to climb 14,014-foot San Luis Peak, but the high incidence of lightning storms in that area can make it a dicey proposition. Be sure to check the cloud patterns and weather before ascending."

Trip Log

Date: _____ Notes: _____

_____

_____

_____

_____

About This Segment

This segment traverses stunning alpine country on the old and appropriately named Skyline Trail. It also has the honor of making the CT's closest approach to a 14,000-foot peak, passing just 1,400 feet below and within 1.3 miles of 14,014-foot San Luis Peak. This mountain was probably christened by members of the Hayden Survey, who were no doubt influenced by the huge valley to the east. At the head of Cochetopa Creek, the trail passes the extreme northwest corner of the La Garita Mountains, a small but unique subset of the immense San Juan Mountains. The interesting gnome-like figures, or "hoodoos," that decorate the mountainsides through here have been eroded out of volcanic ash.

Stewart Creek gets its name from the mountain on whose slopes it begins. Stewart Peak (13,983 feet), which is not visible in this trail segment, was named by the Wheeler Survey for Senator William M. Stewart of Nevada, who was an advocate of the free coinage of silver. Having his name attached to a prominent peak is evidence of the strong feelings Coloradans had for free silver. Stewart Peak also has the dubious distinction of having been demoted from its previous 14,000-foot stature, which occurred when inaccurate early-day triangulations were superseded by more precise modern survey techniques. Since the rather ignominious demotion, this noble mountain is now virtually ignored by peakbaggers who flock into the area to climb San Luis Peak.

Additional Trail Information: From San Luis saddle west to San Luis Pass, the CT stays at or above 12,000 feet and only once barely grazes the upper limits of a spruce forest at the head of Spring Creek. With the exception of the last mile as you approach San Luis Pass, the trail is generally continuous, although obscured at times by talus or thick tundra grasses. Hikers should be aware that snowfields often linger well into the summer on the north slopes beyond San Luis saddle, and mountain bicyclists are reminded of the mandatory detour around La Garita Wilderness.

Backpackers will certainly want to tarry in this segment, which remains almost entirely within the wilderness, and set up camp anywhere along the upper course of Cochetopa Creek or in the headwaters of Spring Creek further west.

Trailhead/Access Points

Eddiesville Trailhead: From Saguache on US-285 in the San Luis Valley, travel west on Colorado Hwy-114 approximately 30 miles to the summit of North Pass. Continue on Hwy-114 west of the pass approximately 5.2 miles and go left (south) on Saguache Co Rd-17GG. Continue on the dirt road approximately 5.2 miles around the southeast side of Cochetopa Dome and go right (west) on Rd-NN14, which is the Cochetopa Pass Road. Drive west 1.3 miles on the pass road and go left on Rd-15GG (which becomes 14DD after a few miles, also FS-794). Follow this main road, which is marked as "Stewart Creek," approximately 21 miles to the Eddiesville Trailhead parking area near the end of the road. The Eddiesville road is a primitive dirt road, generally open to passenger cars with adequate clearance; however, it would be impassable in prolonged rainy weather, and challenging then, even to 4WD vehicles.

San Luis Pass Trail Access: See Segment 21.

Supplies, Services and Accommodations

Available in Creede (see Segment 21).

Maps and Jurisdiction

USFS maps: Gunnison NF, Rio Grande NF, see pages 188-189.
USGS Quadrangle maps: Elk Park, Halfmoon Pass, San Luis Peak.
Trails Illustrated map: # 139.

Jurisdiction: Gunnison Ranger District, Gunnison NF.

Trail Description

From the Eddiesville Trailhead parking area, head south on the road which dips slightly to cross Stewart Creek. Leave the road as it enters private property at **mile 0.2** (10,320) and continue to the right (southwest) 500 feet on a trail which parallels a barbed-wire fence and then passes through a gate. The Cañon Hondo Trail ascends to the right 300 feet beyond. Proceed south at the western edge of the broad, grassy valley which encompasses Cochetopa Creek; a small homestead is visible at left. The trail joins a set of jeep tracks in 0.3 mile and continues south. At **mile 1.1** (10,360), the trail passes through another gate and continues in the La Garita Wilderness. Just a few hundred feet beyond, in a pleasant meadow near the level of the creek, the Machin Basin Trail comes in from the left (east-northeast).

The CT assumes a more southwesterly bearing at **mile 2.0** (10,400) as the valley makes a wide, slow turn to the west. As the trail ascends, it begins to enter small clumps of spruce amid the narrowing valley bottom. Pass through a gate at **mile 3.5** (10,640) and continue through a forest which breaks into grassy meadows from time to time. At **mile 7.2** (11,720) a very obscure side trail ascends to Stewart Creek. Just 200 feet beyond you will ford the headwaters of Cochetopa Creek. Beyond timberline, follow the trail through the willows and enjoy the magnificent views of nearby Organ Mountain. The trail is engulfed by tundra grasses just short of the saddle south of San Luis Peak. Continue to this San Luis saddle at **mile 8.4** (12,600). The summit of 14,014-foot San Luis Peak is only a 1.3-mile ridge walk north of this point.

Pick up the trail again on the opposite side of the saddle and traverse south, then west, into a cirque at the head of Spring Creek. Climb slightly to another saddle at **mile 9.6** (12,360), then descend on the trail, which disappears 200 feet beyond in the grass. A post visible just west of the saddle marks where the trail resumes; follow as it descends slightly into another alpine cirque. An old sign at **mile 10.0** (12,080) identifies where the obscure Spring Creek Trail intersects the CT. Cross a small stream 200 feet beyond and continue to **mile 10.5** (12,000), where the trail briefly enters a upper limit spruce forest.

Proceed 0.4 mile on the trail to another small stream and begin a long ascent. Climb steadily to a switchback then ascend west to **mile 11.3** (12,200), where the trail becomes indistinct in the thick tundra grasses. Continue northwest and aim to the right (north) of the rocky knob which rises prominently above the smooth, grassy ridge of the Continental Divide. Top the divide ridge north of the rocky knob at **mile 11.6** (12,360). The trail is faint or nonexistent for the next 0.7 mile from here to San Luis Pass, and numerous old posts and claim stakes may make the descent confusing. From the grassy divide ridge above, descend slowly 0.3 mile to the northwest. Stay above a mass of short but dense willows below. Continue a slow descent until San Luis Pass comes into view below as a reference point, then descend steeply west maneuvering around the willows to the pass, and the end of this segment, at **mile 12.2** (11,920). Creede is about 10 miles distant, first on a side trail, then on a road (FS-503), which descend south down the valley.

The Fourteeners

The CT has its closest encounter with a 14er when it passes gentle giant, San Luis Peak (14,014 feet), at mile 8.4 of Segment 20. As it turns out, of the 54 peaks in Colorado that rise above the altitude of 14,000 feet, nearly two-thirds sit within twenty miles of the course of the CT. They are a common and an inspiring sight from many a ridgetop on the trail.

It seems remarkable that none of the 14ers exceeds an altitude of 14,433 feet and that all of the peaks lie within a circle having a radius of only 120 miles, centered in the Sawatch Range near Buena Vista. Even more remarkable is that nearby states that share the Rocky Mountains, and presumably share a related geologic history, have no 14ers at all.

The reasons may rest with two geological features unique to Colorado. The *Colorado Mineral Belt* is a northeast-southwest trending band of hot igneous rocks following roughly the same line as the CT. The *Rio Grande Rift* is a narrow rift valley, including the San Luis and Arkansas Valleys. Both of these features tend to push overlaying rocks upward. Interestingly, all but one or two of the 14ers are along these two features; and the highest and most numerous lie at the intersection of the two.

It's thought that although the entire Rocky Mountain region, including Colorado, Wyoming and New Mexico, went through a broad, uniform uplift, the Colorado 14ers seem to be the result of an additional local growth spurt caused by these two trends.

In any case, this happy coincidence has captured the imagination of climbers ever since Carl Blaurock and Bill Ervin became the first to climb them all in 1923. A growing number have followed in their footsteps — the Colorado Mountain Club (CMC) reports that, as of the end of 2001, over 1000 people will have officially finished up the 14ers. But if you choose to climb San Luis Peak while passing by on your trek, you may be lucky enough to have it all for yourself. According to the CMC, San Luis Peak is one of the least climbed of the 14ers.

Camp with San Luis Peak.

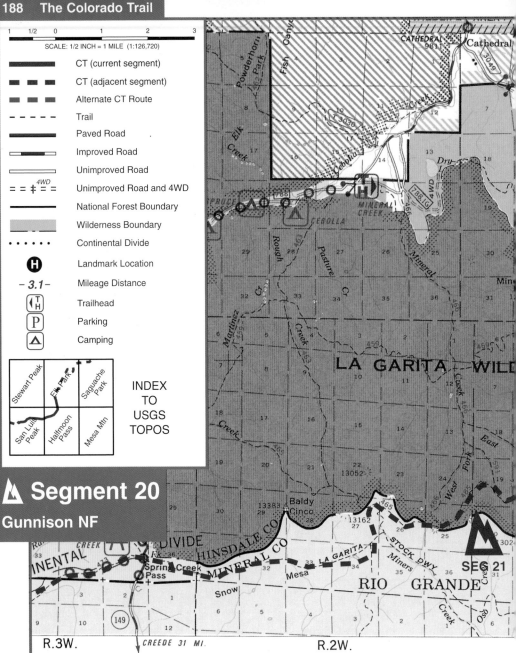

Legend

▬▬▬	CT (current segment)
▬ ▬ ▬	CT (adjacent segment)
▬ ▬ ▬	Alternate CT Route
- - - -	Trail
▬▬▬	Paved Road
▭▬▭	Improved Road
▭▭	Unimproved Road
= = ‡ = = 4WD	Unimproved Road and 4WD
▬▬▬	National Forest Boundary
▨	Wilderness Boundary
• • • • •	Continental Divide
H	Landmark Location
− 3.1 −	Mileage Distance
(T/H)	Trailhead
P	Parking
△	Camping

SCALE: 1/2 INCH = 1 MILE (1:126,720)

INDEX TO USGS TOPOS

(Stewart Peak, Elk Park, Saguache Park, San Luis Peak, Halfmoon Pass, Mesa Mtn)

▲ Segment 20
Gunnison NF

Landmark Location	Mileage	From Denver	Elevation	Latitude	Longitude
A Eddiesville Trailhead	0.0	319.2	10320	38.026639	-106.833799
B San Luis saddle	8.4	327.6	12600	37.971620	-106.923642
C Spring Creek	10.0	329.2	12080	37.961800	-106.939598
D Continental Divide	11.6	330.8	12360	37.969746	-106.961258
E San Luis Pass	12.2	331.4	11920	37.971647	-106.971677

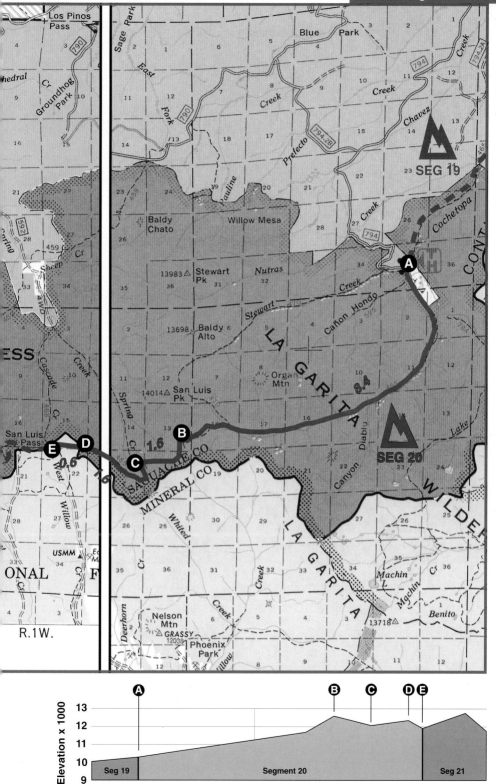

Segment 21
San Luis Pass to Spring Creek Pass

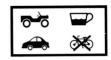

Distance: 14.5 miles
Elevation Gain: approx 2940 ft

Hikers on the Skyline Trail,
La Garita Wilderness.

Gudy's Tip

"Take in the views from Snow Mesa above Spring Creek. You can see the Rio Grande Pyramid and the Uncompahgre Mountains, where Ute Indians once hunted."

Trip Log

Date: _____ Notes: _____

_____

_____

_____

_____

There is something magical about hiking through the La Garita Wilderness, something almost spiritual in its primeval isolation. The Spanish term means "the lookout," most likely named for Indians who used the mountains as signal stations. It was probably among the high ridges of the La Garita Mountains farther east that Colonel John C. Fremont's railroad-route-finding expedition met with disaster during the winter of 1848-49, although no one knows for sure from the sketchy records that remain.

Nicholas Creede probably never dreamed of the rowdy town that would spring up after he staked out his Holy Moses Mine on East Willow Creek in 1889. Creede, like other high-spirited mining communities, had its share of riffraff. The most notorious were Soapy Smith and Bob Ford. Ford, the killer of Jessie James, was himself shot to death while residing in Creede. The town was made famous by Cy Warman's poem of the day, which could have typified many of Colorado's mining towns:

Here's a land where all are equal
Of high or lowly birth,
A land where men make millions
Dug from the dreary earth,
Here meek and mild eyed burros
On mineral mountains feed,
It's day all day in the day time
And there is no night in Creede.

The cliffs of solid silver
With wondrous wealth untold,
And the beds of the running rivers
Are lined with the purest gold,
While the world is filled with sorrow
And hearts must break and bleed,
It's day all day in the day time
And there is no night in Creede.

Additional Trail Information: This segment continues a challenging, but exceedingly rewarding, portion of the CT along the old Skyline Trail. The high-altitude route is poorly identified in places and sometimes without noticeable tread. Map and compass readings may be necessary occasionally to decipher your location in this potentially confusing area of numerous valleys, ridges and mountaintops. North slopes may be snowed in until mid-July, and you might encounter significant lightning hazard on exposed ridges and Snow Mesa.

Much elevation is gained and lost as the CT mounts high ridges and then dives into the headwaters of East and Middle Mineral Creeks, where you can camp in the protection of upper limit spruce forests. Snow Mesa is an alpine experience unlikely to be forgotten as the CT makes its way along the old La Garita Stock Driveway, along which you will find a few remaining historic cairns. Water is available when the trail dips into the upper watersheds of East and Middle Mineral and Willow Creeks; however, be aware that water is not available from the upper drainage of Willow Creek on the east edge of Snow Mesa to the end of the segment at Spring Creek Pass. Mountain bicyclists should refer to Segment 18 for the mandatory detour around the wilderness area.

Trailhead/Access Points

San Luis Pass Trail Access: Travel on Colorado Hwy-149 to Creede and go north on the town's main street. At the north edge of town, proceed into a dramatic, steep-walled, narrow canyon. About 0.5 mile beyond Creede, continue straight ahead on FS-503 as a side road forks to the right. Your car will need a strong first gear and a little extra ground clearance to negotiate these steep and rough roads. Follow the Forest Service road north approximately 6.5 miles to the end of the improved road at the entrance to the Equity Mine. A small parking area is provided here for conventional cars. FS-503 continues as a 4WD road, which you should follow north up the valley for another 1.6 miles, either on foot or in an appropriate vehicle, until it bears to the left (west) and climbs steeply over the high ridge. On foot, continue northward on the sometimes obscure side trail in the narrowing valley bottom another 1.5 miles to San Luis Pass. This access point is popular with people setting off to climb San Luis Peak, so you will probably have some company.

Spring Creek Pass Trailhead: See Segment 22.

Maps and Jurisdiction

USFS maps: Gunnison NF, Rio Grande NF, see pages 198-199.
USGS Quadrangle maps: San Luis Peak, Baldy Cinco, Slumgullion Pass.
Trails Illustrated maps: # 139 and 141.

Jurisdiction: Gunnison Ranger District and Divide Ranger District - Creede.

Trail Description

From the low point at the Forest Service directional signs on the grassy saddle at San Luis Pass, ascend slightly, without aid of any visible trail, a little south of west. After about 500 feet of easy tundra walking, look for a break in a wall of willows which is the start of a short trail section which ascends the steep, willow-covered hillside just southwest of the pass. Ascend this trail south to **mile 0.3** (12,080), where a post marks its end. Make a sharp right (west) here and mount the top of a somewhat broad ridgeline, which becomes more defined as you gain elevation. Follow the ridge west toward the base of rocky summit, Point 13,111, at **mile 1.1** (12,760). A weathered post here signals the beginning of another short trail segment and your entry into the La Garita Wilderness.

Proceed northwest on the rocky trail to the east side of a long, grassy ridge which extends north from the steep slopes of Point 13,111. The trail disappears here, near a post on the grassy ridge at **mile 1.3** (12,840). Massive San Luis Peak

It is about a 10-mile side trip into **Creede** from San Luis Pass. Descend on a side trail south along the headwaters of West Willow Creek until you meet up with FS-503, then continue on it to town. Creede is an old mining town with various watering holes which recall the town's rip-roaring past.

Creede Services

Distance From CT:	
	10 miles
Elevation:	8,852
Zip Code:	81130
Area Code:	719

Supplies, Services and Accommodations

Dining	Several in town		
Gear	San Juan Sports	137 Creede Ave	(719) 658-2359
Groceries	Kentucky Bell Market	2nd & Main	(719) 658-2526
Info	Chamber of Commerce	on Main St	(719) 658-2374
Laundry	Creede Laundromat	101 East Fifth	no phone
Lodging	Several in town		
Medical	Creede Health Clinic	on Loma Ave	(719) 658-2416
Post Office	Creede Post Office	10 S. Main St.	(719) 658-2615
Showers	Snowshoe Lodge & BB	202 La Garita	(719) 658-2315

dominates the eastern horizon from this vantage point. Continue west over the ridge and descend southwest on the wide, grassy slope following a series of cairns and posts. Stay close to the slope's high point at right if you want to follow the dotted route shown on the USGS map. Bear to the left (south) at **mile 1.6** (12,520) and cross a wide erosion course approximately 600 feet beyond. Don't be tempted to follow this channel downhill into East Mineral Creek, but instead cross it and continue south until you pick up the beginnings of a deeply eroded trail at **mile 1.8** (12,320).

Follow the trail as it leaves the grassy slopes to descend the steep walls of an amphitheater; it then continues to the alpine meadow below. Ford a sporadically flowing upper tributary of East Mineral Creek at **mile 2.0** (12,120). Descend gradually another 0.2 mile where the trail becomes poorly defined in a sloppy wet area. Continue west and pick up a better trail as the soil becomes firmer, then descend slightly to **mile 2.4** (11,920), where you will traverse generally southwest across a rockwall with a variety of alpine flowers protruding from every crevice. Enter the trees at **mile 2.5** (11,880) and continue several hundred feet on a descending trail to the lower end of a small open area. The trail descends diagonally through the open area on an east-west axis until it reenters the trees on the opposite side, about 200 feet beyond. Proceed on the trail through a spruce forest to **mile 2.6** (11,840), where the trail again opens out into an inclined, linear clearing. At the eastern edge of this opening, an old directional sign confirms the intersection of the obscure East Mineral Creek Trail with the old Skyline Trail. Continue west 150 feet across the clearing and reenter the trees.

At **mile 2.7** (11,800), the trail abruptly leaves the trees again at the edge of a massive rockslide. Bear to the right (north) here and descend steeply to a stream crossing 250 feet beyond. Make a short but steep ascent after the ford and continue around the foot of the rock avalanche to **mile 2.8** (11,720). Here the trail enters the trees and begins an ascent out of the East Mineral Creek drainage. Exchange the spruce forest for tundra and continue to **mile 3.3** (12,160), where the trail fades out just below the saddle. Bear to the right (west-southwest) here and head for the post 200 feet beyond. This post marks the saddle between East and Middle Mineral Creeks.

From the saddle, descend west through a few willows on a faint trail, which gives out after a few hundred feet. Continue the steep descent westward on a grassy slope, following a posted route which enters the trees just before the crossing of an intermittently flowing stream. Pick up the trail again here and head southwest across the normally dry streambed at **mile 3.6** (11,760) and continue descending southwest through a small clearing in the otherwise dense forest.

Proceed through the spruce forest to the edge of larger, linear clearing at **mile 3.7** (11,720), where the trail fades away again. Descend diagonally west across the inclined meadow, following a posted route, and cross a small seasonal stream near the middle of the opening. Continue west and enter the trees at **mile 3.8** (11,680), where the trail gradually reappears. If you plan to camp, consider using the already established campsite just off the trail here.

Cross the main drainage of Middle Mineral Creek 0.1 mile past this point, just downstream from a large beaver dam. A few steps beyond, the trail bears to the right (northwest) near the remains of a long collapsed cabin. Cross another tributary stream and continue to the trail's low point in this valley at **mile 4.2** (11,480). The very obscure Middle Mineral Creek Trail intersects the CT at a nondescript junction here. Ascend through several switchbacks to the saddle between Middle and West Mineral Creeks at **mile 4.8** (11,840). Notice the evidence of a forest fire which burned long ago in the vicinity.

Continue southwest across the saddle, keeping a sharp eye out for the obscure trail, which is marked by ancient blazes on the trees. From the saddle, the CT, following the old Skyline Trail, continues to ascend, bearing generally southwest through a spruce forest. Cross a prominent avalanche chute at **mile 5.2** (12,000). A snowfield here lingers usually well into the summer. Continue west 0.1 mile to a point where the trail exits the cool, north-facing spruce forest and reorients to a southerly direction onto a west-facing exposed rock expanse which can be uncomfortably warm on sunny summer afternoons.

The trail crosses the rocky area just below some impressive cliffs and continues an ascent to the saddle visible ahead. In a north-facing gully just before the saddle, you may find that you have to cross a steep snowfield in early summer. Cross over the saddle at **mile 5.7** (12,240) and continue on the faint trail, which generally follows the contour around an upper side drainage of West Mineral Creek onto another north-facing slope with another potential steep snowfield crossing in early to mid-summer.

Enter a field of willows at **mile 6.0** (12,280) and maneuver between the bushes, bearing generally west-southwest on a vague path which eventually is overwhelmed by the willows. A broken-down directional sign at **mile 6.1** stands alone, protruding above the sea of willows and pointing out the junction of the West Mineral Creek

Trail and the old Skyline Trail (which the CT follows in this area). The West Mineral Creek Trail descends to the right (north) at this point and may be better marked with posts than the Skyline, so check your bearings before continuing. Some CT through-hikers have found themselves happily marching down into West Mineral Creek from this obscure trail intersection. From the sign, continue west through the willows, following the wandering route of the old Skyline around patches in the willows, to the broad grassy saddle between West Mineral and Miners Creek at **mile 6.3** (12,280). The saddle is marked with a solitary, slender post. Ascend west-northwest on the broad ridge which extends upward from the saddle, following a posted route, and a faint footpath. Navigate as necessary through the willow patches and pick up a better footpath again at **mile 6.7** (12,480) near the bottom of a talus slope. Bear to the left and continue ascending generally southward on a re-emerging trail marked with an occasional post. As the trail bends to the right (west then west-northwest) and levels out slightly it becomes fainter, but a posted route continues through lush alpine tundra just below the crest of the broad Continental Divide ridge.

Odd rock formations below Snow Mesa.

At **mile 7.4** (12,760), near the high point of the route you will be following the faint but recognizable trail which then begins a descent gradually to the west-northwest. The distinctive profile of Uncompahgre Peak is visible through the notch ahead. On the opposite side of the valley, to your left and below, is a curious rock formation reminiscent of the Wheeler Geologic Area.

The trail continues a descent, the last part across a rocky area, to the notch saddle at **mile 8.1** (12,560). Here, the CT and the Skyline Trail diverge. The Skyline Trail descends northwest into Rough Creek and is more recognizable at the saddle than the recently built CT, which bends left (south). Some CT hikers have continued mindlessly ahead here on the old Skyline, so again watch your bearings. You will want to bend to the left (south) at the saddle and follow the CT, which stays in the upper drainage of Miners Creek. Snowfields often cover the trail here until mid-summer, and water is usually plentiful in the upper basins of the creek just below the trail. The CT continues to bear generally south as it clings to the steep and sometimes rocky mountainside far above Miners Creek. Take time to enjoy the panoramas down the valley and of Table Mountain to the south from this scenic section of trail.

The trail tread comes to an end at **mile 9.3** (12,320) at the extreme eastern edge of Snow Mesa, northeast of the small pond which forms the headwaters of Willow Creek. Continue around the east, then south, side of the pond. From the south side of the pond, strike out almost due west across expansive Snow Mesa following infrequent old cairns of the La Garita Stock Driveway, and more recent carsonite post trail markers, as you gently dip into and out of several shallow branches of Willow Creek. You will pick up a faint trail the closer you get to the western edge of the

Panorama from above Miners Creek.

mesa. If the weather is clear at **mile 11.5** (12,360), the cairns and posts marking the southern boundary of the stock driveway, and the route of the CT, can be seen to stretch westward in front of you for more than a mile to the edge of the mesa.

Visible to the south, far beyond the Rio Grande Valley below, are the rugged peak tops of the southeastern San Juan. These peaks carry the Continental Divide on a large, meandering "U" which forms the huge watershed of the mighty Rio Grande. Most prominent in the distance is the Rio Grande Pyramid. Can you identify its distinctive profile?

Continue west, following the southern line of a few remaining and historic stock driveway cairns, to **mile 12.6** (12,280), where a final cairn marks your approach to the western edge of Snow Mesa. Proceed west-southwest to the head of a prominent drainage which plunges off the western edge of the mesa. An obscure but important post at **mile 12.7** (12,240) signals the beginning of a better trail which descends southerly into the drainage. The rocky trail makes a gradual bend to the right (west), then rises a little on the north side of the drainage and enters an area of scattered trees at **mile 13.0** (11,840). The trail descends here through a spruce forest, bearing generally west to west-northwest, marked with old blazes.

The CT then descends in a seasonal drainage that is usually flowing only in early summer but nevertheless causes yearly trail erosion problems. The trail exits the trees at **mile 13.4** (11,640) and opens up into a gently rolling meadow dotted with a few stands of spruce. Angle to the right here (northwest) and continue across the meadow following a series of carsonite posts and rock cairns. Views ahead are of Jarosa Mesa and the lopsided summit of Uncompahgre Peak. The rocky trail enters a stand of spruce at **mile 13.6** (11,600), bends to the right and takes on a more northerly bearing for approximately 200 feet as it dips slightly into a shallow gully. Bear to the left (west) and descend in a small clearing ringed with spruce to **mile 13.7** (11,560). Here the trail enters the trees again and bears to the right as it traverses about 200 feet to the Continental Divide, which is broad and forested here and barely recognizable as the backbone of the continent. You may also notice a trail-less swath cut in the trees here which may be a convenient access for snowmobilers descending to their trailhead parking area near the highway.

Descend on the crest of the divide due west on a steep, rocky and eroded trail that might provide a difficult footing in places. As you approach Spring Creek Pass, Colorado Hwy-149 is visible below through the spruce and aspen. Exit the trees just above the highway and cross over the buried diversion ditch ahead. This ditch sends water from the headwaters of Cebolla Creek to the eastern slope. This ditch may be flowing or shut off, and is not a reliable source of water. This segment ends at **mile 14.5** (10,898), where Hwy-149 tops the Continental Divide at Spring Creek Pass.

White-tailed
ptarmigan.

Viewing Ptarmigan

White-tailed ptarmigan are small alpine grouse that inhabit open tundra slopes in summer, resorting to willows and other sheltered areas in winter. They are the only bird species in Colorado to spend the entire year above treeline. The extensive alpine terrain along the old Skyline Trail is perfect habitat for viewing these hardy ground birds — if only you can spot them!

With their near-perfect seasonal camouflage, the birds attempt to escape detection from predators. Their mottled-brown summer plumage makes them almost invisible among the scattered rocks and alpine plants. In winter, only the black eyes and bill stand out against their pure white coloration.

Ptarmigan are weak flyers, as likely to scurry away when disturbed, as to burst into a short, low sail over the tundra. Despite that, they still manage to travel over surprising distances in early winter, to congregate in areas that harbor their favorite winter sustenance, dormant willow buds. In summer, they add insects, seeds, and berries to their diet.

Nesting occurs in June with 4-8 buff, spotted eggs laid in a lined depression in open ground. During breeding, males are sometimes aggressive toward any interlopers passing through their territory, flying around erratically, accompanied by hooting noises, or approaching to peck comically at the boot of a resting hiker.

A recent study by ecologist James Larison of Cornell University raises a warning flag about the future for these fascinating birds. In areas of Colorado where metals from mining operations have leached into the soil, ptarmigan have accumulated high levels of cadmium in their bodies. Ultimately this causes calcium loss and many birds suffer broken bones from brittle wings and legs.

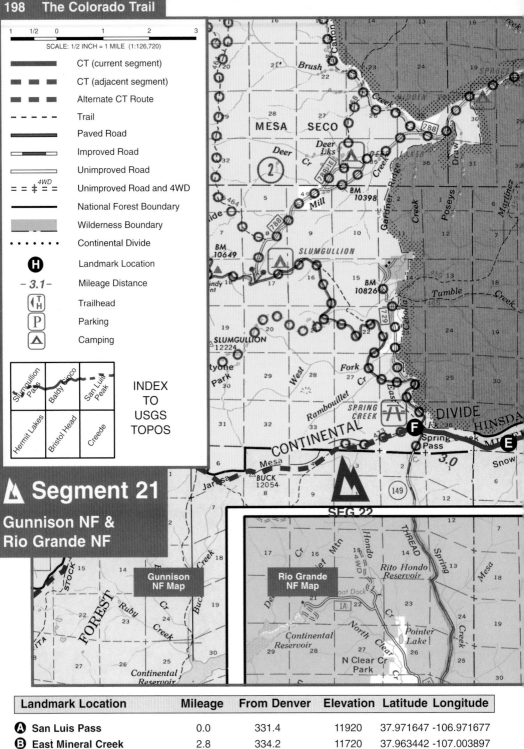

Segment 21

Gunnison NF & Rio Grande NF

Landmark Location	Mileage	From Denver	Elevation	Latitude	Longitude
Ⓐ San Luis Pass	0.0	331.4	11920	37.971647	-106.971677
Ⓑ East Mineral Creek	2.8	334.2	11720	37.963442	-107.003897
Ⓒ Middle Mineral Creek	4.2	335.6	11480	37.961716	-107.021510
Ⓓ Continental Divide crest	7.4	338.8	12760	37.953269	-107.059431
Ⓔ Snow Mesa	11.5	342.9	12360	37.936643	-107.109107
Ⓕ Spring Creek Pass	14.5	345.9	10898	37.940151	-107.158399

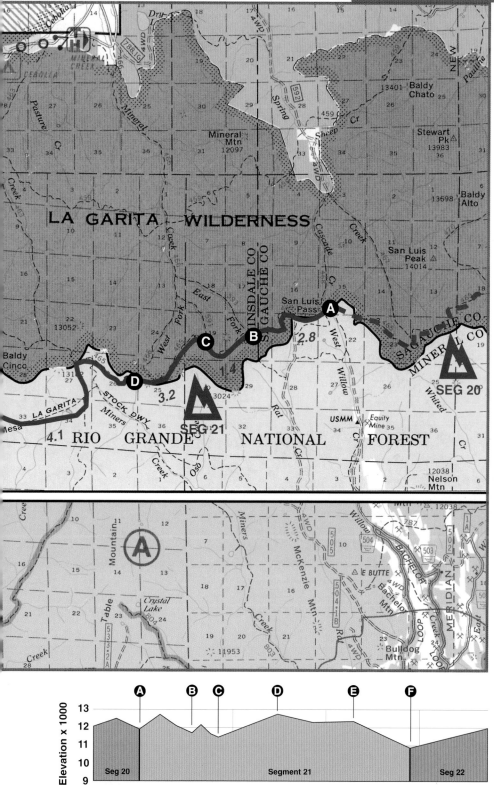

Segment 22
Spring Creek Pass to Carson Saddle

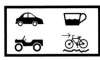

Distance: 16.2 miles
Elevation Gain: approx 3680 ft

Trail crew member working on the CT near Big Buck Creek.

Gudy's Tip

"Don't miss the panoramas from Antenna Summit, just after Jarosa Mesa. The view overlooking the Uncompahgre Mountains is worth the climb. Then from Coney Summit to Carson Saddle there is an incredibly steep descent on a rutted four-wheel-drive road. If your boot tread is worn, you'll probably slip and slide here."

Trip Log

Date: _____ Notes: _____

_____

_____

_____

About This Segment

With an average elevation in excess of 12,000 feet, this segment has the distinction of being the loftiest single portion of the CT. Not surprisingly, it also tops out at the trail's high point, just below 13,334 foot Coney Summit. The trail winds its way along the broad, grassy alpine ridges of the Continental Divide and only once drops down into a suitable camping near the headwaters at Big Buck Creek. Otherwise the entire route is waterless, but you can drop short distances into the headwaters of either Rambouillet Park or Ruby Creek for water and a more protected campsite.

This segment, like the previous one, follows an exhilarating alpine route. The CT is generally well delineated and follows jeep roads in places, however, map and compass readings might be necessary on occasion. Mountain bicyclists are given the option of detouring this segment. This exposed alpine ridge walk abounds with views nearly every step of the way. To the southwest are the Needle Mountains and Grenadier Range, while to the west, in a confusing jumble of summits, are three popular fourteeners, Handies, Redcloud and Sunshine Peaks. To the north, down the valley of the Lake Fork, is Colorado's second largest natural body of water, Lake San Cristobal.

Although there is some controversy over the naming of the lake, there is no question as to how it was formed. Somewhere between 700 and 350 years ago, the still active Slumgullion Earthflow (a massive landslide earth mud flow complex, called slumgullion because its brightly colored, mineralized contents reminded New Englanders of the discarded entrails of a slaughtered whale) detached itself from Cannibal Plateau and flowed down to dam the valley, creating the emerald green Lake San Cristobal. The great cliff forming escarpments through here were formerly thought to be lava flows extruded on the surface, but are now recognized to have been formed out of airborne ash so hot that it was welded together upon deposition, forming a dense, crystalline rock layer.

The most likely, if not the most romantic, tale of the naming of Lake San Cristobal recalls the H. G. Prout Ute Reservation survey of 1873. It seems one of the engineers, a Cornishman, was a great admirer of Tennyson, and one night around the campfire persuaded his colleagues to bestow on the lake the name of one of the poet's fictional landscapes.

Additional Trail Information: Hiking on this segment's grassy, rolling highlands and extensive rockfields is not particularly dangerous in itself, but lingering summer snowfields can turn the route into a threatening obstacle course in some places due to steep drop-offs and cliffs. If you pass this way before early July, be prepared for crossing snowfields which may cover portions of the trail on the shady north sides of Coney and the high points north of it. Likewise, frequent summer thunderstorms may pose a significant lightning hazard.

Trailhead/Access Points

Spring Creek Pass Trailhead: This obvious trailhead is located where Colorado Hwy-149 tops the Continental Divide at Spring Creek Pass. The pass is approximately 17 miles southeast of Lake City and 33 miles northwest of Creede. There are a few pullouts and picnic tables here, but this is not an official campground

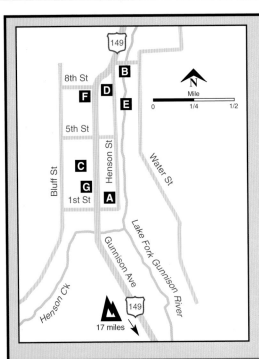

Lake City Services

Distance From CT:	
	17 miles
Elevation:	8,671
Zip Code:	81235
Area Code:	970

It is approximately 17 miles north and west to **Lake City** on Colorado Hwy-149 from Spring Creek Pass, probably too far for most backpackers to travel to resupply, although a trailhead shuttle service is available from Cannibal Outdoors (970) 944-2559.

Supplies, Services and Accommodations

Dining		Several in town		
Gear	**A**	The Sportsman	238 S Gunnison Ave	(970) 944-2526
Groceries	**B**	The Country Store	916 Hwy 149 North	(970) 944-2387
Info	**C**	Chamber of Commerce	3rd & Silver	(970) 944-2527
Laundry	**D**	The Lost Sock	808 N Gunnison	(970) 944-5009
Lodging		Several in town		
Medical	**E**	Lake City Medical Center	700 Henson	(970) 944-2331
Post Office	**F**	Lake City Post Office	803 Gunnison Ave	(970) 944-2560
Showers	**G**	San Juan Base Camp	355 S Gunnison Ave	(970) 944-2559

and facilities are minimal. A jeep road, FS-550, continues west from the top of the pass near the divide and serves as the CT route for the first several miles of this segment. The CT goes directly east from this point across Hwy-149 into Segment 21.

Carson Saddle, Wager Gulch Road Trail Access: See Segment 23.

Maps and Jurisdiction

USFS maps: Gunnison NF, Rio Grande NF, see pages 208-209.
USGS Quadrangle maps: Slumgullion Pass, Lake San Cristobal, Finger Mesa.
Trails Illustrated maps: # 141 and 504.

Jurisdiction: Gunnison Ranger District and Divide Ranger District - Creede.

Begin at the cul-de-sac pullout parking area on the west side of Colorado Hwy-149 at Spring Creek Pass. The CT follows a jeep road as it ascends west from the cul-de-sac, then levels off in a spruce forest punctuated with meandering meadows. Continue on the jeep road and notice the headwaters of Rito Hondo Creek off to the left (south) and below at **mile 1.6** (11,040).

The CT bears right off the jeep road near the crossing of a small stream at **mile 2.5** (11,320). Follow posts west through the ascending meadow. Top out on a grassy field at **mile 2.7** (11,480) east of wide, rolling Jarosa Mesa, which appears velvety green because of its extensive covering of willows. Bear to the right (northwest) following the posts at the edge of the willows. In 0.2 mile, the posts take you up to a swath bearing generally west that was cut through the willows and a spruce forest for the stock driveway. Break out of the willow swath and top out near the broad summit of the mesa at **mile 3.8** (12,000), and descend 1.5 miles west to join up again with the jeep road at an important intersection. Those considering a camp in this area will have to descend into the headwaters of Buck Creek to the south or Rambouillet Park to the north to find water and some protection from the extreme exposure on this alpine highland.

At the intersection, the right fork goes north and drops into Rambouillet Park, continuing eventually to rejoin Hwy-149. The jeep track at left continues the CT as it goes west around the south side of Antenna Summit (12,305), so called because of the radio tower array at its top. Following the jeep track at left will take you on the CT to the saddle at mile 6.6 southwest of Antenna Summit as described below. If you want to follow the high divide route over Antenna Summit which adds some distance and elevation, head northwest on the grassy tundra between the two jeep tracks toward a very obvious swath cut in the willows. This swath ascends to the smooth, rounded top of Antenna Summit. Climb northwest, then west, to the summit using the convenient corridor cleared through the willows. The photovoltaic antenna array on top seems strangely out of place here in this remote location. Five fourteeners are visible from this lofty point. Can you identify them? Also clearly visible is the path of the Slumgullion Slide which dammed Lake San Cristobal in the valley below. Bear generally south-southwest from the summit to pick up the CT at the saddle.

From the saddle just southwest of Antenna Summit at **mile 6.6** (12,040), the CT continues to follow the jeep track 0.2 mile uphill (southwest) to another grassy knob on the divide. From this knob, descend southwest on the jeep track approximately 0.5 mile and look for a short section of trail which leaves the jeep track at right (southwest) and ducks into an upper limit spruce forest. Follow this trail through the trees to a meadow at **mile 8.2** (11,720) and continue ahead (south)

Yurt by Big Buck Creek being used by CT trail crew.

600 feet across the grassy marsh. This is an extreme upper headwater point for a tributary stream of Big Buck Creek. Pick up another old jeep track as you enter a spruce forest on the opposite side of the grassy marsh and continue a sometimes steep ascent through the forest bearing generally south.

At **mile 8.9** (12,000), break out of the trees onto the lower end of a broad, slightly inclined, willow covered ridge which extends west toward the grassy crest of the Continental Divide. Follow the indistinct jeep track in a more westerly direction through the willows. As you progress, an unmistakable swath and trail develops in the willows. This swath becomes patchy as you head for the two barely recognizable switchbacks beyond the willows on the grassy tundra ahead. The trail bears to the left (south) as it exits the willows at **mile 9.5** (12,200), and turns through a couple of switchbacks. From here, the CT continues as a narrow alpine footpath which bears generally south-southwest near the edge of the willows.

At **mile 10.5** (12,440) the CT heads for an indistinct, rocky saddle on the divide approximately 0.4 mile beyond. From this saddle, begin a curvilinear ascent into a grassy upper bowl to the right of the impressive cirque which forms the main headwater drainage of Ruby Creek. The trail climbs steeply through several switchbacks to a rocky point on the divide at **mile 11.9** (13,040). Weather permitting, take a few minutes to observe the dramatic, rarified surroundings and your route along the divide to this lofty position. Follow a route marked with carsonite posts as it traverses generally south-southwest, detouring around patches of talus and rock where necessary near the crest of this huge, rolling highland. Views extend all the way to San Luis Peak on the northeast horizon. At **mile 12.4** (13,000), as the route bends to the southwest, then west, look for the beginning of a recently built trail as a saddle to the west becomes visible.

Descend to the saddle at **mile 12.9** (12,840) on the trail then begin a diagonal ascent generally to the south-southwest, crossing an inclined rock field to the gentle slopes of another, though smaller and rockier, alpine highland. Continuing on the comfortable trail, contour to the right (southwest) at about 13,000'. At **mile 13.4** (12,960), yet another saddle comes into view to the southwest. Descend to this saddle at **mile 13.8** (12,840) and begin an ascent generally to the south-southwest to the CT's high point at 13,240', just below and just east of 13,334 foot Coney Summit.

From the saddle at mile 13.8, take a few minutes to ponder your route to Coney. Early in the season, it is possible that the trail can be covered by steep and potentially dangerous snowfields. If the trail is snowed in, it is possible that a narrow, grassy corridor between the snowfield and a steep drop-off at the very crest of the divide (west of and above the trail) might be thawed out at an earlier date. However, if this alternative is also snowed in, it is much more dangerous because of the steep

Hiking the tundra near Coney Peak.

drop-off west of Coney. In a situation such as this, mountaineering experience is invaluable.

Hopefully, however, you will be unencumbered by vexing snowfields. If so, ascend on the well-built trail from the saddle at mile 13.8 through two switchbacks to a point just east of Coney at **mile 14.5** (13,240). It is worth taking a few steps west of here to the top of Coney Summit at 13,334'. Don't be too alarmed if you meet a rental jeep loaded with flat-landers from Lake City here, Coney is a popular tourist destination.

From the trail's high point, descend south, then west around Coney to a point southwest of its summit at **mile 15.0** (13,160). From this point, you will drop quickly through several switchbacks parallel to a steep jeep road that leads over the divide to

Trekking With Llamas

Llamas have been raised in South America for centuries as pack animals, as well as for their fiber and meat. Increasingly on long distance trails, such as the CT, hikers are enjoying the advantages of these unique personal porters.

Llamas may be used for short hikes or may be fully loaded for traveling through the mountains on a week-long outing. An adult animal (3 years or more) can carry about 20% of its body weight in rough terrain, or about 70 pounds. They have two-toed padded feet, which do much less damage to the environment because they do not tear into or dent the ground the way hooves do. Llamas are browsers, not grazers — a style that limits over-grazing of delicate backcountry meadows.

As highly social animals, llamas travel well in a string and are easy to train. Most importantly, they are calm and trusting with people. The common stigma, that llamas spit, is true in the sense that they use that to gain advantage in their social structure — just don't get stuck between two angry

llamas.

With their panniers fully loaded, and in the mountains, you should expect to go 5 to 9 miles per day. Smaller and far more maneuverable than other pack animals, their pace is perfectly suited for comfortable hiking.

In Colorado, several outfitters offer trekking services on the CT using llamas. But as the price of pack stock continues to drop dramatically, they are coming into use by individuals, as well as by the Forest Service. Check with land management agencies, in the segments that you wish to travel, about any restrictions regarding pack animals. A good web site for learning more about using llamas for pack stock is *www.llamapaedia.com.*

a destination at beautiful Heart Lake, about 3 miles away. At **mile 15.5** (12,800) the trail connects into the jeep road and continues a steep descend into the old Carson mining district. Go right (west-northwest) on an intersecting jeep road at **mile 16.0** (12,320). Continue to a three-cornered jeep road intersection at a saddle on the divide at **mile 16.2** (12,360). This obscure point is given the name Carson Saddle to identify it as the end of this segment. The difficult jeep road which descends northward from Carson Saddle into Wager Gulch eventually ties into Hwy-149 near Lake City. The route of the CT follows the jeep road which bends to the left (south) here and descends into the upper headwaters of Lost Trail Creek.

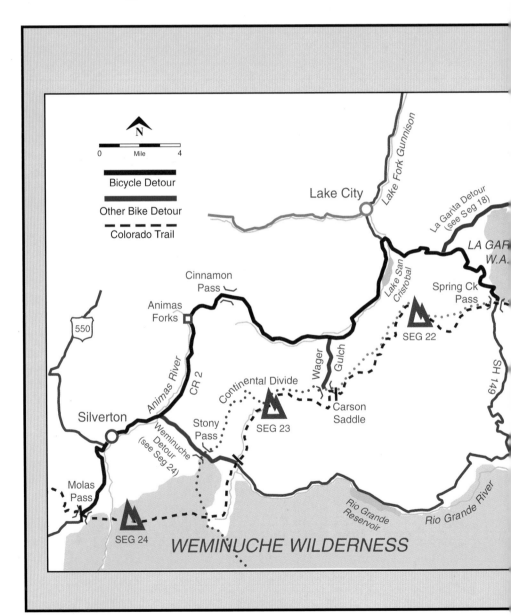

Mountain Bicycle Detour

Coney Summit Detour — *Segment 22, 23 and 24 (Gunnison NF, San Juan NF):* This optional, lengthy detour from Colorado Hwy-149 to Molas Pass avoids Segments 22, 23 and 24. It is intended to be a continuation of the La Garita Wilderness detour. Mountain bicyclists are encouraged to continue the detour here around Segment 22 because of the difficulty of the official route in the vicinity of 13,334 foot Coney Summit and because of the alpine tundra's sensitivity to tire tracks. Starting at Carson Saddle in Segment 23, the CT is still rough but somewhat less difficult. Purists who insist on rejoining the official CT here may do so by leaving this detour description about half way up the Lake Fork Road at Wager Gulch.

Cyclists using this route will not be deprived of stunning scenery. This detour passes Lake San Cristobal, continues up the valley of the Lake Fork which is ringed with 14,000 foot peaks, and then ascends 12,640 foot Cinnamon Pass. The pass is a well known 4WD road that was originally constructed by Otto Mears and Enos Hotchkiss as part of the Saguache-San Juan Toll Road in the 1870s. The story goes that it received its name because of the glistening alpine grasses on the surrounding mountainsides.

Detour Description: Continue the La Garita Wilderness detour by turning right onto Colorado Hwy-149 from the Los Piños-Cebolla Road and descending the steep highway toward Lake City. Turn left off the highway at **mile 7.1** (8880) and follow a paved road to Lake San Cristobal. Continue beyond the lake, and past the side road up Wager Gulch to Carson Saddle, and pedal up the narrow valley following the signs to Cinnamon Pass as the road gets progressively rougher. Top out on Cinnamon Pass at **mile 28.9** (12,640). Descend 2.2 miles from the pass and make a sharp left (south) onto an intersecting jeep road just above the ruins of the old mining town of Animas Forks. Continue south, then southwest, down the upper Animas Valley on San Juan Co Rd-2 until you reach Silverton. Pedal through town and join US-550 at **mile 43.9** (9240). Go south on busy US-550 and carefully ascend to **mile 50.0** (10,880) just 600 feet north of the highway's summit on Molas Pass where you will pick up the CT going west. This point is the beginning of Segment 25.

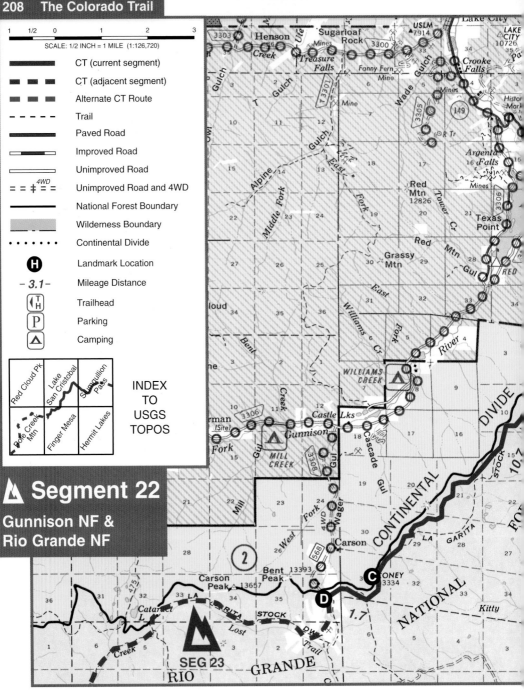

Legend

———	CT (current segment)
– – –	CT (adjacent segment)
– – –	Alternate CT Route
- - - - -	Trail
———	Paved Road
▭▬▭	Improved Road
▭▭	Unimproved Road
= = ‡ = =	Unimproved Road and 4WD
———	National Forest Boundary
▨▨▨	Wilderness Boundary
• • • • •	Continental Divide
Ⓗ	Landmark Location
– *3.1* –	Mileage Distance
🚩	Trailhead
Ⓟ	Parking
⛺	Camping

INDEX TO USGS TOPOS

Red Cloud Pk	Lake San Cristobal	Slumgullion Pass
Pole Creek Mtn	Finger Mesa	Hermit Lakes

▲ Segment 22

Gunnison NF & Rio Grande NF

Landmark Location	Mileage	From Denver	Elevation	Latitude	Longitude
Ⓐ Spring Creek Pass	0.0	345.9	10898	37.940151	-107.158399
Ⓑ Jarosa Mesa	3.8	349.7	12000	37.927860	-107.230050
Ⓒ Coney Summit	14.5	360.4	13240	37.857868	-107.344449
Ⓓ Carson Saddle	16.2	362.1	12360	37.856104	-107.367161

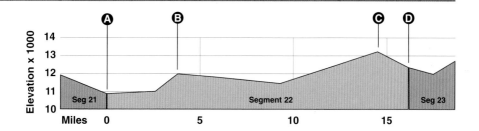

Gunnison
NF Map

Rio Grande
NF Map

Seg 21

Segment 22

Seg 23

Elevation x 1000

14

13

12

11

10

Miles   0   5   10   15

Segment 23
Carson Saddle to
Rio Grande Reservoir Road

Distance: 12.0 miles
Elevation Gain: approx 1040 ft

Sunset, Lost Trail Creek.

Gudy's Tip

"Carson Saddle has a surprising number of people in four-wheel-drive vehicles, which can be a shock after the previous isolation of the trail. Most of these folks will never see Pole Creek Falls, just a few hundred yards off the trail in a spectacular setting below the double crossing of Pole Creek."

Trip Log

Date: _____ Notes: _____

_____

_____

_____

About This Segment

The challenging high-altitude route of the CT continues into this segment, although the way is on established trails in more protected water drainages which make the going a little easier. You may have to bushwhack through thick and sometimes marshy tundra grasses in brief stretches on the upper parts of Lost Trail and Pole Creeks. In the case of Pole Creek, it is important that you carefully maintain your bearings at the head of Cataract Gulch or you may find yourself incorrectly marching down the trail to Cataract Lake. As in the previous segments, you should have a map and compass handy to confirm your location.

The old Carson mining district began when Christopher J. Carson discovered gold-bearing ores here in the early 1880s. The town of Carson, which still exists as a well-preserved ghost town, developed at the head of Wager Gulch about a mile north of the mining district. Most of the supplies, however, were sent in from the south via the road, built in 1887, up Lost Trail Creek. The most prolific producers here were the Bonanza King and the St. Jacob's Mines, but by the early 1900s even these properties had been abandoned.

Additional Trail Information: This segment may be one of the most isolated of any on the CT. Vehicle access on either end is long and difficult up forlorn roads, and 4WD vehicles are mandatory for the bumpy grind up to Carson Saddle via Wager Gulch and up the Stony Pass Road beyond Rio Grande Reservoir to Pole Creek. However, once in this remote area, hikers will find campsites abounding along Lost Trail Creek and the broad, grassy meadows of upper Pole Creek, where trout splash in the meandering watercourse. However, grazing cattle and sheep may be cause for chagrin, especially in Pole Creek. This segment is outside of any wilderness area; nevertheless, mountain bicyclists may opt to detour around this segment using the historic Cinnamon Pass Road.

Trailhead/Access Points

Carson Saddle, Wager Gulch Trail Access: From Lake City, travel south on Colorado Hwy-149 approximately 1.5 miles to a turnoff which leads right to Lake San Cristobal. Continue 9.3 miles on the road up the valley of the Lake Fork to the 4WD road turnoff at left, which leads to Wager Gulch and Carson. It is approximately 5 miles up this rough, steep road to Carson Saddle, so called because it is a low point on the Continental Divide about a mile beyond the old townsite of Carson.

Rio Grande Reservoir - Stony Pass Road: See Segment 24.

Maps and Jurisdiction

USFS maps: Gunnison NF, Rio Grande NF, see pages 214-215.
USGS Quadrangle maps: Finger Mesa, Pole Creek Mountain.
Trails Illustrated maps: # 140, 141 and 504.

Jurisdiction: Gunnison Ranger District and Divide Ranger District - Creede.

Supplies, Services and Accommodations

Available in Lake City (see Segment 22).

Trail Description

From the three-cornered jeep road intersection at Carson Saddle on the divide, gradually descend southward on the road past the ruins of the old mining district. Be alert for the trail to bear right (south-southwest) off the jeep road at **mile 0.5** (12,200) just before the road turns east for a steep descent into the deep valley ahead. The trail angles away from the road, then quickly rounds a ridgeline and assumes a westerly heading high above Lost Trail Creek. The trail descends slowly to a side stream and a low point at **mile 1.5** (12,000), though still well above the wide, marshy valley bottom of the main creek drainage. Dead ahead is a formidable-looking rock outcropping, through which the trail weaves its way for the next 0.3 mile. This area of rock and talus is notorious for remaining heavily snowed-in during early summer.

Once through the rocky obstacle course, the CT opens into the upper portion of a wide, gently inclined, grassy meadow at the head of Lost Trail Creek and trends a few degrees north of west. The trail stays in the upper part of the meadow away from the tangled mass of willows closer to the creek and ascends to the right of the rather ominous cliffs visible at the head of the valley.

As you progress, the CT bears west-northwest as it gains elevation on the hillside, pulling away from the wide valley floor. At **mile 3.0** (12,560), the trail makes a quick double switchback and continues an ascent past the unusual gnome-like figures so typical of the geology in this part of the San Juans. Your ascent ends at the unnamed pass at **mile 3.6** (12,920), referred to here as the Lost Trail/Pole Creek Pass. Perhaps someone in the future will give it a more appropriate name.

From the pass, the trail makes a gradual descent to the west, high above the headwaters of Pole Creek. Follow the trail southwest as it settles onto a broad, descending ridge of the Continental Divide and approaches a prominent cliff at the head of the cirque which forms Cataract Gulch. Reach an important point and trail intersection at **mile 5.0** (12,360) near the prominent cliff above Cataract Lake. The CT bears to the left (southwest) here as another trail continues to the right eventually to descend northward into Cataract Gulch. Proceed south-southwest, descending into the headwaters of Pole Creek across a broad, marshy alpine meadow. The trail continues approximately 0.5 mile on the north side of the creek at a sometimes steep descent into the long and spacious upper valley, which is carpeted with fringed gentian in late summer.

Continue southwest to south-southwest on a nearly flat and sometimes faint trail which follows the meandering of Pole Creek. The broad valley narrows into a tighter V-shaped gap beyond **mile 6.9** (11,680). At a deep and difficult ford, cross briefly to the east side of Pole Creek at **mile 7.8** (11,480), then return to the west side 800 feet beyond.

The trail leaves the narrow gap at **mile 8.3** (11,280) and leads into another rolling meadow at timberline. A side trail forks sharply to the right (northwest) here and ascends the Middle Fork of Pole Creek. Another trail forks to the right in this area and crosses to the west side of the Middle Fork. Continue south-southeast a few steps beyond the trail junctions and make a final deep ford to the east side of Pole Creek. The trail follows a grassy bench south-southeast slightly above the creek. Another intersecting side trail at **mile 9.0** (11,200) forks sharply to the right (west) and ascends the West Fork of Pole Creek. Continue south 400 feet beyond this trail junction and be sure to take a short walk off the trail to view scenic Pole Creek Falls, concealed by a deep gorge.

The CT continues a gradual descent to the south, staying on a grassy, spruce-lined bench while Pole Creek drops off further and further below. Several intersecting side streams provide water for those wishing to camp along the way. The trail drops to the level of Pole Creek at **mile 10.4** (10,960) and enters another long, grassy meadow ringed with willow and spruce. Pass through a gate at **mile 11.1** (10,920) and pause briefly to check out the CT's route up the valley of Bear Creek, visible for several miles to the south-southwest. Begin a short but steep descent from the elevated meadows. Pole Creek roars as it accelerates in the cascade at right. Avoid an intersecting side trail which forks to the right at **mile 11.7** (10,600) and continue ahead (south) through a grassy meadow. This segment ends where the trail intersects the Rio Grande Reservoir - Stony Pass Road at **mile 12.0** (10,560). A sign here indicates that the reservoir is down the road to the left (southeast and east) and Stony Pass (and eventually Silverton via Cunningham Gulch and Howardsville) to the right (northwest and west).

Treasure of Timber Hill

Colorado has an exciting history, one that has spawned its share of tall tales about fabulous lost riches. But often there is a kernel of truth behind these stories. One of them centers on the area of meadows and marsh at the end of Segment 23, where the historic Stony Pass Road meets the CT.

The road was constructed in 1879 as a route to transport supplies in and ore out of the booming Silverton mining district. It seems that along the road at Timber Hill, near the intersection with the modern CT, there was a large rock where road agents used to lie in wait for the Silverton stage, or for loaded ore wagons, to pass by.

One day, three wagons loaded with sacks stuffed with rich silver ore were being brought down, escorted by guards.

The guards rode ahead, discovered the robbers hiding behind the rock and in the ensuing gunfight, one guard was killed. The surviving guard galloped back to the wagons to raise the alarm, whereupon the drivers quickly hid the silver in a swamp close at hand. Before they could unload the third wagon though, the road agents came on the scene, killed everyone and fled with the lone wagon.

According to the legend, the silver treasure remains buried to this day, somewhere alongside the CT. While the tale may be true or not, you can start your search by visiting the bandits' lair. Turn left (southeast) onto the Stony Pass Road at the sign that indicates the way to Rio Grande Reservoir. In 0.5 mile, you come to Timber Hill and the infamous big rock can be seen halfway down the hill.

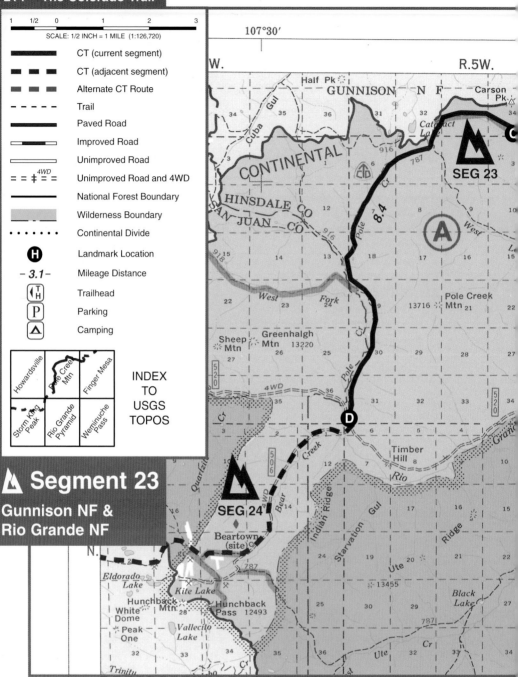

| 1 | 1/2 | 0 | 1 | 2 | 3 |
SCALE: 1/2 INCH = 1 MILE (1:126,720)

▬▬▬▬	CT (current segment)
▬ ▬ ▬	CT (adjacent segment)
▬ ▬ ▬	Alternate CT Route
- - - - -	Trail
▬▬▬▬	Paved Road
▭▬▭	Improved Road
▭▭▭	Unimproved Road
= = ‡ = =	Unimproved Road and 4WD
▬▬▬▬	National Forest Boundary
▬▬▬	Wilderness Boundary
• • • • • •	Continental Divide
H	Landmark Location
– *3.1* –	Mileage Distance
[T/H]	Trailhead
[P]	Parking
[A]	Camping

INDEX TO USGS TOPOS

Index grid:
| Howardsville | Pole Creek Mtn | Finger Mesa |
| Storm King Peak | Rio Grande Pyramid | Weminuche Pass |

▲ Segment 23

Gunnison NF & Rio Grande NF

Landmark Location	Mileage	From Denver	Elevation	Latitude	Longitude
A Carson Saddle	0.0	362.1	12360	37.856104	-107.367161
B Lost Trail Creek	1.5	363.6	12000	37.848590	-107.387578
C Lost Trail/Pole Creek Pass	3.6	365.7	12920	37.853371	-107.419062
D Rio Grande Reservoir Road	12.0	374.1	10560	37.761895	-107.466016

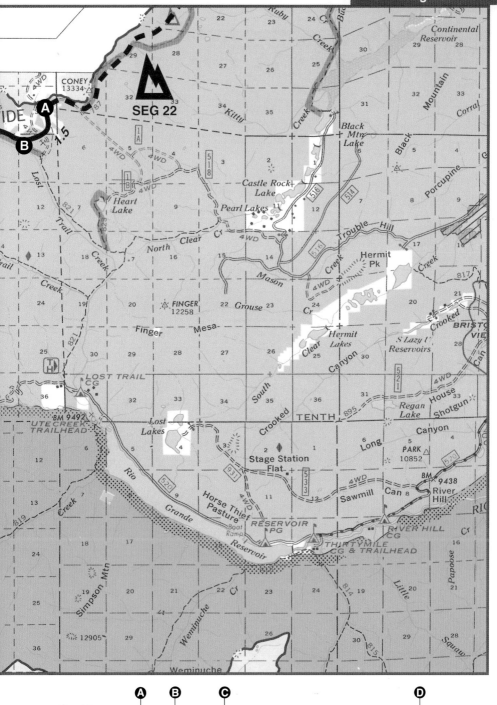

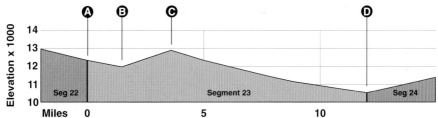

Segment 24
Rio Grande Reservoir Road to Molas Pass

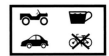

Distance: 21.1 miles
Elevation Gain: approx 4460 ft

Preparing to cross the Rio Grande River.

Gudy's Tip

"All major water crossings have bridges spanning them except for Pole Creek and the Rio Grande. Both can be extremely fast during high water, so use caution. Once over the Divide and in the Weminuche Wilderness, the Elk Creek drainage and its dramatic geologic walls are topped off with views of Arrow and Vestal peaks."

Trip Log

Date: _____ Notes: _____

_____

_____

_____

About This Segment

The mystical San Juan Mountains reach a crescendo in the rugged and beautiful Needle Mountains and Grenadier Range. This 21.1-mile segment penetrates much of this spectacular scenery and, for the last time, crosses the Continental Divide. Mountain bicyclists will have to bypass this segment, which passes through the Weminuche Wilderness.

Hikers have plenty of challenges in this segment, starting with the crossing of the Rio Grande. This is the longest ford on the entire CT. It is precarious, deep and frigid. Another possible difficulty is the extreme, almost dizzying, steepness of the trail in the headwaters of Elk Creek. Snowfields here may linger well into summer, and could be a hazardous obstacle, even for experienced mountaineers.

The first 4 miles of this segment follow the 4WD road up Bear Creek. Kite Lake, at the head of the creek, is a popular destination for jeepers, and you may be able to hitch a ride across the Rio Grande, and perhaps all the way to Beartown. With the exception of a few mine dumps, nothing remains today of Beartown, which was a bustling mining community in the 1890s.

The enthusiasm that Captain Charles Baker had for the San Juans was unfortunately never justified by the quantity of gold he panned from its rivers. But after the Confederate's untimely death at the hands of the Utes on whose land he was trespassing, other prospectors discovered a bonanza in the area's silver lodes. Eventually, enough pressure was exerted on the Utes to force them to cede a large portion of their reservation in the infamous Brunot Treaty of 1873. Soon after, the valleys around Bakers Park echoed with activity. The little town of Silverton sprang up in the park and thrived for nearly 20 years until the Sherman Silver Purchase Act was repealed in 1893, devastating the economy of the area. By then, however, the region had received its legendary nickname, by which it is still known by many today: the Silvery San Juan.

Additional Trail Information: Some CT trekkers have reported disorientations on the rolling divide highlands above Beartown where the trail is obscure in places, and not well marked. There are other trails and markers here that compound the confusion. A few trekkers have gone almost as far north as Stony Pass before realizing their mistake. Therefore, be attentive in this area.

Once backpackers arrive at the Animas River, they will be confronted with a unique choice—either to finish the last 70 miles of the CT or to take a nostalgic shortcut to Durango via the narrow gauge railroad. This curious remnant of the past was constructed in 1882 by the D&RG and remained part of the system into the early 1980s when it was sold to a company that maintains the line as one of Colorado's historical highlights. Don't be tempted to hike down the railroad tracks in the narrow Animas River canyon as a shortcut to Silverton; locomotives can appear quickly around blind corners, and it is illegal anyway.

Trailhead/Access Points

Rio Grande Reservoir - Stony Pass Road: From Creede, drive west on Colorado Hwy-149 for 21 miles and turn left on the side road marked "Rio Grande Reservoir." Continue approximately 19 miles to Lost Trail Campground (beyond the reservoir) where the graded road ends and the 4WD road begins. From here on, the road is rough, occasionally steep, often muddy and sometimes impassable. Continue approximately 7 miles to where the CT crosses the road at a sign reading "Pole Creek Trail." This rough 4WD road continues to Silverton via Stony Pass.

US-550 - Molas Trail Trailhead: See Segment 25.

Supplies, Services and Accommodations

Available in Silverton (see Segment 25).

Maps and Jurisdiction

USFS maps: Rio Grande NF, San Juan NF, see pages 222-223.
USGS Quadrangle maps: Pole Creek Mountain, Rio Grande Reservoir, Storm King Peak, Snowdon Peak.
Trails Illustrated maps: # 140 and 504.

Jurisdiction: Columbine Ranger District - West, Divide Ranger District - Creede.

Trail Description

Starting from where The Colorado Trail joins the Rio Grande Reservoir Road near Pole Creek, go right (northwest) on the road about 150 feet, then make a sharp left (south) on the intersecting jeep road. A sign here marks this as the way to Beartown. Gradually descend south on the jeep road to the long ford of the Rio Grande at **mile 0.4** (10,440). If you are lucky, you will catch a ride across the river, which runs deep and cold, especially so in early summer.

Once across the Rio Grande, follow the jeep road as it ascends west, then southwest, through a grassy, inclined valley bordered by a thick spruce forest. Pass through a gate at **mile 3.1** (10,920) and ascend 0.5 mile further to the lower end of a large meadow. As the jeep road enters several scattered groups of spruce and begins an ascent out of the upper end of the meadow at **mile 4.5** (11,320), it passes through the townsite of Beartown. The only signs of human habitation here are a few long-abandoned mine dumps. Fields of columbine now bloom on these slopes which were once trampled by the feet of fortune seekers.

Be on the lookout here for the trail to leave the road at right (north). It rises quickly through a series of switchbacks to timberline. The trail then traverses west at about the 11,880-foot level into a lovely little side drainage covered with wildflowers until early August. After a few more switchbacks, the CT ties into a wider trail at **mile 6.1** (12,080) in a larger side drainage. Across the drainage are the remains of several cabins which might provide shelter during one of the frequent San Juan showers. Continue at right (northwest) a few hundred feet to a fork in the trail. This is where the CT route gets confusing as reported by some past trail trekkers. From here, your objective is to get to the top of the Continental Divide (the long, flat, grassy ridge visible about 0.5 mile to the west), where the trail then descends west into Elk Creek. This point on the divide is visible from where you now stand by looking almost due west. If you have sharp eyes, or field glasses, you may even be able to pick out the signpost on the divide marking this spot.

Alpine sunflowers near Eldorado Lake.

The source of the confusion stems at least in part from the variety of routes in this area, and the lack of markings. From the fork in the trail above, continue ahead (northwest) and avoid the old jeep track at left that descends slightly into the drainage. Proceed about 0.3 mile to the head of the drainage. Here, the trail ascends into a short but very pronounced "V" shaped gully.

PLEASE NOTE THE FOLLOWING — VERY IMPORTANT.
THIS IS WHERE PEOPLE GET CONFUSED.

At the top of the pronounced gully, where you open into the rolling divide highland country, you want to leave the trail (which continues ahead to Stony Pass) and bear left, trending to the west-southwest, until you pick up an obscure jeep track that will shortly take you to a more southwesterly heading toward the crest of the Continental Divide.

Follow the jeep track as it bends to the southwest, and slowly mounts the divide at **mile 6.9** (12,600). Lingering snowfields here might obscure the route in places in early summer. The jeep track eventually bears due south as it follows the wide, rolling crest of the Continental Divide. The divide here is covered with marsh marigolds that bloom where the tundra has been saturated by melting snowfields. On a clear day, it is possible to pick out massive San Luis Peak and the long, horizontal profile of Snow Mesa to the east-northeast.

At **mile 7.3** (12,680), the CT makes a sharp right (west), leaving the jeep track which continues south along the divide. The CT here begins a long descent into Elk Creek. The trail immediately loses 500 feet of elevation as it maneuvers through nearly 30 consecutive switchbacks, on an extremely steep mountainside seemingly held in place by the intertwining roots of an exquisite alpine flower garden.

The trail levels out briefly near an old mine cabin in the headwaters of Elk Creek at **mile 8.3** (12,080), where a convenient camp could be set up. Below the cabin, the valley narrows dramatically into a tight gorge bordered by sheer cliffs which feature numerous precipitous waterfalls. The descent from the Continental Divide through this gorge could be extremely dangerous, even impassable, if blocked by snowfields.

The trail briefly crosses to the south side of upper Elk Creek at **mile 8.6** (11,800), then returns to the north bank 0.2 mile beyond. As you continue, the creek plunges further down the gorge, leaving the trail perched ledge-like and isolated a dizzying distance above. Enter the security of a spruce forest at **mile 9.3** (11,400) and continue a steep descent bearing generally west. The trail levels off and takes on a northwesterly heading somewhat nearer the creek at **mile 9.8** (10,720). Campsites become more frequent here in the roomier valley below the narrow gorge.

Ford a large side stream at **mile 10.7** (10,320) as the CT swings to the west and gradually pulls away from the creek. Descend a rocky trail in a sunny Douglas fir and aspen forest at **mile 12.6** (10,000), where the impressive vertical faces of Vestal and Arrow Peaks are reflected in a picturesque pond at trailside. The trail continues its descent, steeply at times, to **mile 14.0** (9360), where it parallels the creek in a narrowing canyon. Listen for the whistle of the narrow gauge locomotive as the CT ascends slightly and pulls away from Elk Creek.

A sign and register at **mile 15.5** (9040) mark your exit from the Weminuche Wilderness. There are two trails to choose from here. The left fork descends to a whistle-stop on the D&SRR at the Elk Park siding for those who would like a shortcut to Durango. If you are continuing on the CT, take the right fork, which traverses northwest slightly above the Animas River and Elk Park. Descend to and cross the tracks at **mile 16.1** (8940), then continue north 700 feet to a convenient footbridge spanning the river.

About 600 feet beyond the bridge, ford Molas Creek and begin a monotonous 1,300-foot ascent on a zigzagging trail with more than 30 switchbacks. One benefit of this ascending section is watching the spectacular Animas Canyon and Grenadier Range come into perspective. Notice the dramatic metamorphic folds in the huge rock wall just opposite the trail.

The trail tops out finally at **mile 18.6** (10,280) and leaves the trees behind in a gently sloping meadow. Climb steeply through two switchbacks at **mile 19.3** (10,360) as Molas Creek rushes down a nearby deep ravine. Take the left fork as the trail levels off just beyond. Ascend to the edge of a spruce forest at **mile 19.8** (10,600) where the trail splits. The right (north) fork goes 0.2 mile further to the Molas Trail parking area just off US-550. To stay on the CT, bear to the left (west) and follow the trail as it curves around and assumes a southerly bearing, then ford Molas Creek at **mile 20.1** (10,520). The trail makes several wide, meandering switchbacks as it ascends, at times following a posted route through an alpine meadow. This segment ends at **mile 21.1** (10,880) as the CT crosses US-550 just 600 feet north of the highway's summit on Molas Pass.

Mountain Bicycle Detour

Weminuche Wilderness Detour *(Rio Grande NF, San Juan NF):* Mountain bicyclists who do make their way along Segment 22 and Segment 23 will have to detour Segment 24, which makes its way through the Weminuche Wilderness. This detour crosses the Continental Divide at 12,600-foot Stony Pass, and then joins up with the official trail route at Molas Pass, as does the Coney Summit detour. The Stony Pass route, like Cinnamon Pass, is a historic and scenic bypass, originally built in 1879. Originally, the burro trail over Stony Pass carried most of the traffic into Silverton, primarily because it was one of the few routes into the area that did not cross Ute reservation lands.

Detour Description: The CT intersects the Rio Grande Reservoir Road at the end of Segment 23 where this detour leaves the official route. Pedal ahead (northwest) on the road toward Stony Pass. The ford of Pole Creek a short distance beyond can be deep and swift until late summer. Top out on Stony Pass at **mile 6.3** (12,600). Descend steeply to Cunningham Gulch Road at **mile 10.3** (10,120) and continue 2.5 miles north to an intersection at the old site of Howardsville. Turn left (west) onto San Juan Co Rd-2, which follows the broad Animas River Valley. Descend into Silverton and pick up busy US-550 on the opposite end of town at **mile 17.7** (9240). Carefully ascend south on US-550 to **mile 23.8** (10,880) just 600 feet north of the highway's summit on Molas Pass where you will join the official CT going west. This point is the beginning of Segment 25.

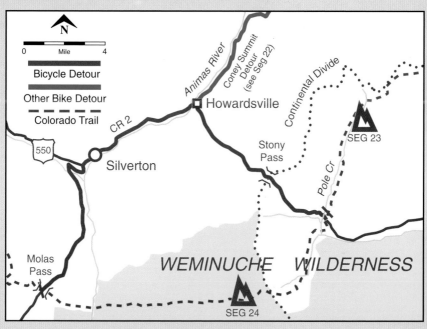

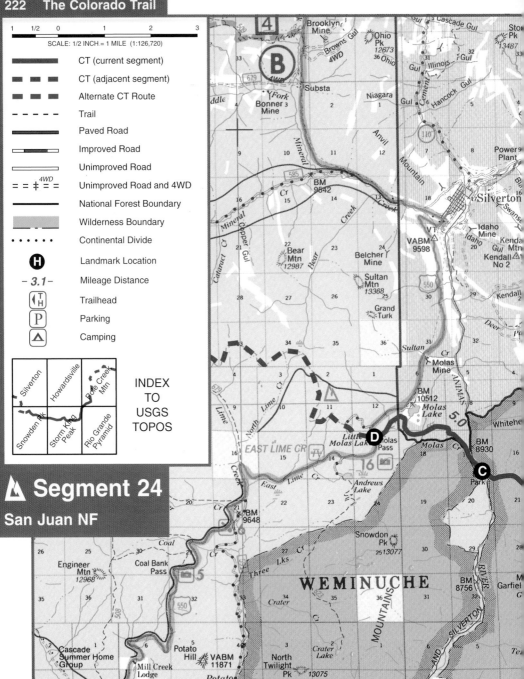

1   1/2   0   1   2   3
SCALE: 1/2 INCH = 1 MILE (1:126,720)

━━━━━	CT (current segment)
▬ ▬ ▬	CT (adjacent segment)
▬▬ ▬▬	Alternate CT Route
– – – –	Trail
━━━━━	Paved Road
▭▭▭	Improved Road
▭▭▭	Unimproved Road
= = ‡ = = *4WD*	Unimproved Road and 4WD
━━━━━	National Forest Boundary
▬▬▬▬	Wilderness Boundary
• • • • • •	Continental Divide
H	Landmark Location
– *3.1* –	Mileage Distance
Ⓣ⒣	Trailhead
P	Parking
⃤	Camping

INDEX
TO
USGS
TOPOS

▲ **Segment 24**
San Juan NF

Landmark Location	Mileage	From Denver	Elevation	Latitude	Longitude
Ⓐ Rio Grande Reservoir Road	0.0	374.1	10560	37.761895	-107.466016
Ⓑ Continental Divide	7.3	381.4	12680	37.718395	-107.535471
Ⓒ Animas River	16.1	390.2	8940	37.732034	-107.658861
Ⓓ Molas Pass	21.1	395.2	10880	37.739553	-107.697626

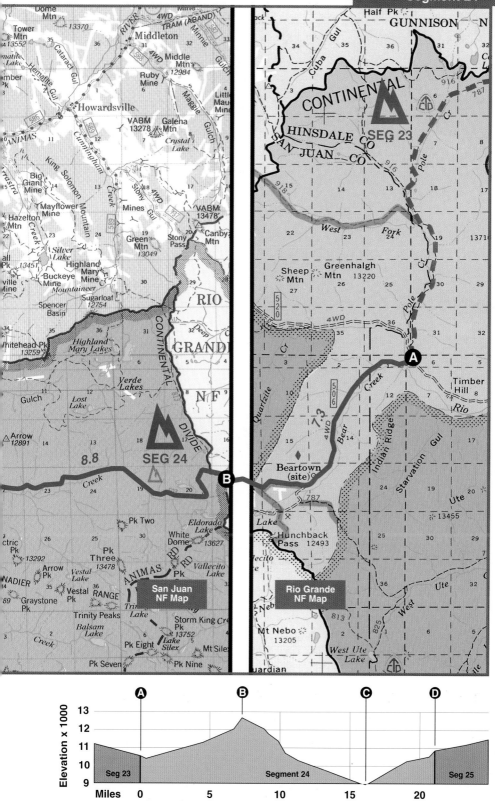

Segment 25
Molas Pass to
Bolam Pass Road

Distance: 19.9 miles
Elevation Gain: approx 3120 ft

Rolling Mountain (13,693')
from an unnamed alpine lake.

Gudy's Tip

"*Along the southern reaches of the trail, towns and local services are few and far between. There is a little store at Molas Pass (by Big Molas Lake) that offers showers and a good variety of staples. Don't miss it. Then between Little Molas Lake and Lime Creek, wildflowers grow knee high in a kaleidoscope of colors.*"

Trip Log

Date: _____ Notes: _____

_____

_____

_____

About This Segment

The CT traverses a unique, rolling highland in this segment. Once heavily forested, the terrain was cleared by a devastating fire in 1879 and has not yet recovered, despite efforts at reforestation. One result of the fire is the unequalled panoramas south to the La Plata Mountains and west to the Needle Mountains and Grenadiers. Prominent in the initial portion of this segment are 12,968-foot Engineer Mountain, known as Station 31 to the Hayden Survey, and 13,077-foot Snowdon Peak, which was named after the founder of Silverton, Francis Marion Snowdon.

From US-550, the CT gradually climbs and then contours above Lime, North Lime and West Lime Creeks under an impressive pediment of cliffs high above the trail. Large portions of this segment have no forest cover, and snowfields may linger here well into July. Backpackers will want to tarry in this attractive segment and perhaps set up a high-altitude camp in the shadow of the Twin Sisters or Rolling Mountain. Mountain bicyclists can rejoin the official route of the CT at Molas Pass after their long detour.

Additional Trail Information: Some trekkers have been confused by the two Molas Lakes in the vicinity of Molas Pass at the beginning of this segment. Molas Lake is east of US-550 near the Molas Trail Trailhead. It is privately owned and encircled with attractive camping sites. Some limited services are available at the general store here. Little Molas Lake is west of US-550 and is located on Forest Service property. There is no official campground here, although many use it for dispersed, primitive car-camping. Little Molas Lake is popular with fishermen, campers and picnickers.

Trailhead/Access Points

US-550 - Molas Trail Trailhead: This segment begins near the summit of Molas Pass where there is a scenic pullout but where overnight parking is not allowed. However, long-term parking is available nearby at the Molas Trail Trailhead. From Molas Pass on US-550, drive north about a mile to a dirt road on the right marked as "Molas Trail." This point is about 5.5 miles south on US-550 from Silverton. From the parking area, an unmaintained road (the beginning of the Molas Trail) leads south 0.2 mile to the CT.

Little Molas Lake Trailhead: From Molas Pass on US-550, go north 0.4 mile and turn left (west) on a dirt road. Continue a mile to the Little Molas Lake fisherman parking area. The CT passes on the west side of the lake.

Bolam Pass Trail Access: See Segment 26

Maps and Jurisdiction

USFS map: San Juan National Forest, see pages 230-231.
USGS Quadrangle maps: Snowdon Peak, Silverton, Ophir, Engineer Mountain, Hermosa Peak.
Trails Illustrated maps: # 140 and 504.

Jurisdiction: Columbine Ranger District - West, Mancos/Dolores Ranger District.

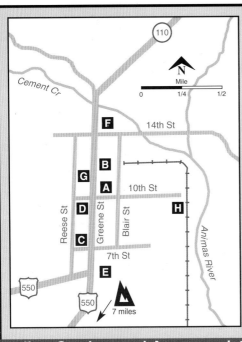

Silverton Services

Distance From CT:	
	7 miles
Elevation:	9,318
Zip Code:	81433
Area Code:	970

Silverton is located approximately 7 miles north of Molas Pass on US-550. Molas Lake Campground, near Molas Trail Trailhead, carries some limited grocery items. But they do seem to have an accommodating supply of the essentials for backpackers just emerging from the wilderness, cold beer and hot showers.

Supplies, Services and Accommodations

Bus	A	at The Lunch Box	1150 Greene St	(970) 387-5658
Dining		Several in town		
Gear	B	Outdoor World	1234 Greene St	(970) 387-5628
Groceries	C	Silverton Grocery	717 Greene St	(970) 387-5652
	D	T&T Market	959 Greene St	(970) 387-5341
Info	E	Chamber of Commerce	414 Greene St	(970) 387-5654
Laundry		The Silverton Wash Tub	on Greene St	(970) 387-9981
Lodging		Several in town		
Medical	F	Silverton Clinic	1450 Greene St	(970) 387-5354
Post Office	G	Silverton Post Office	138 W 12th	(970) 387-5402
Train Depot	H	D&SNGRR	at the east end of 10th St	

Trail Description

This segment begins on US-550, about 600 feet north of the sign and scenic pullout which reads "Molas Pass Summit, Elevation 10,910." Look for the trail on the west side of the highway. The CT soon crosses a cut in an old snow fence and meanders through gently rolling terrain, at times following a posted route, toward Little Molas Lake less than a mile away.

The trail travels around to the west side of the lake, coming closely to the shoreline at times. At **mile 0.6** (10,940) you'll cross another trail that heads north several hundred feet to the fisherman parking area. Proceed northwest then north-northwest on the CT as it drops into a small group of trees, and then travels west to cross a road. From here, the CT ascends the terraced terrain on a series of gentle switchbacks. Notice that the lodgepole pines planted after the 1879 fire have not done well as reforestation plantings.

At **mile 1.5** (11,120) go right and uphill on the intersecting old road, bearing southwest then west. In 0.5 mile, a short section of trail leaves the old road at right and ascends to an old jeep track which continues the ascent to the north-northeast. After about 0.8 mile, and as you approach the gray cliffs of 12,849-foot West Turkshead Peak, the jeep track gives way to a well-built trail that reorients to the north-northwest. A side trail ties in from the east at this point.

Approach the saddle between North Lime and Bear Creeks at **mile 3.9** (11,480). To the north are views of Bear Mountain on the left and Sultan Mountain on the right. About 0.4 mile west of the saddle, an old obscure pack trail comes in from the right, although it is difficult to find. This side trail will take you down Bear Creek to US-550 northwest of Silverton. There is a good viewpoint at **mile 5.0** (11,520). As you face the valley below, visible from right to left are Twin Sisters, Jura Knob, Engineer Mountain, Potato Hill, Snowdon Peak and the Needle Mountains.

Descending from Rolling Mountain pass.

Descend a few switchbacks and cross upper Lime Creek at **mile 6.1** (11,340). The next couple of miles take you generally west to southwest as you progress into the upper West Lime Creek drainage. You will notice large conglomerate rocks that appear to have broken off the cliffs above and scatter the area you are traveling through. There are many cascades and waterfalls descending from above and, in mid-summer, wildflowers everywhere. At **mile 9.6** (11,920), just before you reach a small lake on your right, a stream gushes out of the side of the mountain. Continue an ascent to the southwest.

At **mile 10.3** (12,120), near an attractive alpine lake hidden from view by a willowy rise, the CT intersects the Engineer Mountain Trail and the Engine Creek Trail which go south eventually to connect with a trailhead on US-550 at Coal Bank Pass. Make a sharp right turn here (north then northwest) and continue on the CT. As you rise above the lake, the extensive ridge system of appropriately named Rolling Mountain is visible ahead. Shortly, the CT bears left (west-northwest to west) and bounces over a rocky hummock which may be drifted with snow into August. At **mile 11.0** (12,320), the CT joins up with the old, historic Rico-Silverton Trail, an early mine trail which has its beginning before the railroad connected the two towns. From this point, you could descend north on the Rico-Silverton to the South Fork Mineral Creek road (FS-585), and eventually, to Silverton. At this intersection with the Rico-Silverton Trail, the CT ascends 0.2 mile southwest over a 12,490-foot unnamed pass south of Rolling Mountain. From this Rolling Mountain pass, the CT descends into the Cascade Creek drainage on several comfortable, newly built switchbacks before entering the protection of the trees.

At **mile 12.3** (11,640), there are two consecutive trail intersections where care must be taken. At the first, avoid the trail coming in from your right which leads to a nearby lake nestled in the trees and excellent for an overnight camp—to continue on the CT here, you want to bear downhill to your left (southwest). About 200 feet beyond at the second trail intersection, go right (west) to stay on the CT—the left (south-southwest) fork here is the White Creek Trail, which takes you to the Engineer Mountain Trail and the Engine Creek Trail, and eventually to the trailhead on US-550 at Coal Bank Pass. For the rest of this segment, you may see old signposts marking the way as the Rico-Silverton Trail, which coincides for several miles with the CT. The trail descends through several switchbacks to **mile 13.3** (10,920), where the trail makes a cumbersome crossing of the cascades on White Creek.

Cross Cascade Creek at **mile 13.8** (10,800), where the falls plunge into a seemingly bottomless gorge below. Until this sturdy bridge was built in the mid-1990s, the pre-existing ford just below the new bridge crossing was undoubtedly the most dangerous on the entire CT. Many loaded-down backpackers lost their footing here in the deep, forceful current, and were nearly washed over the falls. A sad story recalls a hiker's dog who was lost at this point. And an old friend and trail crew buddy backpacking this way in the swift runoff of early summer barely caught himself on the rocks before taking the plunge, but in the chaos and turmoil lost his false teeth!

At this point, you may notice that the valley is squeezed together into a narrow cleft by the basement rocks of towering Grizzly Peak to the west and massive Rolling Mountain to the east. This is one of the aesthetic highlights of the Cascade Creek Valley. Just beyond the creek crossing, the trail precariously hangs on the edge of the gorge before assuming a more responsible position higher on the canyon walls.

The Cascade Creek Trail comes in from the left at **mile 14.2** (10,840). Stay right (south) and ascend at this point on the CT. If you take the Cascade Creek Trail, it will lead you down the valley to US-550 just north of Purgatory Ski Resort. The trail now begins an ascent on the west side of Cascade Creek valley, contouring in and out of several side drainages. At **mile 16.3** (11,280), a short side trail descends to the end of the Cascade Divide Road (FS-579) visible below. This long, rough 4WD road provides a mid-segment trail access to the sturdiest vehicles and drivers by exiting the Hermosa Park Road above Purgatory Ski Area (see Bolam Pass Trail Access, Segment 26). From the Cascade Divide Road side trail, continue an ascent generally south, then west, on the CT.

At **mile 18.1** (11,760) the trail tops out near timberline and crosses a saddle, the divide between Cascade and Hermosa Creeks, then drops into the upper part of Tin Can Basin in the Hermosa Creek drainage. Almost due west, and about 2 miles distant, is Hermosa Peak, a prominent landmark visible for many miles around. Lizard Head and the San Miguel Mountains are visible to the northwest.

Parry's primrose and Cascade Creek.

From the saddle, descend to the north, following posts and the trail through the meadow. In about 0.3 mile you'll come to an old road that is closed to vehicular traffic. Bend left here (west) and follow the old road about 0.5 mile downhill to the timber where you'll come to another road (FS-578B) which is open to vehicles. Turn left (south then west) on this road and in 0.6 mile look for a cairn on your left (south-southwest) which marks the trail as it leaves the road. From the cairn, the trail goes deep in the forest for less than 0.2 mile and emerges on FS-578, the Bolam Pass Road, at **mile 19.9** (11,120) near the south end of Celebration Lake, where this segment ends.

Safe Drinking Water

In times past, one of the great outdoor pleasures for a hiker was to dip a Sierra cup in a fast-flowing stream, like Cascade Creek, for a long drink of ice-cold water. Today, hikers know that this can be an invitation for a nasty pathogen to enter your system.

While day-hikers on the CT typically carry water for their needs, it is a constant daily bother for through-hikers to meet the need for safe drinking water. Most likely possibilities for contamination in the Colorado backcountry include *giardia lamblia*, *cryptosporidium*, and occasionally, some strains of bacteria and viruses in areas closer to towns.

While agricultural runoff is seldom a backcountry problem, chemical discharge from old mines is common in Colorado. The rule of thumb here is to look in the stream for plants, insects, and ample signs of life.

There are three proven methods that CT backpackers can use to treat water. Boiling is the simplest, if you have the additional fuel, and kills all known pathogens. While there is debate about shortest boil times, a minimum of 5 minutes at a rolling boil is recommended. Iodine (or less effective chlorine) disinfectant is not as reliable, providing some protection against giardia, and most bacteria, but not crypto. Very cold water should be left to treat overnight. Filters are the latest rage in backcountry water purification, if not a bit confusing. Check the specifications before you buy. A filter with pores larger than 0.2 microns will let bacteria through. A system with an iodine matrix will kill viruses.

Choose your water sources carefully, away from obvious animal hosts like beaver and cattle. Take water from as close to the ultimate source as possible, such as a spring.

Arnold Haak filtering water along the CT.

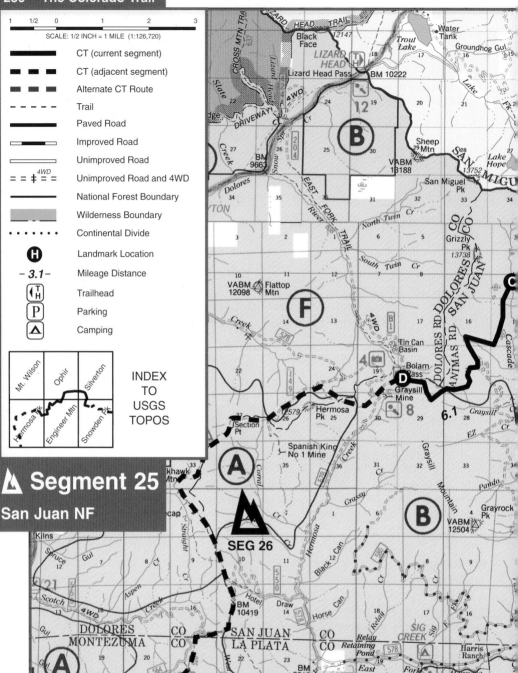

Landmark Location	Mileage	From Denver	Elevation	Latitude	Longitude
Ⓐ Molas Pass	0.0	395.2	10880	37.739553	-107.697626
Ⓑ Rolling Mountain Pass	11.3	406.5	12490	37.749356	-107.816043
Ⓒ Cascade Creek	13.8	409.0	10820	37.746929	-107.847689
Ⓓ Bolam Pass Road	19.9	415.1	11120	37.713227	-107.902880

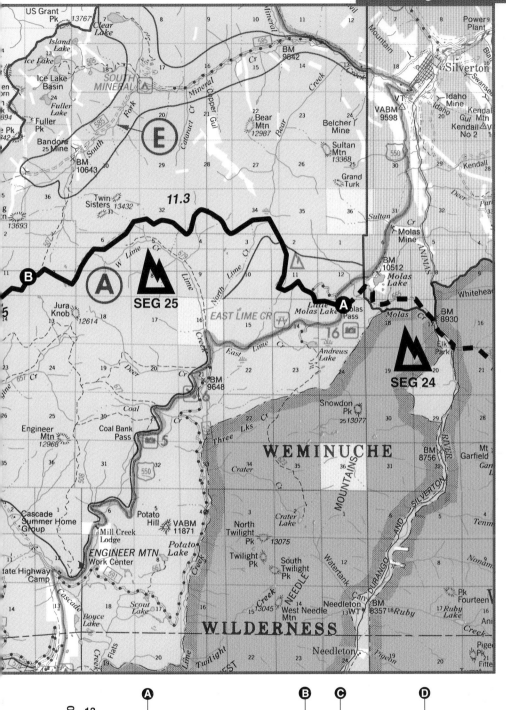

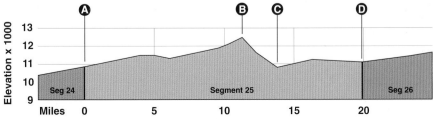

Segment 26
Bolam Pass Road to Hotel Draw Road

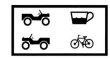

Tarn below Blackhawk Pass.

Distance: 11.0 miles
Elevation Gain: approx 1480 ft

Gudy's Tip

"The north side of Blackhawk Pass is a valley of enchantment with vast herds of elk."

Trip Log

Date: _____ Notes: _____

_____

_____

_____

_____

About This Segment

These isolated ramparts were explored by a Hayden Survey team in 1874, one year after the Utes ceded a large part of their mineral-rich reservation. The expedition, led by the well-respected geographer Allen Wilson and the articulate topographer Franklin Rhoda, ascended many peaks in the area, including Hermosa Peak, Blackhawk Mountain, Mount Wilson, Engineer Mountain and Vermillion Peak. This early team of surveyors can at least be partially credited with making sense out of the rugged jumble of mountains and valleys in southwestern Colorado.

Trespassing prospectors were testing the soil in the headwaters of the Dolores River long before the Brunot Treaty actually wrestled the land from the Utes. But the boom did not come until 1879 when lead carbonates rich in silver were discovered. So optimistic were the miners that they named their town and the surrounding mountains Rico, which means "rich" in Spanish.

Additional Trail Information: Hikers along this segment will continue to enjoy exceptional views as they make their way through the little-known Rico Mountains, but will not encounter as many water stops as in the previous segment. This is so primarily because the CT route follows at or near the crest of the scenic divide between the Animas and Dolores Rivers for most of this segment. However, headwater flows for either drainage can be found by descending slightly down the hillsides. Here, also, snowfields may linger well into July.

Trailhead/Access Points

Bolam Pass Road (FS-578) Trail Access: The trail access point on the Bolam Pass Road is accessible from two directions, US-550 near Purgatory Ski area and Colorado Hwy-145 just south of Lizard Head Pass and just north of Rico. Both require a 4WD, or at least a strong, high-clearance, pickup-type vehicle. For the US-550 approach, travel approximately 28 miles north of Durango to the Purgatory Ski Area entrance. At the upper parking area, bear right onto FS-578 and follow the road as it ascends through several switchbacks. At the top of the ridge, the road heads north briefly, then forks left where marked for Sig Creek Campground and Hermosa Park. (FS-579, the Cascade Divide Road, continues ahead here as a long, rough 4WD approach into Segment 25.) Follow FS-578 west, then north to a long, deep ford at Hermosa Creek. This ford is substantial enough to drown a conventional car, and perhaps inundate a 4WD vehicle in times of high runoff. Just beyond the ford, take the right fork as the road splits. Continue about 7 miles up the rough road to Celebration Lake about a mile before the road tops out at the pass. The CT skirts the south end of the lake. There is room to park a few cars here. For the approach from Hwy-145, travel 6 miles north from Rico and turn right on FS-578, Barlow Creek Road. The road climbs steadily for 7 rough, steep miles then levels off. Go left where the road forks, continue to Bolam Pass, then descend to Celebration Lake mentioned above, where the trail crosses the road.

Hotel Draw Trail Access: See Segment 27.

Supplies, Services and Accommodations

No convenient supply point.

Maps and Jurisdiction

USFS map: San Juan National Forest, see pages 236-237.
USGS Quadrangle map: Hermosa Peak.
Trails Illustrated map: # 504.

Jurisdiction: Mancos/Dolores Ranger District, San Juan NF.

Trail Description

This segment begins at Celebration Lake on the west side of FS-578. The trail crosses the road on the south end of the lake on something of an east-northeast to west-southwest diagonal. The trail begins a gradual ascent west-southwest then northwest as it goes around an extended ridge which reaches east from Hermosa Peak. At **mile 0.9** (11,520) the CT heads over a flat spot in the ridge. From here, the trail dips a bit and follows blazed posts bearing generally west-northwest along the edge of the talus coming off the north slope of Hermosa Peak. In about 0.4 mile, the trail turns abruptly to the right (north) ascending slightly through a skunk cabbage field. Shortly, the trail bears northwest then west and comes to a jeep track, where you turn right (north-northwest) and proceed for 0.1 mile to a jeep road (FS-149) that has been closed to vehicles. Turn left (west-southwest to west) here and follow the road as it continues approximately 1.6 miles around the north side of Hermosa Peak, passing in a few places some upper headwater springs that form Barlow Creek lower in the valley. As the road ascends through a switchback, and just before it tops out at an open saddle west of the peak, look for the faint trail to leave the road to the right (west) at **mile 2.9** (11,560). The first several hundred feet of the trail might be difficult to find if the markers were vandalized, but in a few steps the trail picks up a reliable tread.

The trail continues west from the road at the saddle, staying very near the crest of the Animas-Dolores divide. As you maneuver through the switchback near Section Point, do not be misled by the trail which heads west to northwest down the ridge. The CT goes southwest after leaving the turn.

The trail soon enters a lush basin and begins climbing toward Blackhawk Pass. About 0.3 mile below the pass, a spring bubbles out of a rock cliff. Top out on Blackhawk Pass at **mile 6.9** (11,970). The wind can be uncomfortable as it funnels through this notch in the Rico Mountains. Even so, the views from here are worth the extra time spent at this point. To the south are the La Plata Mountains and Indian Trail Ridge, where the CT will continue into the next trail segment; to the north is the unmistakable Lizard Head.

From the pass, the CT begins a descent into the Straight Creek drainage. Once the trail enters the trees, it makes several wide, swinging switchbacks on the west side of the valley to maintain a comfortable grade. At **mile 8.5** (10,980), the trail crosses to the east side of Straight Creek. Just before the crossing, a short side trail leads uphill to a viewpoint for a six-cascade waterfall. Long-distance trekkers should note that this creek crossing is the last reliable, flowing water point on the trail until Taylor Lake at the end of the next trail segment, about 20 miles away.

The CT follows the valley south for about a mile, while slowly pulling away from the creek. It then bears southeast, away from the drainage and heads back to the broad, forested ridge crest of the Animas-Dolores divide. As you reach the almost flat ridge crest, the trail seems to end at a cairn. At this point, look for an old road which begins here and follows the crest southward. This road has been closed to vehicles and reseeded, and is therefore quickly losing its road-like appearance. Some very alert hikers may notice an aged Forest Service sign that marks this section of trail as the old "Highline Trail." Stay on this old road as it continues nearly a mile south, on or near the divide crest. This segment ends at **mile 11.0** (10,400), where there is a green closure gate for the old road you just traveled, and an intersection with FS-550. The CT continues south on the Forest Service road into the next trail segment.

Trail Crews

What makes the CT unique is that it was developed with the efforts of thousands of committed volunteers. If you walk any significant length of the trail, you will undoubtedly meet one of the dozen or more organized volunteer work crews that toil on the CT system each year.

Each volunteer on a crew typically spends a week of his/her summer in creating trails, improving and restoring existing trails, and providing signage and information. The CTF estimates the cost of building the CT at $500 a mile, mostly to feed the volunteers. Trail crews work four days out of the week, with Wednesday free for hiking, fishing, climbing a 14er, or just resting in camp. Weekends are for training and camp setup and removal.

Volunteers come from every state and several foreign countries. They must be at least 16 years old, in good physical shape, and provide their own sleeping bag, tent, utensils, and clothing. The CTF, in partnership with the Forest Service (USFS), furnishes food, tools, and supplies.

The next level beyond volunteering for a trail crew is the CTF's *Adopt-A-Trail Maintenance Program*, where individuals or groups take responsibility for a section of the trail. The trail currently is divided into 53 sections for maintenance purposes, varying in length from 3 to 20 miles. Besides maintaining the tread (walking surface) and signage, adopters provide status reports and advise the CTF and USFS.

To check out the volunteer opportunities helping to create and maintain the CT, contact The Colorado Trail Foundation.

CTF volunteer trail crew assembled in Hotel Draw.

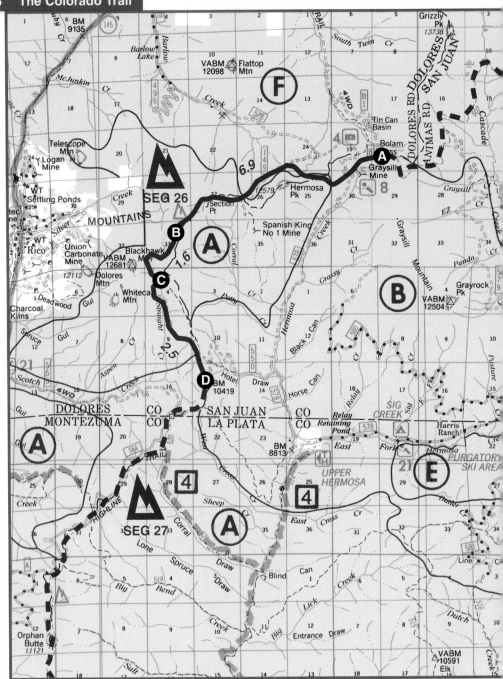

Landmark Location	Mileage	From Denver	Elevation	Latitude	Longitude
Ⓐ Bolam Pass Road	0.0	415.1	11120	37.713227	-107.902880
Ⓑ Blackhawk Pass	6.9	422.0	11970	37.684485	-107.979727
Ⓒ Straight Creek	8.5	423.6	10980	37.675856	-107.974546
Ⓓ FS-550 Hotel Draw Road	11.0	426.1	10400	37.649571	-107.956351

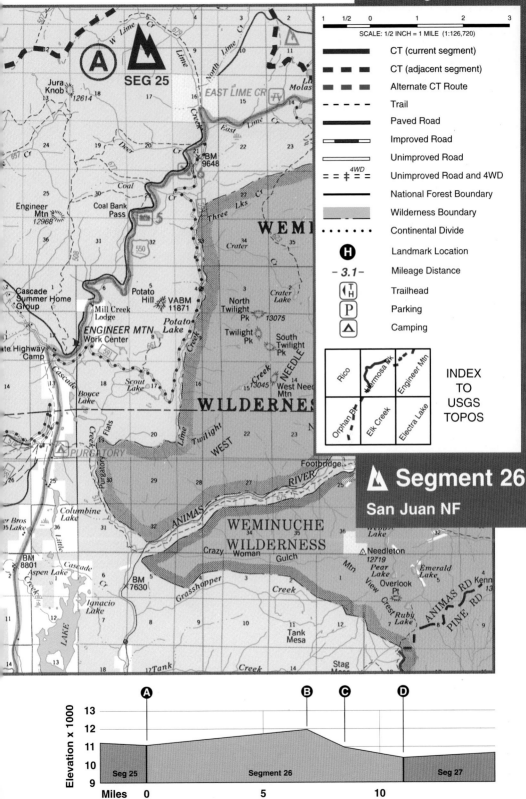

Scale: 1/2 inch = 1 mile (1:126,720)

Legend

CT (current segment)
CT (adjacent segment)
Alternate CT Route
Trail
Paved Road
Improved Road
Unimproved Road
Unimproved Road and 4WD
National Forest Boundary
Wilderness Boundary
Continental Divide
H Landmark Location
– *3.1* – Mileage Distance
Trailhead
P Parking
△ Camping

INDEX TO USGS TOPOS

| Rico | Hermosa Pk | Engineer Mtn |
| Orphan Pk | Elk Creek | Electra Lake |

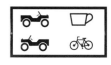

Segment 27
Hotel Draw Road to Cumberland Basin

A hiker rests among an abundance of alpine flowers on Indian Trail Ridge.

Distance: 20.1 miles
Elevation Gain: approx 3640 ft

Gudy's Tip

"From Indian Trail Ridge, a crest of cascading wildflowers, the views of Hermosa Valley and the La Plata Mountains are extraordinary."

Trip Log

Date: _____ Notes: _____

_____

_____

_____

_____

From the start of this segment at FS-550, the CT continues to follow the divide between the Animas and Dolores Rivers. Elevation is gained in a series of steps, with some little ups and downs in between. Your reward is the dramatic alpine finale on Indian Trail Ridge. Much of the trail in this segment is new, re-routed by volunteers from 1989 to 1991 around areas of extensive logging, which obliterated much of the historic and pre-existing Highline Trail. The CT still follows this historic old trail in numerous places and many old Highline Trail (Trail 1520) signs still exist along the way. However, the CT unavoidably crosses some old clear-cut zones, at the beginning of the segment and around Orphan Butte. But those open areas only serve to accentuate the panoramas from all angles that are a primary highlight of traversing this little-known San Juan divide.

FS-550, on top and on either side of the Animas-Dolores divide, follows the approximate route of the historic Rico-Rockwood Toll Road. Completed in 1881, it connected the mining town of Rico to the smelter in Durango. It was heavily used until Otto Mears built his Rio Grande Southern up the Dolores River to Rico in 1891. At the mouth of Hotel Draw, weary travelers on the Rico-Rockwood Road could rest at an inn operated by Hans Aspaas. Evidence indicates that even these early-day pioneers were not the first to use the rambling Animas-Dolores divide. Indian Trail Ridge further south, as the name suggests, was very likely traversed not only by the Utes but perhaps by people of pre-Columbian cultures.

Additional Trail Information: Scenic camping spots abound in this segment, but water may be difficult to find. Unless you are willing to scamper down off the broad divide crest to find the headwater springs forming the considerable flows of Hermosa Creek (a tributary of the Animas River) or the Dolores River, you will have to content yourself with a few muddy springs along the way, or hold your thirst until Taylor Lake at the end of this segment. The most likely place to look for nearby water on the ridge is west of and below Orphan Butte, and in the extreme headwaters of Deer, Roaring Forks, and Rough Canyon creeks, as noted in the text below. Another strategy would be to tank up, camel-like, at Straight Creek at mile 8.5 in the previous Segment 26, and trudge all the way to Taylor Lake.

This segment begins where FS-550A enters into FS-550, the Hotel Draw and Scotch Creek Road, at the top of the Animas-Dolores divide. FS-550A is a short side road permanently closed to vehicles by a locked green gate. It has been reseeded and now is suitable only for foot and hoof traffic. It leads north into Segment 26. From the beginning of this segment, FS-550 heads in a southerly direction about 1.2 miles along the Animas-Dolores divide, then descends Scotch Creek drainage to intersect Colorado Hwy-145 about 2 miles south of Rico. Until 1991, the CT followed FS-550 for this 1.2 miles along the divide to its intersection with FS-564. The official route of the CT now avoids most of FS-550 by following abandoned logging roads west of the divide through an old clear-cut which gives magnificent views north to Blackhawk Mountain and Pass, the route of the CT in the previous segment.

Trailhead/Access Points

Hotel Draw Trail Access: Travel north from Durango on US-550 approximately 28 miles to the Purgatory Ski Area entrance. At the upper parking area, turn right onto FS-578, and follow the dirt road as it ascends through several switchbacks. At the top of the ridge, follow the road as it turns north briefly, then take the left fork as marked for Sig Creek Campground and Hermosa Park. Follow FS-578 west and then north to the long, deep ford on Hermosa Creek. This ford is substantial enough to drown a conventional car, and perhaps inundate a 4WD vehicle in times of high runoff. About a mile after the ford, take a sharp left at the fork onto FS-550. A sign, usually shot full of holes, indicates this as the way to Scotch Creek and Hotel Draw. Ascend steadily approximately 3.5 miles on FS-550 to a point where the road levels out near the crest of the Animas-Dolores divide. Look for a side road blocked with a green closure gate on your right (north) which is marked as FS-550A; it indicates the beginning of this segment. The CT leads north along the ridge beyond the gate into Segment 26. To the south, the CT follows FS-550 a short ways. This spot is also accessible from Colorado Hwy-145 about 2 miles south of Rico. Follow FS-550, Scotch Creek Road, about 5 steep and rocky miles (4WD vehicle recommended) to the Animas-Dolores divide, then continue on FS-550 to the start of the segment mentioned above.

FS-435/FS-564 Trail Access: From Colorado Hwy-145 about 9 miles south of Rico, turn onto FS-435, Roaring Fork Road. After approximately 6 miles, avoid the right fork and continue ahead on FS-564 which continues the ascent to the Animas-Dolores divide. FS-564 is mostly a good dirt road with gradual grades that eventually intersects with FS-550 at the crest of the divide. It is a long drive but does reach several access points along the CT (see the trail description). Near Orphan Butte, there are numerous logging roads (closed to vehicles) that leave FS-564 and meander over to the CT.

Cumberland Basin Trailhead: See Segment 28.

Supplies, Services and Accommodations

No convenient supply point.

Maps and Jurisdiction

USFS map: San Juan National Forest, see pages 246-247.
USGS Quadrangle maps: Hermosa Peak, Elk Creek, Orphan Butte, La Plata.
Trails Illustrated map: # 504

Jurisdiction: Columbine Ranger District - West, San Juan NF.

From the beginning of this segment, at the green gate for FS-550A, go south on FS-550 about 300 feet. Here, another locked gate at right prevents motorized access to an abandoned logging road. Leave FS-550 here and head southwest on this road. In 500 feet, pass a minor fork at right and stay straight ahead. Shortly, you will enter the clear-cut giving a panorama of the Straight Creek valley you descended in the previous segment. At **mile 0.6** (10,400), ascend the side road steeply at left (west). This will take you over a small ridge and reorient you in a few steps to a descent bearing generally south-southeast. In 0.2 mile, the logging road you are following will begin a mild ascent and then assume a southwesterly heading. At **mile 1.2** (10,440), the old log road appears to end at a narrow crest on the divide ridge. Notice that FS-550 runs in a deep road cut just below you on your left, and that a rough trail continues ahead (west) from the end of the old log road. This short trail extension will tie into FS-550 in 450 feet. Continue ahead (west) on FS-550 for about 350 feet to the intersection of FS-550 and FS-564. Here, FS-550 descends at right into Scotch Creek and FS-564 goes left to stay near the divide crest and the CT for several more miles. If you are desperate for water at this point, there is a meager seep several hundred feet west-northwest of this intersection. To find it, descend from the intersection to a visible old logging road below and then descend on it a few steps to a switchback. The seep, if it is flowing, should be visible here.

The CT goes left (south-southwest) on FS-564 from the intersection and follows it only about 350 feet, where a faint tread leaves the Forest Service road at left (west-southwest). This is the beginning of a long pull, as the CT again follows the route of an abandoned log road for nearly 0.5 mile up the east side of the divide crest. Near the end of this log road, the CT, as a trail, bears to the right (southwest then west) and continues a steep ascent another 0.2 mile to the top of the divide ridge at **mile 2.1** (10,760). From here, the CT mostly follows the route of the old Highline Trail, bearing from west to south as it meanders along the divide offering spectacular views from time to time of the Needle and West Needle Mountains to the east and the La Plata Mountains to the south.

Pass the Corral Draw Trail at **mile 2.8** (10,840). The CT ties into FS-564 at **mile 3.4** (10,760) and follows it south to south-southwest about 700 feet, where the trail resumes at left (south). The trail will cross FS-564 twice in the next 600 feet, then pull away from the Forest Service road to an open area just south of the divide crest with more spectacular views. The trail again descends to FS-564 at **mile 4.7** (10,720) and follows it briefly a few hundred feet southwest, then leaves the road to the left (south). In another 0.6 mile, the trail again ties into FS-564 for 300 feet, then leaves it, again, to the left (southwest). After a short ascent, the trail will level off on the divide with more panoramas, then descend to a

Hikers in Hotel Draw.

The CT winds along the crest of Indian Trail Ridge.

saddle which is a popular car-camping area. The trail disappears into the grassy meadow here but resumes in a few steps as you proceed south.

From another shallow saddle on the divide at **mile 6.3** (10,600), the Big Bend Trail descends at left into the Hermosa Creek drainage. A short side trail goes right here to FS-564. In 0.5 mile, the CT passes close to FS-564, then joins up with an abandoned log road in another 750 feet. Go left (south-southeast) on this road. The trail bears generally south as it continues through an old logged-over area, then ascends to an open section of the divide ridge with a view north to the San Miguel Mountains.

Pass the Salt Creek Trail at **mile 7.8** (10,840). About 0.2 mile beyond, the trail joins up with an abandoned log road just north of Orphan Butte. For the next mile, the CT route will follow a potentially confusing combination of roads through the logged area surrounding Orphan Butte. However, trail maintainer Zea Beaver notes that the trail has become easier to follow over the years due to the growing over of the unused log roads and the increased use of the trail. She also notes that several springs exist on the west side of, and below, Orphan Butte for those in search of nearby water. Nevertheless, be aware of the many critical junctions to come in the next mile. Orphan Butte itself is a curious molehill on the divide crest, now highlighted because of its "crew-cut" appearance from the logging activity.

Follow the log road south, around the east, and then south, side of the butte to a fork in the road at **mile 8.7** (10,880). Take the right fork here (south-southwest), and follow 200 feet to a section of trail that leaves the old road behind and continues ahead (south). In about 800 feet, re-enter the forest as the trail joins an obscure old jeep track going generally south-southwest. About 0.2 miles beyond, be on the lookout for a post to mark the point at left (south-southeast) where the trail will leave the old jeep track. From here, the trail continues bearing generally south in and out of old logged-over sections, usually on the broad divide crest or slightly below it on the east side.

The trail begins a long ascent to the Cape of Good Hope at **mile 11.1** (10,800). In the next 0.5 mile, the CT climbs steadily, then levels out briefly below a sloping rockfield to your right. The trail is usually damp at this point until mid-summer because of seeps that form Deer Creek lower in the drainage. If you need water, there is the likelihood that these seeps will be dribbling until then, or perhaps longer. About 200 feet beyond the seep is the first in a series of three switchbacks that take you to a mid-level bench and sunny meadow at **mile 12.1** (11,320). Just as the trail orients from north to west and re-enters the trees, there is a faint side trail to the right which leads in about 200 feet to a magnificent view area where you can visually survey your route to this point. This view area, with its many flat areas among the trees, makes a good campsite if the seeps mentioned are flowing; otherwise you would have to plan on a dry camp.

Masses of heart-leaved arnica on Indian Trail Ridge.

The trail continues from the mid-level bench and crosses a few more sporadically flowing seeps that form the Roaring Forks Creek lower in the drainage. It then switchbacks left (south-southeast) and tops out on the Cape of Good Hope (which extends east from this point) at **mile 13.0** (11,600). Here, in an inviting meadow, the trail intersects the Good Hope Stock Trail and the Flag Point Trail, which are not too noticeable for lack of use. From the meadow, the CT will descend slightly as it continues a southerly course. Again, if you are searching for water, trail maintainer Larry Mack says that about 0.7 mile past the above meadow, and just before the trail begins to climb, a very indistinct side trail at right will descend shortly to some headwater springs that form the upper drainage of the creek through Rough Canyon.

Intersect the Grindstone/Bear Creek Trail at **mile 14.6** (11,600) in an inclined meadow which reaches down from the heights of Indian Trail Ridge. The Highline Loop Trail #608 descends at right (west) here, but you want to go left (east-southeast) to continue on the CT and Highline Trail. In a few hundred feet the trail will re-orient to the right (south-southwest) and continue an ascent out of the trees and onto the expansive tundra of the ridge.

In the next several miles, the trail will go through sequential and exasperating elevation gains and losses as it passes over several summits, the last two of which are the most identifiable and dramatic. However, if you pass this way during the end of July or the first part of August, you will be rewarded with an exquisite display of alpine flowers and a backdrop of incredible mountain scenery. A few places have steep dropoffs to the east side, but the trail is wide enough that it presents no real hazard, at least in good weather. This ridge walk would be very dangerous, however, during afternoon thunderstorms, high winds, or if lingering snowfields are present. These snowfields could hamper travel in some years until mid-July. From the high point on the ridge, 12,338 feet in elevation, you can survey the La Plata Mountains close-up, as well as the San Miguel Mountains to the north and the Needle Mountains to the northeast.

After passing Point 12,258, **mile 18.4**, on the southern end of Indian Trail Ridge, you will come to an old sign reading "Trail 1520." The CT turns east here and descends steeply into Cumberland Basin. Below is Taylor Lake, and visible across the basin are three peaks of the eastern La Platas: Cumberland Mountain, Snowstorm Peak and Lewis Mountain. Approximately 0.5 mile beyond at a trail junction near the lake, the CT continues on the left (east) fork. The right fork here goes south of Taylor Lake and drops into upper Bear Creek, where you can continue on the Highline Loop Trail, or go west on the Sharkstooth and West Mancos Trails all the way to Transfer Campground.

At **mile 20.1** (11,600) you will reach the Cumberland Basin trailhead parking area, where an informational bulletin board is posted. FS-571 descends as a steep, rough 4WD road a couple of miles into La Plata Canyon, and then as a better road through the canyon to US-160.

Mancos Spur

The Mancos Spur is an alternative start or finish to the Colorado Trail. Instead of taking Segment 28 to Durango, this trail terminates in Boyle Park in the town of Mancos. There is a sign in the park with information about the spur and The Colorado Trail. Take Main Street through town, across Highway 160, and pick up Highway 184. Continue on Hwy. 184 for about 1/4 mile, and turn right on County Road 42. Follow CR 42 for about 4 miles to Mancos State Park (also known as Jackson Reservoir). Cross the dam at the reservoir until you reach Chicken Creek Trail, Trail #615. Go 8 miles on Chicken Creek Trail until you reach Transfer Campground. From Transfer Campground, the spur follows the West Mancos River. Where the river splits into the North Fork and the South Fork, the spur follows the North Fork. It ties into the Sharkstooth trail head #565. It may be difficult to follow where the spur follows some logging roads but when you reach Sharkstooth trail head (10 miles) you will know that your are on the right trail. Follow Sharsktooth until you reach the Colorado Trail in the vicinity of Taylor Lake (7 miles). The spur section from Transfer Campground to the Sharkstooth trail head does not show on the Forest Service map of the San Juan Forest, but Paul Peck (former Ranger of the Mancos District, USFS), said that the spur was well marked. He also said it is easier to follow the spur from Taylor Lake to Mancos than from Mancos to Taylor Lake. Nobody is maintaining this spur except for what the Forest Service can get done.

Photographing Wildflowers

If you are lucky enough to traverse Indian Trail Ridge in mid-summer, you will be rewarded with a spectacular display of alpine flowers, including arnica, indian paintbrush, bistort, and columbine. Taking photographs that provide results good enough to enlarge and display requires the right equipment, knowledge and patience. Here are five basic tips offered by the CT hikers whose photos appear in this guide:

✔ Enjoy the control of a full-featured SLR, rather than a point-and-shoot or one of the newer digital cameras.

✔ Invest in a "macro" lens for close focusing ability.

✔ Always use a tripod and a cable shutter release. Have a piece of cardboard handy for a wind block.

✔ Use slower, finer-grained film. Transparency film is preferred by pros over print film.

✔ Shoot early or late in the day to avoid intense mid-day light. Often, overcast or even rainy days are best for subtle color saturation or for the effects of raindrops on petals (see the columbine below).

A hiker photographing wildflowers along the CT.

Alpine blue columbine.

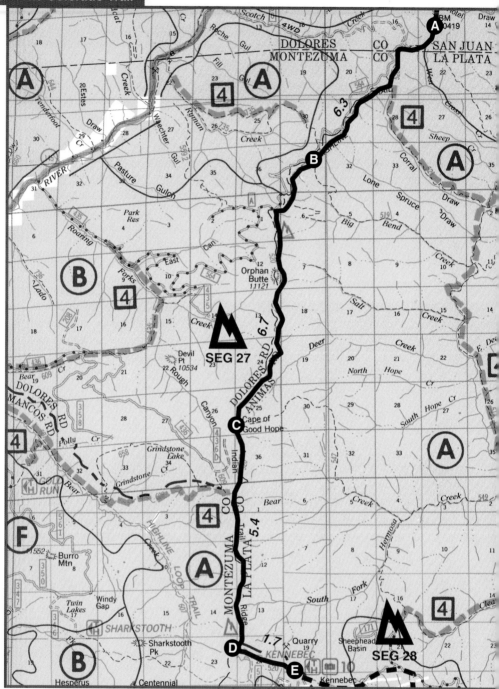

Landmark Location	Mileage	From Denver	Elevation	Latitude	Longitude
Ⓐ FS-550 Hotel Draw Road	0.0	426.1	10400	37.649571	-107.956351
Ⓑ Big Bend Trail	6.3	432.4	10600	37.595673	-108.013977
Ⓒ Cape of Good Hope	13.0	439.1	11600	37.526278	-108.032393
Ⓓ Point 12,258	18.4	444.5	12258	37.460550	-108.034361
Ⓔ Cumberland Basin Trailhead	20.1	446.2	11600	37.451508	-108.010588

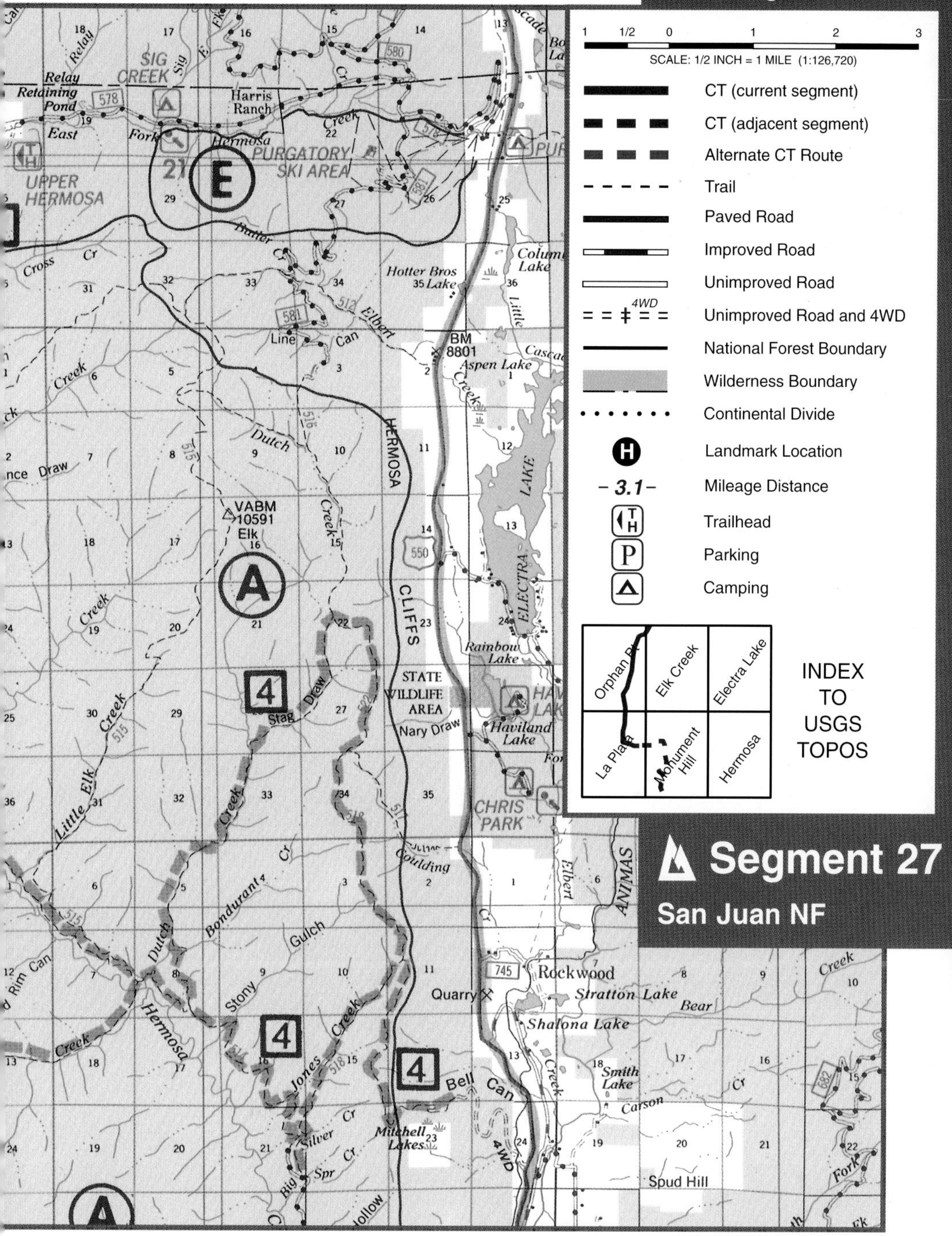

SCALE: 1/2 INCH = 1 MILE (1:126,720)

CT (current segment)
CT (adjacent segment)
Alternate CT Route
Trail
Paved Road
Improved Road
Unimproved Road
4WD
Unimproved Road and 4WD
National Forest Boundary
Wilderness Boundary
Continental Divide

H Landmark Location

– **3.1** – Mileage Distance

Trailhead

P Parking

Camping

INDEX TO USGS TOPOS

Orphan P. | Elk Creek | Electra Lake
La Plata | Monument Hill | Hermosa

▲ Segment 27
San Juan NF

Relay Retaining Pond
Relay
SIG CREEK
Harris Ranch
PURGATORY SKI AREA
East Fork
Hermosa
UPPER HERMOSA
Cross Cr
Hotter Bros Lake
Columbine Lake
Little
BM 8801
Aspen Lake
Cascade
Dutch
VABM 10591 Elk
HERMOSA
Line Can
Elbert
Creek
CLIFFS
ELECTRA LAKE
Rainbow Lake
STATE WILDLIFE AREA
Nary Draw
Haviland Lake
Stag Draw
Little Elk Creek
Bonduran
Gulch
CHRIS PARK
Goulding
ANIMAS
Rockwood
Quarry
Stratton Lake
Bear
Shalona Lake
Smith Lake
Stony Creek
Jones Creek
Bell Can
Carson
Silver Cr
Mitchell Lakes
Big Spr
Spud Hill

Elevation x 1000

13
12
11
10
9

Seg 26   Segment 27   Seg 28

Miles   0   5   10   15   20

A   B   C   D   E

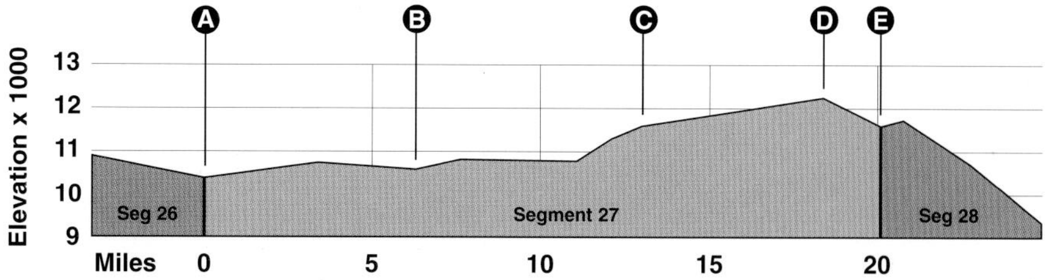

Segment 28
Cumberland Basin to Junction Creek Trailhead

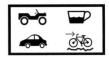

Distance: 21.4 miles
Elevation Gain: approx 1400 ft

Otis Teets sitting on the bench at Gudy's Rest.

Gudy's Tip

"If you didn't stop for a shower in one of the falls of Junction Canyon, then grab one at the Rec Center, just north of where the Junction Creek Road dead ends into Main Street in Durango."

Trip Log

Date: _____ Notes: _____

_____

_____

_____

_____

About This Segment

This segment is the final leg of the 468-mile trip from Denver. The trail tops out at scenic 11,760-foot Kennebec Pass and then begins its long descent to Junction Creek Trailhead. The drop from Kennebec Pass to the trailhead is 4,790 feet, the single greatest altitude change on the entire trail. In addition, hikers must contend with more than a thousand feet of ascent with along the way, making the total elevation drop in this segment nearly 6,000 feet.

The trail generally follows the canyon of Junction Creek, winding in and out of numerous steep side drainages, where setting up camp could be challenging. Beyond Walls Gulch, the trail clings to the side of the gorge far above the creek, and water is scarce for 12 miles, until you descend again into the canyon.

Portions of the CT in the upper end of the canyon use the historic Oro Fino Trail, which supplied the mining district of the same name during the early 1900s. This trail had almost totally surrendered itself to the forest when volunteer trail crews began working in the Junction Creek area in 1986. It took two difficult summers for the volunteers to build new trail and to reconstruct the old Oro Fino for the nearly 18 miles between Junction Creek Trailhead and the upper end of the canyon.

Additional Trail Information: Through-hikers are usually anxious at this point to get back to civilization, and have an extra incentive to propel themselves through this last segment. Unfortunately, it is rugged and not particularly conducive for a swift passage. Flat camping spots with water are also rare in the craggy canyon, although ironically, water is most plentiful where the terrain is the roughest and camping spots the fewest. A few flat spots exist at creekside near Walls Gulch and another about a half mile north, but you may have to share them with others. You may want to consider stocking up with water at the Walls Gulch creek crossing and camp at the grassy, but usually dry, Road End Canyon, or the rounded, sunny foothills further south. If you are desperate to get down quick, consider taking the bike route descent on the Forest Service road just below Kennebec Pass. Also note that this segment, particularly the last portion nearer town, is extremely popular with mountain bicyclists, who may appear quickly around curves in the trail.

Trailhead/Access Points

Cumberland Basin Trailhead: From Durango, travel west on US-160 approximately 0.5 mile beyond Hesperus and turn right (north) on FS-571. A sign here points out the turn as La Plata Canyon. The trailhead is approximately 14 miles north from US-160. The road gets rougher and steeper as you progress. The last 2 miles continue as a tough 4WD road, and may be snowed-in until late June. Please note that the last few miles of this road cross private property and may be subject to closure in the future.

Junction Creek Trailhead: Go north on Main Avenue in Durango and turn left (west) on 25th Street. Drive approximately 3 miles and go left where the road splits. Continue approximately 0.4 mile to a cattle guard and a sign announcing your entrance into San Juan National Forest. The CT begins on the left, a hundred feet past the cattle guard. There is room for only a few cars here. The road continues beyond this point as FS-171. There is additional parking about a mile up from the official

Junction Creek Trailhead at a switchback to the right. A short side trail from the switchback here takes you to the CT. Trail access to the upper part of this segment near Kennebec Pass is possible by continuing on FS-171 for 17.5 miles beyond the cattle guard to a side road on the left (west), whose portal is identified with two large-diameter wooden posts. Continue up the side road 0.7 mile to where the CT crosses the road and ascends at right toward Kennebec Pass.

Maps and Jurisdiction

USFS map: San Juan National Forest, see pages 254-255.
USGS Quadrangle maps: La Plata, Monument Hill, Durango West.
Trails Illustrated map: # 504.

Jurisdiction: Columbine Ranger District - West, San Juan NF.

Trail Description

From the Cumberland Basin Trailhead, follow the trail east then southeast 0.2 mile where it connects into an old mine road, and continue east-southeast to Kennebec Pass. At **mile 0.7** (11,760), you will arrive at the pass and have views east to the Needle Mountains and south down the Junction Creek drainage. Cumberland Mountain towers as a grassy cone nearby to the south. At the pass, the CT begins an immediate descent toward the south-southeast; the ruins of the Muldoon Mine are visible a short distance ahead. A few hundred feet beyond the pass, look for the trail to veer left off the mine road, and descend rapidly, with redrock cliffs above and the headwaters of Junction Creek below. Early in the season, use caution when crossing lingering snowfields here, as the drop-offs are precipitous in places. At **mile 1.3** (11,000) the trail enters a spruce forest and drops quickly through several switchbacks.

At **mile 2.5** (10,340), the trail crosses an unmarked Forest Service road, which connects at left to FS-171 in 0.7 mile, and eventually descends all the way to Durango. A sign here at this crossing reads "Sliderock Trail, Kennebec Pass." The trail continues on the opposite side of the unmarked Forest Service road as a well-built new trail, descending slowly in and out of several side gullies. Approximately a mile beyond the road crossing, the trail will ascend slightly to a meadow just below FS-171, then drop steeply to the south into Fassbinder Gulch.

This section of trail is out of character with the portions on either side of it, which are evenly graded and well-built. The explanation for this anomaly is that this section of trail is a temporary detour to avoid a patchwork of patented mining claims. Until necessary rights-of-way can be obtained through here, this awkward section of trail will remain. The CT continues to descend into Fassbinder until you again connect with a comfortable tread, well below the mining property.

The newly constructed trail continues down Fassbinder Gulch on even grades past the confluence of the Flagler Fork. The CT makes a brief easterly swing into Gaines Gulch, passing a 50-foot waterfall. Once back in the main canyon, the trail crosses to the west side of the Flagler Fork. For the next mile, the trail stays close to

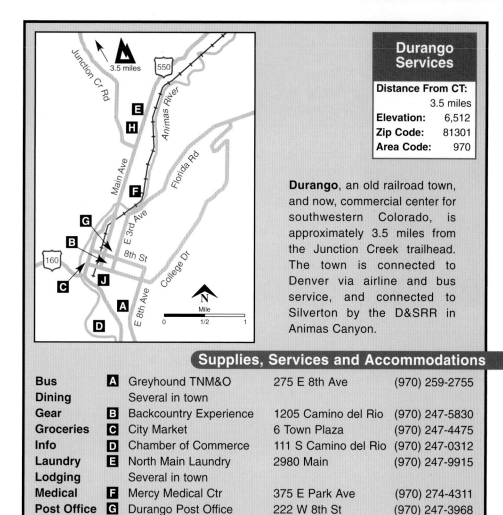

Durango Services

Distance From CT:

3.5 miles

Elevation:	6,512
Zip Code:	81301
Area Code:	970

Durango, an old railroad town, and now, commercial center for southwestern Colorado, is approximately 3.5 miles from the Junction Creek trailhead. The town is connected to Denver via airline and bus service, and connected to Silverton by the D&SRR in Animas Canyon.

Supplies, Services and Accommodations

Service		Name	Address	Phone
Bus	A	Greyhound TNM&O	275 E 8th Ave	(970) 259-2755
Dining		Several in town		
Gear	B	Backcountry Experience	1205 Camino del Rio	(970) 247-5830
Groceries	C	City Market	6 Town Plaza	(970) 247-4475
Info	D	Chamber of Commerce	111 S Camino del Rio	(970) 247-0312
Laundry	E	North Main Laundry	2980 Main	(970) 247-9915
Lodging		Several in town		
Medical	F	Mercy Medical Ctr	375 E Park Ave	(970) 274-4311
Post Office	G	Durango Post Office	222 W 8th St	(970) 247-3968
Showers	H	Recreation Center	2700 Main	
Train Depot	J	Durango & Silverton RR	479 Main Ave	(970) 247-2733

the creek and crosses it several more times. The canyon is narrow and awkward here, the vegetation is jungle-like in places, and each ford is difficult and deep. There are some places where the trail is within the flood plain and may be partially washed out. Camping in this section of the narrow canyon is challenging because of the lack of flat spots, although water is plentiful.

The last crossing of upper Junction Creek, on a convenient bridge at **mile 7.0** (8520), is near the mouth of Walls Gulch, where there are multiple flat, however rocky, places for camping. The trail here crosses to the west side of the creek and begins a 4-mile ascent, gaining about 1,000 feet as it winds in and out of side drainages. This is rugged terrain with steep slopes down into the Junction Creek gorge. Water flows in the side drainages are meager if at all, and most likely to be

Waterfall on Junction Creek.

found in Sliderock and First Trail Canyons early in the season.

About 0.5 mile before Road End Canyon, the CT tops out at one last rise and begins the final descent to the Junction Creek Trailhead. At Road End Canyon, the trail gradually turns into an old 4WD road, which it follows for the next 3 miles. As the road slowly changes its direction from southwest to east, you will pass through a red gate on the road. Continue 0.2 mile past the gate; be alert for the trail to leave the road at left (east). This point might be difficult to spot if the small trail sign is vandalized.

Once it leaves the road, the CT contours east almost on the level for a mile through a sunny ponderosa forest. If you walk quietly here, you might see some grazing elk. Toward the end of this pleasant contour, the trail goes over a ridge and drops into a small drainage then passes through another gate.

The trail continues 400 feet down the trail through an aspen grove and passes through a third gate. There are remnants of an old brush fence here, which suggests that the area must have been grazed for many years. The CT takes on the appearance of an old road in places as it descends east to east-southeast in the sunny forest. About a mile beyond the gate, the Hoffhiens Connection Trail intersects the CT at right. This side trail goes a couple of miles to the Dry Fork Road and beyond to US-160; it is very popular with mountain bicyclists doing a loop on the CT from Durango. From this trail intersection, the CT resumes an easterly bearing. In about 0.3 mile, you will come to an overlook at the edge of a rock cliff that gives a dramatic bird's-eye view of the last few miles of the trail as it descends Junction Creek Canyon. This striking overlook has been named Gudy's Rest in honor of Gudy Gaskill, builder of The Colorado Trail.

Beyond Gudy's Rest, the trail ambles through several switchbacks on its descent to Junction Creek. Building these switchbacks required a laborious summer of toil in the steep canyon by volunteer trail crews in 1987. A wide bridge takes you to the east side of Junction Creek at **mile 18.8** (7390). Bear to the right (south) on the trail just beyond the bridge and continue to the tiny side tributary of Quinn Creek, then begin a short ascent which takes you nearly 200 feet above Junction Creek. This area is lush with vegetation and hosts many birds. You may see a Western tanager here, or perhaps a dipper diving into the whirling pools along the creek.

Hikers should be aware of several hazards along this section of the trail in Junction Creek. First, the creek is subject to flash floods, and camps should not be set up in the flood plain. Second, this area promotes the growth of much poison ivy and poison oak, which at times is camouflaged on the side of the trail. Be careful where you walk and sit—trail crew volunteers learned about this hazard the hard way. Third, there are two areas where mudslides on the steep canyon side have caused serious damage to the trail during spring rains. Crossing these sections before trail maintenance crews have cleaned them up could be a little precarious and unnerving. Also, keep in mind that this area is popular with mountain bicyclists, some of whom come booming down the switchbacks. You will most likely see many along this stretch.

About 1.3 miles after the bridge crossing, you will again descend to the level of the creek and then come to a fork in the trail where the CT continues straight ahead. The short side trail to the left leads in 200 feet to a switchback on FS-171 about a mile up from the Junction Creek Trailhead. This is a good alternate starting point for hikers. Continuing on the CT at this fork takes you down the final mile of the trail. There are several side trails along here which ascend to the Forest Service road. Along this narrow stretch of the cliffy canyon, there are many cascading pools perfect for dipping on hot summer afternoons. It is a summer paradise, with lots of sun, shade, grasses, flowers, birds and, unfortunately, poison ivy.

Soon, the canyon widens and you cross a small irrigation ditch which takes you through the flood plain for 0.3 mile to the trailhead and the official western terminus of The Colorado Trail at **mile 21.4** (6960). Turn right (southeast) onto the road which takes you across the cattle guard and out of the San Juan National Forest. It is a 3.4-mile walk on the blacktop into town. Welcome to Durango!

Viewing Dippers

A chunky, drab, wren-like bird, the water ouzel, or *dipper*, would hardly attract anyone's attention if it were not for its very unusual manner of earning a living. Dippers reside along rushing mountain streams, often perched atop a rock in the foaming center of the torrent. From this vantage point, it constantly bobs up and down, looking for aquatic insects. Spotting a tasty morsel, it then dives headlong into the water, opens its wings, and "flies" submerged through the flow.

Birds stake out a 75- to 200- meter length of stream for their territory, rarely venturing any distance from its banks. Disturbed, they fly low and rapidly, back up or down the stream, with a high, ringing alarm. During winter, dippers move to lower levels.

Nests are a bulky ball of moss, one side open, built just above the waterline in inaccessible places, such as on a rock wall or behind a waterfall.

Dippers can be found throughout the streams and rivers of western Colorado. In Segment 28, you are as likely to spot one along the lush banks of little Quinn Creek as perched on a boulder in the middle of the Animas River in downtown Durango.

Landmark Location	Mileage	From Denver	Elevation	Latitude	Longitude
Ⓐ Cumberland Basin Trailhead	0.0	446.2	11600	37.451508	-108.010588
Ⓑ Kennebec Pass	0.7	446.9	11760	37.449171	-108.003737
Ⓒ Walls Gulch	7.0	453.2	8520	37.416366	-107.972348
Ⓓ Sliderock Canyon	9.4	455.6	9140	37.396970	-107.969608
Ⓔ Junction Creek	18.8	465.0	7390	37.354797	-107.927158
Ⓕ Junction Creek Trailhead	21.4	467.6	6960	37.331382	-107.902081

SCALE: 1/2 INCH = 1 MILE (1:126,720)

	CT (current segment)
	CT (adjacent segment)
	Alternate CT Route
	Trail
	Paved Road
	Improved Road
	Unimproved Road
4WD	Unimproved Road and 4WD
	National Forest Boundary
	Wilderness Boundary
	Continental Divide
H	Landmark Location
– 3.1 –	Mileage Distance
T H	Trailhead
P	Parking
▲	Camping

INDEX TO USGS TOPOS

La Plata | Monument Hill | Hermosa
Herperus | Durango West | Durango East

▲ **Segment 28**

San Juan NF

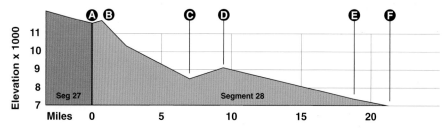

Mountain Bicycle Detour

Junction Creek Canyon Detour — *Segment 28 (San Juan NF):* The portion of the official CT in Junction Creek is mostly on good trail, but it does traverse some precipitous spots in rough terrain, particularly in the upper end of the canyon. By contrast, there is a very good road that begins just east of Kennebec Pass and descends at the edge of the canyon to the trailhead on Junction Creek. This bypass is intended for those cyclists who are anxious for a speedy descent to Durango, or for those interested in making a long loop trip up Junction Creek and then down the road to their starting point.

Detour Description: This detour begins at **mile 2.5** (10,340) in Segment 28 just east of Kennebec Pass where the trail crosses a side road. Descend at left 0.7 mile on the side road, then turn right at an intersection onto FS-171. Continue downhill, dropping quickly through several life zones. Do not be so distracted by the scenery that you fail to notice the many hazardous cattle guards on the road. Pass the entrance to Junction Creek Campground and continue 1.4 miles to the National Forest boundary and Junction Creek Trailhead, the western terminus of the CT. This is the end of Segment 28; Durango is 3.4 miles down the road.

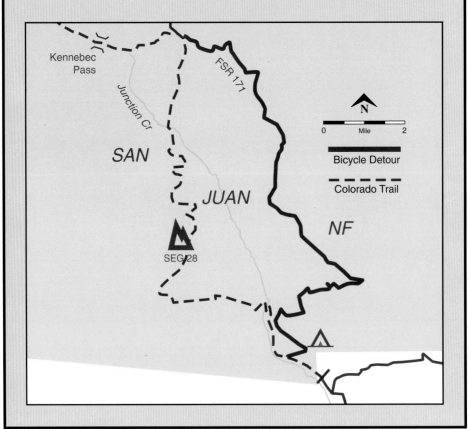

Notes

Notes

REFERENCE ◣

△ CT Summary

Paved or graded dirt access road

Rough, dirt access road

4-wheel-drive access road

Seg	Starting Access Point	Ending Access Point
1	Kassler	South Platte Canyon
2	South Platte Canyon	Colorado TH FS-550
3	Colorado TH FS-550	FS-560
4	FS-560	Long Gulch
5	Long Gulch	Kenosha Pass
6	Kenosha Pass	Goldhill Trailhead
7	Goldhill Trailhead	Copper Mountain
8	Copper Mountain	Tennessee Pass
9	Tennessee Pass	Hagerman Pass Road
10	Hagerman Pass Road	Halfmoon Creek
11	Halfmoon Creek	Clear Creek Road
12	Clear Creek Road	North Cottonwood Creek
13	North Cottonwood Creek	Chalk Creek TH
14	Chalk Creek TH	US-50 (Fooses Creek TH)
15	US-50 (Fooses Creek TH)	Marshall Pass
16	Marshall Pass	Sargents Mesa
17	Sargents Mesa	Colorado Hwy-114
18	Colorado Hwy-114	Saguache Park Road
19	Saguache Park Road	Eddiesville TH
20	Eddiesville TH	San Luis Pass
21	San Luis Pass	Spring Creek Pass
22	Spring Creek Pass	Carson Saddle
23	Carson Saddle	Rio Grande Reservoir Road
24	Rio Grande Reservoir Road	Molas Pass
25	Molas Pass	Bolam Pass Road
26	Bolam Pass Road	Hotel Draw
27	Hotel Draw	Cumberland Basin
28	Cumberland Basin	Junction Creek TH

☕ Plentiful water sources				Suitable for mtn. bikes 🚲		
☕ Scattered water sources				Recommended detour		
☕ Water is difficult to obtain				Mandatory detour		

Distance	Elev. Gain	Water	Mtn. Biking	Description	Map	Seg
15.4	2160	Plentiful	Suitable	46-49	50-51	1
10.8	2200	Difficult	Suitable	52-55	56-57	2
12.1	1520	Scattered	Suitable	58-61	62-63	3
16.2	2840	Plentiful	Mandatory detour	64-69	70-71	4
14	1540	Scattered	Mandatory detour	72-75	76-77	5
32	4520	Scattered	Suitable	78-83	84-85	6
12.5	3600	Scattered	Recommended detour	86-91	92-93	7
24.4	4020	Plentiful	Suitable	94-101	102-103	8
14.9	2120	Plentiful	Mandatory detour	104-109	110-111	9
11.4	1760	Scattered	Mandatory detour	112-117	118-119	10
19.9	1520	Plentiful	Suitable	120-125	126-127	11
18.2	4520	Plentiful	Mandatory detour	128-133	134-135	12
22.2	3720	Plentiful	Mandatory detour	136-141	142-143	13
20.0	3320	Scattered	Recommended detour	144-149	150-151	14
14.0	3440	Scattered	Suitable	152-155	156-157	15
14.5	3080	Difficult	Suitable	158-161	162-163	16
20.3	2440	Difficult	Suitable	164-167	168-169	17
12.9	1220	Difficult	Mandatory detour	170-175	176-177	18
13.5	1660	Scattered	Mandatory detour	178-181	182-183	19
12.2	2960	Scattered	Mandatory detour	184-187	188-189	20
14.5	2940	Scattered	Mandatory detour	190-197	198-199	21
16.2	3680	Scattered	Recommended detour	200-207	208-209	22
12.0	1040	Plentiful	Recommended detour	210-213	214-215	23
21.1	4460	Scattered	Mandatory detour	216-221	222-223	24
19.9	3120	Plentiful	Suitable	224-229	230-231	25
11.0	1480	Scattered	Suitable	232-235	236-237	26
20.1	3640	Difficult	Suitable	238-245	246-247	27
21.4	1400	Scattered	Recommended detour	248-253	254-255	28

⚠ Equipment Checklists

Note: When preparing for a hike on the CT, always start with the *Ten Essentials* as your foundation. Boots should be light but sturdy (no tennis shoes). Backpackers will want heavier, stiffer boots for good support. For clothing, modern synthetics, like polypropylene and pile, are light, insulate well and dry quickly. But traditional wool clothing is still effective, even when damp. Avoid cotton entirely, as it loses all insulating ability when wet. Effective, good-quality clothing and other gear will often determine the difference between a safe, enjoyable day in the mountains and an unpleasant, or even potentially disastrous, experience.

The Ten Essentials

Food
Water
Emergency shelter
Extra clothing
First aid kit
Flashlight
Map and compass
Matches/fire starter
Pocket knife
Sunglasses/sunscreen

For Day Hikes

❑ Day-pack:1500 to 3000 cubic inches
❑ Insulating layer: poly tops and bottoms
❑ Shirt or sweater: poly or wool
❑ Pants: poly or wool
❑ Parka shell: waterproof, windproof
❑ Pants shell: waterproof, windproof
❑ Hat: stocking cap or balaclava
❑ Gloves: poly or wool
❑ Extra socks

For Backpacking

❑ Backpack: 3500 cubic inches or more
❑ Pack cover: waterproof
❑ Sleeping bag
❑ Sleeping pad
❑ Extra clothing
❑ Stove and fuel
❑ Cooking gear
❑ Eating utensils
❑ Food and food bags
❑ Tent or bivy sack
❑ Groundcloth: waterproof
❑ Personal toiletries
❑ Camp shoes
❑ Headlamp
❑ Repair kit and sewing kit

❑ Water filter and/or iodine tablets
❑ Plastic trowel: for catholes
❑ Plastic bags: for garbage
❑ Rope or cord

Optional Gear:
Pillow
Camera gear and film
Reading material and/or journal
Fishing gear
Binoculars
Camp chair
Radio and cell phone
Walking stick

USFS Ranger Districts ⚠

USDA Forest Service
Rocky Mountain Regional Office
740 Simms, PO Box 25127
Lakewood, CO 80225
303-275-5350

Gunnison National Forest
Gunnison Ranger District
216 N. Colorado
Gunnison, CO 81230
970-641-0471

Pike National Forest
South Park Ranger District
320 Hwy. 285, Box 219
Fairplay, CO 80440
719-836-2031
South Platte Ranger District
19316 Goddard Ranch Ct.
Morrison, CO 80465
303-275-5610

Rio Grande National Forest
Divide Ranger District - Creede
3rd & Creede Ave., Box 270
Creede, CO 81130
719-658-2556
Saguache Ranger District
46525 State Hwy. 114, Box 67
Saguache, CO 81149
719-655-2547

San Isabel National Forest
Leadville Ranger District
2015 N. Poplar
Leadville, CO 80461
719-486-0749
Salida Ranger District
325 W. Rainbow Blvd.
Salida, CO 81201
719-539-3591

San Juan National Forest
Columbine Ranger District - West
110 W. 11th St.
Durango, CO 81301
970-385-1283
Mancos/Dolores Ranger District
100 N. Sixth, Box 210
Dolores, CO 81323
970-882-7296

White River National Forest
Dillon Ranger District
680 Blue River Parkway, Box 620
Silverthorne, CO 80498
970-468-5400
Holy Cross Ranger District
24747 US Hwy. 24, Box 190
Minturn, CO 81645
970-827-5715

Useful Phone Numbers

Colorado Trail Foundation
(303) 384-3729 x113
Statewide road conditions:
(303) 639-1111
Statewide weather reports
(303) 398-3964
Colorado Division of Wildlife
(303) 297-1192
To activate a rescue group, contact the nearest county sheriff:

Seg 1-3	Jefferson (303) 277-0211
Seg 4-6	Park (719) 836-2494
Seg 6-8	Summit (970) 453-6222
Seg 8	Eagle (970) 328-6611
Seg 9-11	Lake (719) 486-1249
Seg 12-15	Chaffee (970) 539-2814
Seg 15-20	Saguache (970) 655-2544
Seg 21	Mineral (719) 658-2600
Seg 21-23	Hinsdale (970) 944-2291
Seg 24-25	San Juan (970) 387-5531
Seg 26	Dolores (970) 677-2257
Seg 27-28	La Plata (970) 247-1157

▲ Bibliography

Note: This bibliography is only a partial listing of the references and guidebooks to those portions of Colorado's mountains touched by the CT. Because most of the guides are updated with new printings or editions every few years, the publication dates given are those of the first edition, unless otherwise noted.

General References

Bueler, William M. *Roof of the Rockies: A History of Colorado Mountaineering.* Colorado Mountain Club Press, Golden, Colorado, 2000, third edition.
   Definitive history of Colorado mountaineering.

Chronic, Halka. *Roadside Geology of Colorado.* Mountain Press, Missoula, Montana. 1980.
   Best overall introduction to Colorado's geology.

Griffiths, Mel, and Rubright, Lynnell. *Colorado: A Geography.* Westview Press, Boulder, Colorado, 1983.
   General treatment of the geography of the whole state.

Hart, John L. Jerome. *Fourteen Thousand Feet: A History of the Naming and Early Ascents of the High Colorado Peaks.* Colorado Mountain Club, Denver, Colorado, 1972.
   The 1931 history of Colorado's 14,000-foot peaks; still available in a 1972 reprint.

Wolle, Muriel Sibell. *Stampede to Timberline.* Artcraft Press, Denver, Colorado, 1949.
   Classic account of the mining era in Colorado.

Zwinger, Ann H., and Willard, Beatrice E. *Land Above the Trees.* Harper & Row Publishers, New York, New York, 1972.
   Comprehensive guide to alpine ecology, including the Colorado Rockies.

Other Readings on the CT

Fayhee, M. John, and Fielder, John. *Along the Colorado Trail.* Westcliffe Publishers, Englewood, Colorado, 1992.
   Journal account with photos of a summer on the CT.

Sumner, David. "The Colorado Trail Takes Shape." *Colorado Magazine*, July-August 1974.
   Account of the CT during its beginnings.

Boddie, Caryn and Peter. *Hiking Colorado*. Falcon Press, Helena, Montana, 1997.
A guide to 100 hikes throughout Colorado.

Borneman, Walter R., and Lampert, Lyndon J. *A Climbing Guide to Colorado's Fourteeners*. Pruett Publishing Company, Boulder, Colorado, 1978, 1989, 1998.
A climbing guide to the 54 Colorado summits above 14,000 feet.

Fielder, John and Pearson. *The Complete Guide to Colorado's Wilderness Areas*. Westcliffe Publishers, Englewood, Colorado, 1998.
Includes coverage of the six wilderness areas that the CT traverses.

Gebhardt, Dennis. *A Backpacking Guide to the Weminuche Wilderness in the San Juan Mountains of Colorado*. Basin Reproduction and Printing Company, Durango, Colorado, 1976.
Backpacking guide to Weminuche Wilderness with pocket maps.

Jacobs, Randy, and Ormes, Robert M. *Guide to The Colorado Mountains*. Colorado Mountain Club Press, Golden, Colorado, 2000, tenth edition.
Definitive guide to all areas of the Colorado mountains.

Jones, Tom Lorang. *Colorado's Continental Divide Trail*. Westcliffe Publishers, Englewood, Colorado, 1997.
Comprehensive guide to the Colorado portion of the trail.

Martin, Bob. *Hiking the Highest Passes*. Pruett Publishing Company, Boulder, Colorado, 1984.
A guide to hiking 50 popular passes in the state.

Pixler, Paul. *Hiking Trails of Southwestern Colorado*. Pruett Publishing Company, Boulder, Colorado, 1981.
Day hikes in the San Juan Mountains.

Savage, Ania. *Colorado Mountain Club Pocket Guide to the Colorado Fourteeners*. Johnson Books, Boulder, Colorado, 1997.
Brief guide to the standard routes on the fourteeners.

Wolf, James R. *Guide to the Continental Divide Trail*. Volumes 4 and 5. Continental Divide Trail Society, Bethesda, Maryland, 1982.
A guide to the divide trail from Canada to Mexico, including Colorado.

⚠ Leave No Trace

The Leave No Trace program is a message to promote and inspire responsible outdoor recreation through education, research, and partnerships. Managed as a non-profit educational organization and authorized by the U.S. Forest Service, LNT is about enjoying places like the CT, while traveling and camping with care. The 7 LNT Principles of outdoor ethics form the framework of LNT's message:

✔ *Plan Ahead and Prepare*
Know the regulations and special concerns for the area you'll visit.
Prepare for extreme weather, hazards, and emergencies.
Schedule your trip to avoid times of high use.
Visit in small groups. Split larger parties into groups of 4-6.
Repackage food to minimize waste.
Use a map and compass to eliminate the use of marking paint, rock cairns or
    flagging.

✔ *Travel and Camp on Durable Surfaces*
Durable surfaces include established trails and campsites, rock, gravel, dry
    grasses or snow.
Protect riparian areas by camping at least 200 feet from lakes and streams.
Good campsites are found, not made. Altering a site is not necessary.
In popular areas:
    Concentrate use on existing trails and campsites.
    Walk single file in the middle of the trail, even when wet or muddy.
    Keep campsites small. Focus activity in areas where vegetation is absent.
In pristine areas:
    Disperse use to prevent the creation of campsites and trails.
    Avoid places where impacts are just beginning.

✔ *Dispose of Waste Properly*
Pack it in, pack it out. Inspect your campsite and rest areas for trash or spilled
    foods. Pack out all trash, leftover food, and litter.
Deposit solid human waste in catholes dug 6 to 8 inches deep at least 200 feet
    from water, camp, and trails. Cover and disguise the cathole when finished.
Pack out toilet paper and hygiene products.
To wash yourself or your dishes, carry water 200 feet away from streams or lakes
    and use small amounts of biodegradable soap. Scatter strained dishwater.

✔ *Leave What You Find*
Preserve the past: examine, but do not touch, cultural or historic structures and
    artifacts.
Leave rocks, plants and other natural objects as you find them.
Avoid introducing or transporting non-native species.
Do not build structures, furniture, or dig trenches.

✔ *Minimize Campfire Impacts*

Campfires can cause lasting impacts to the backcountry. Use a lightweight stove
for cooking and enjoy a candle lantern for light.

Where fires are permitted, use established fire rings, fire pans, or mound fires.

Keep fires small. Only use sticks from the ground that can be broken by hand.

Burn all wood and coals to ash, put out campfires completely, then scatter cool
ashes.

✔ *Respect Wildlife*

Observe wildlife from a distance. Do not follow or approach them.

Never feed animals. Feeding wildlife damages their health, alters natural
behaviors, and exposes them to predators and other dangers.

Protect wildlife and your food by storing rations and trash securely.

Control pets at all times, or leave them at home.

Avoid wildlife during sensitive times: mating, nesting, raising young, or winter.

✔ *Be Considerate of Other Visitors*

Respect other visitors and protect the quality of their experience.

Be courteous. Yield to other users on the trail.

Step to the downhill side of the trail when encountering pack stock.

Take breaks and camp away from trails and other visitors.

Let nature's sounds prevail. Avoid loud voices and noises.

Leave No Trace publishes an educational booklet, *Outdoor Skills and Ethics*,
that specifically covers backcountry recreation in the Rocky Mountains. To obtain a
copy of this, or for more information about the LNT program, contact:

Leave No Trace, Inc.
P.O. Box 997
Boulder, CO 80306
Ph: 1 (800) 332-4100
Fax: (303) 442-8217
Website: www.lnt.org

▲ Global Positioning System

The following coordinate list is given in decimal degrees of Latitiude and Longitude. Mileages are expressed with an implied decimal point: 055M = 5.5 miles. The letter(s) before the mileage identifies a "waypoint," established and recorded for the *Official Colorado Trail GIS Reference Map Series*, available on CD ROM. Contact the CTF office for availability. The letter(s) after the mileage refers to the following feature code: M (mileage), XR (trail intersects road), XT (trail intersects trail), GT (gate), WT (water source), RT (ridge top, pass, or top of climb), WB (Wilderness Boundary), PL (power line), BR (brdige). Additional short descriptive annotations and elevations follow selected waypoints. Set you GPS settings to match both the coordinate format (D.ddd) and NAD27 CONUS datum before hand entering coordinates. You can download the latest coordinate sets by visiting *www.bearcreeksurvey.com*.

The mileages recorded here by a professional grade GPS unit differ in some degree from those recorded in the segment chapters of this book (which were derived from field use of a "rolotape" device.) While both methods of collection introduce some error into the mileage calculation, the CTF believes the mileage figures generated by the GPS survey are the most accurate available. Also please note that the GPS survey choose to start Segment 3 from the crossing of Hwy-126 instead of the Colorado Trailhead on FS-550. Likewise, the GPS survey began Segment 8 from the bridge crossing of Ten Mile Creek instead of at Hwy-91. Both these changes result in slightly different mileages for those segments than those published in the segment chapters of this guide. GPS elevations are up to 5 times less accurate than horizontal and should be considered approximate.

SEGMENT 1
39.4912790 -105.0944650; A000TH
    WATERTON TRAILHEAD; 5495
39.4840860 -105.1092370; A010M
39.4805710 -105.1182260; A020M
39.4732610 -105.1307530; A030M
39.4614590 -105.1322790; A040M
39.4502440 -105.1219900; A050M
39.4370720 -105.1241950; A060M
39.4347330 -105.1223100; A062XR
    DAM ROAD INTERSECTION; 5812
39.4306610 -105.1182730; A066XR
    LEAVE MAIN ROAD; 5984
39.4287670 -105.1190290; A067XT
    BEGIN SINGLE TRACK; 6069
39.4256740 -105.1181180; A070M
39.4240340 -105.1202820; A079FT
    LENNYS REST; 6555
39.4177580 -105.1241540; A090M
39.4133460 -105.1251110; A096XT
    JOIN MC TRAIL 692; 6661
39.4096760 -105.1302560; A100M
39.4079540 -105.1292350; A102XT
    INT MC TRAIL 692; 6908
39.4112150 -105.1336380; A108XT
    FINAL INT. MC 692; 7220
39.4096250 -105.1472660; A120M
39.4058190 -105.1523250; A126RT
    HIGH POINT ON HILL; 7512
39.4019410 -105.1501930; A130M
39.4066250 -105.1586720; A140M
39.4065950 -105.1626660; A150M
39.4020020 -105.1640460; A160M
39.4003720 -105.1671740; A165TH
    AT S. PLATTE; 6113
SEGMENT 2
39.4003720 -105.1671740; B000TH
    AT S. PLATTE; 6113
39.4001930 -105.1677660; B001XR
    LOOP UNDER BRIDGE TO SE; 6113

39.3959330 -105.1704750; B010M
39.3994430 -105.1836440; B020M
39.4002250 -105.1849480; B021M
    FOLLOW TRAIL TO LEFT
39.4014500 -105.1969030; B030M
39.4062530 -105.2094990; B040M
39.4055460 -105.2133680; B043XT
    CROSS JEEP TRAIL; 7374
39.4045000 -105.2211410; B050M
39.4004840 -105.2318280; B060XR
    FS538 TOW CG RD; 7706
39.3902020 -105.2375080; B070M
39.3868440 -105.2396210; B073XR
    CROSS ROAD; 7613
39.3795220 -105.2387490; B080XT
    PASS TOW CG; 7604
39.3679970 -105.2383410; B090M
39.3598570 -105.2449740; B100TH
    AT CR126; 7615
SEGMENT 3
39.3598570 -105.2449740; C000TH
    AT CR126; 7615
39.3585010 -105.2450670; C001XR
    SPRING CR RD.; 7630
39.3562830 -105.2458910; C003XR
    SPR CR RD 2; 7637
39.3558960 -105.2470770; C004XR
    CR 126; 7655
39.3517620 -105.2547410; C010M
39.3451910 -105.2572730; C015TH
    BUFFALO CREEK; 7847
39.3426420 -105.2650290; C021XR
    FS RD 550; 7830
39.3401270 -105.2774960; C030M
39.3421400 -105.2827000; C034XT
    SHINGLE MILL TRAIL; 7763
39.3361120 -105.2838840; C040M
39.3317890 -105.2848690; C044XR
    JEEP TRAIL AND CREEK; 7740
39.3297910 -105.2879030; C050M

39.3266830 -105.2954990; C060M
39.3339240 -105.3090220; C071XT
    TRAMWAY BIKE PATH; 7745
39.3337800 -105.3174620; C078XT
    GREEN MTN TRAIL; 7640
39.3366830 -105.3279200; C085XT
    CROSS TRAIL; 7543
39.3395570 -105.3338140; C090XT
    GREEN MTN LOOP; 7458
39.3401860 -105.3366650; C092XR
    MEADOWS CG ROAD; 7398
39.3405700 -105.3463630; C100M
39.3411250 -105.3634800; C110M
39.3446550 -105.3789050; C120M
39.3370990 -105.3901110; C130M
39.3384140 -105.4006050; C137TH
    AT FS543; 8259

SEGMENT 4
39.3384140 -105.4006050; D000TH
    AT FS543; 8259
39.3358770 -105.4022660; D003TH
    PARKING AREA; 8322
39.3400390 -105.4117120; D010XT
    JOIN TRAIL TO S; 8565
39.3326080 -105.4215740; D019WB
    WILDERNESS BOUNDARY; 9009
39.3286950 -105.4372900; D030M
39.3291370 -105.4426010; D033XT
    TRAIL FORKS TO S; 9327
39.3229050 -105.4513590; D040M
39.3163080 -105.4639730; D050M
39.3134730 -105.4729730; D056XT
    LEAVE ROAD; 9924
39.3094600 -105.4732400; D060M
39.3033360 -105.4865380; D070M
39.3052940 -105.4918830; D074XR
    REJOIN OLD RD; 10467
39.3065290 -105.5018700; D080M
39.3076730 -105.5048730; D082WB
    WILDERNESS BOUNDARY; 10285
39.3066930 -105.5145000; D089XT
    LOST CREEK TRAIL; 10185
39.3144210 -105.5311850; D100M
39.3225550 -105.5458360; D110M
39.3301510 -105.5610990; D120M
39.3388210 -105.5746220; D130M
39.3445030 -105.5897100; D140M
39.3477910 -105.6068230; D150M
39.3453800 -105.6119450; D160M
39.3484200 -105.6159090; D166TH
    AT ACCESS TRAIL; 10179

SEGMENT 5
39.3484200 -105.6159090; E000TH
    AT ACCESS TRAIL; 10179
39.3482080 -105.6191530; E002XT
    TRAIL TO PARKING; 10205
39.3480070 -105.6204600; E003WB
    WILDERNESS BOUNDARY; 10226
39.3502010 -105.6269540; E010M
39.3553230 -105.6384840; E020M
39.3630390 -105.6344940; E029WT
    CROSS STREAM; 10369
39.3649720 -105.6350100; E031WT
    MARSHY AREA; 10384
39.3742190 -105.6413140; E039WT
    CREEK; 10322
39.3753940 -105.6546940; E050M
39.3789930 -105.6561980; E053WT
    STREAM; 10163
39.3738630 -105.6667340; E060M
39.3692160 -105.6758180; E066WB
    WILDERNESS BOUNDARY; 9800

39.3652190 -105.6786830; E070M
39.3644300 -105.6834650; E073WT
    STREAM; 9537
39.3641670 -105.6834390; E074XT
    BEN TYLER TRAIL; 9544
39.3623790 -105.6869060; E080TH
    ROCK CREEK TH; 9715
39.3612620 -105.6928320; E084FT
    JOHNSON GULCH; 9597
39.3650430 -105.7036790; E090M
39.3712840 -105.7194730; E100M
39.3757840 -105.7256190; E106XR
    T_ROAD INTERSECTION; 9995
39.3811670 -105.7279730; E110M
39.3921690 -105.7314210; E120M
39.4015510 -105.7433410; E130M
39.4120030 -105.7537920; E140M
39.4135740 -105.7542930; E141XR
    JOIN ROAD; 10008
39.4124970 -105.7576680; E143TH
    AT HWY 285; 9998

SEGMENT 6
39.4124970 -105.7576680; F000TH
    AT HWY 285; 9998
39.4179070 -105.7732590; F010M
39.4231370 -105.7892900; F020M
39.4276770 -105.8010070; F030XR
    CROSS ROAD; 9852
39.4284420 -105.8192880; F040M
39.4287740 -105.8256910; F044XR
    CROSS ROAD; 10127
39.4298190 -105.8349500; F050M
39.4296140 -105.8444150; F059XR
    CROSS ROAD; 10010
39.4281050 -105.8470440; F061XT
    W JEFFERSON TRAIL; 10034
39.4291120 -105.8479870; F062XT
    TRAILS SPLITS OFF; 10028
39.4275460 -105.8614720; F070M
39.4302800 -105.8680650; F076XT
    MICH CR TRAIL; 10684
39.4341990 -105.8660710; F080M
39.4342840 -105.8784510; F090M
39.4389850 -105.8922750; F100M
39.4514690 -105.8998400; F110M
39.4540820 -105.9017370; F112XT
    W JEFFERSON TRAIL; 11656
39.4567880 -105.9077850; F116XR
    CROSS JEEP ROAD; 11828
39.4579980 -105.9104120; F118RT
    SUMMIT OF RIDGE; 11856
39.4611130 -105.9096600; F120XR
    CROSS PASS ROAD; 11774
39.4731630 -105.9050380; F130M
39.4825790 -105.9107150; F140M
39.4839370 -105.9197030; F149XR
    T ROAD INTERSECTION; 11137
39.4934440 -105.9227550; F160M
39.4978190 -105.9250790; F167XR
    ROAD INTERSECTION; 10191
39.4983090 -105.9298110; F170M
39.5055960 -105.9409750; F180M
39.5154350 -105.9347530; F190M
39.5165700 -105.9340400; F192XR
    C CROSS ROAD; 10046
39.5191370 -105.9377980; F196XT
    CROSS TRAIL; 10066
39.5203560 -105.9354560; F200M
39.5307830 -105.9327790; F210M
39.5372360 -105.9399660; F217RT
    SUMMIT OF RIDGE; 11175

39.5413520 -105.9446700; F221XT
CROSS RIDGE LOOP; 11122
39.5476560 -105.9563060; F230M
39.5509800 -105.9576380; F233XT
W. RIDGE TR.; 11022
39.5478550 -105.9617130; F240M
39.5439580 -105.9687700; F250M
39.5421360 -105.9708990; F256XR
T ROAD INT; 10037
39.5402160 -105.9742210; F260M
39.5396210 -105.9844600; F270M
39.5365860 -105.9970310; F280M
39.5416080 -106.0057000; F290M
39.5405550 -106.0198100; F300M
39.5421690 -106.0334590; F311M
39.5422300 -106.0352100; F314XR
HIT ROAD IN SUBD; 9174
39.5380270 -106.0416870; F320XR
HIT HIGHWAY 9; 9195
39.5412220 -106.0415710; F323TH
AT GOLD HILL TH; 9200

SEGMENT 7
39.5412220 -106.0415710; G000TH
GOLD HILL TH; 9200
39.5423260 -106.0576400; G010M
39.5369900 -106.0653850; G020M
39.5381150 -106.0695270; G023XR
OLD JEEP ROAD; 10315
39.5395060 -106.0753610; G027XT
INTERSECT JEEP TRAIL; 10164
39.5374940 -106.0810880; G032XT
INTERSECT TRAIL; 9962
39.5335830 -106.0801800; G034XT
JOIN PEAKS TRAIL; 10013
39.5302280 -106.0885120; G040M
39.5330560 -106.0970550; G048XT
MINERS CREEK TRAIL; 10558
39.5273540 -106.1085390; G060M
39.5161520 -106.1088630; G070M
39.5045860 -106.1134160; G080RT
TOP OF RIDGE; 12511
39.4910690 -106.1131700; G090M
39.4802030 -106.1154440; G100M
39.4756080 -106.1148450; G104XT
HOOSIER TRAIL; 11243
39.4806720 -106.1219250; G110M
39.4925880 -106.1299440; G120M
39.4973910 -106.1349950; G125XL
LEFT OVER BRIDGE; 9755

SEGMENT 8
39.4973870 -106.1349820; H00WT
AT BRIDGE; 9765
39.4972100 -106.1353140; H00XL
LEFT ON TRAIL; 9763
24.4925120 -106.1352570; H04XT
CROSS HWY 91; 9815
39.4932350 -106.1411460; H010M
39.4953910 -106.1441000; H013XT
BRIDGE DRY; 10172
39.4974040 -106.1480440; H016XL
TURN LEFT; 9856
39.4976400 -106.1500100; H017XT
CROSS TRAIL; 9839
39.4978830 -106.1507390; H018XT
CROSS TRAIL; 9824
39.4994040 -106.1522800; H020XL
LEFT ON TRAIL; 9770
39.4986580 -106.1554200; H022XL
FOLLOW ROAD LEFT; 9845
39.4976160 -106.1621750; H025XL
LEAVE ROAD; 10014
39.4977380 -106.1648590; H027XL; LEFT; 10026

39.4956450 -106.1678690; H031WT; STREAM; 10124
39.4961900 -106.1685540; H032XL; LEFT; 10129
39.4954380 -106.1694720; H033XR; RIGHT; 10179
39.4953770 -106.1700490; H034XL; LEFT; 10205
39.4945950 -106.1699560; H035XL; LEFT; 10289
39.4937770 -106.1709830; H037XR; RIGHT; 10342
39.4934230 -106.1712950; H037X1; RIGHT; 10411
39.4923510 -106.1857710; H050M
39.4906400 -106.1859520; H052XR; RIGHT; 10622
39.4903260 -106.1860520; H053XR; RIGHT; 10634
39.4887690 -106.1879080; H054XR; RIGHT; 10550
39.4880200 -106.1898070; H056XL
LEFT ON TRAIL; 10484
39.4827420 -106.1960770; H061XL
39.4774420 -106.2129310; H071M
39.4690050 -106.2255210; H081M
39.4667700 -106.2315500; H091M
39.4584970 -106.2277060; H101M
39.4582470 -106.2276830; H101RT
SEARLE PASS; 12037
39.4458930 -106.2273000; H111M
39.4371750 -106.2188980; H121M
39.4321490 -106.2181060; H128RT
ELK RIDGE; 12277
39.4303460 -106.2227340; H131M
39.4287620 -106.2263420; H133RT
KOKYMO PASS; 12022
39.4356530 -106.2354750; H141XT
BEAR LEFT DOWN; 11636
39.4329340 -106.2477810; H151M
39.4305150 -106.2650680; H161M
39.4244030 -106.2689460; H169XR
JEEP TRAIL; 10065
39.4211520 -106.2674150; H172M
39.4218940 -106.2710460; H175XT
BEAR R TO CREEK; 9649
39.4219630 -106.2816730; H181M
39.4212860 -106.2849820; H183XR
JOIN ROAD; 9414
39.4218700 -106.2875610; H184XT
LEAVE ROAD; 9398
39.4241420 -106.2979790; H191TH
CAMP HALE ROAD; 9354
39.4243130 -106.3004790; H192XR
TURN S ON T_RD; 9336
39.4196320 -106.3018140; H196XR; S AT INT; 9325
39.4164800 -106.3098460; H202M
39.4130790 -106.3136720; H205XR
CROSS ROAD; 9678
39.4053590 -106.3155090; H211M
39.3996690 -106.3163970; H216XR
OLD ROAD; 9908
39.3942440 -106.3145650; H221M
39.3888550 -106.3167500; H225XR
CROSS HWY 24; 9972
39.3854760 -106.3220270; H231M
39.3792970 -106.3273680; H240XR
JOIN JEEP ROAD; 10199
39.3683190 -106.3228970; H251M
39.3633090 -106.3113320; H259TH
TENNESSEE PASS; 10426

SEGMENT 9
39.3633090 -106.3113320; I000TH
TENNESSEE PASS; 10426
39.3553730 -106.3232070; I010M
39.3537700 -106.3402100; I020M
39.3479560 -106.3535510; I031XR
JEEP TRAIL; 10381
39.3450360 -106.3561850; I034XR
JEEP TRAIL; 10359
39.3423460 -106.3608900; I037XR
JEEP TRAIL; 10366

39.3426090 -106.3655100; I040M
39.3408760 -106.3816070; I050M
39.3334460 -106.3949110; I060M
39.3285280 -106.4058630; I067WT
    CROSS STREAM; 10931
39.3260870 -106.4099040; I070M
39.3212550 -106.4129240; I076WT
    LAKE; 11457
39.3179960 -106.4083360; I080M
39.3101440 -106.4024220; I088RT
    TOP OF RIDGE; 11718
39.3023680 -106.4071050; I096WB
    WILDERNESS BOUNDARY; 11288
39.3008990 -106.4072810; I097TH; FS 107; 11241
39.3023870 -106.4112490; I100M
39.2994960 -106.4170700; I105XT; TRAIL INT; 11114
39.2964520 -106.4235380; I109WT; LAKE; 11096
39.2958490 -106.4298580; I114RT
    TOP OF SADDLE; 11421
39.2938420 -106.4376530; I120M
39.2905540 -106.4418160; I126WB
    WILDERNESS BOUNDARY; 10558
39.2877900 -106.4389910; I129PL
    POWERLINE; 10409
39.2848990 -106.4439360; I133PL
    POWERLINE; 10112
39.2848930 -106.4465570; I135BR
    MILL CREEK; 10060
39.2813030 -106.4460930; I140M
39.2722140 -106.4357310; I150M
39.2696210 -106.4324350; I154TH
    HAGERMAN ROAD; 10379

SEGMENT 10
39.2696210 -106.4324350; J000TH
    HAGERMAN ROAD; 10379
39.2623300 -106.4239090; J010M
39.2504320 -106.4223320; J020M
39.2389910 -106.4205870; J030M
39.2307680 -106.4204690; J036XT
    INTERSECT FISHING TRAIL; 10663
39.2310710 -106.4221140; J037XT
    FISHING TRAIL; 10655
39.2292470 -106.4255140; J040M
39.2255030 -106.4233140; J045WT
    CROSS ROCK CREEK; 10289
39.2191770 -106.4245850; J050M
39.2083230 -106.4267960; J061XT
    HIGHLINE TRAIL; 10942
39.1948630 -106.4301490; J071WT
    N WILLOW CREEK; 11104
39.1895610 -106.4277420; J076RT
    TOP OF RIDGE; 11326
39.1844660 -106.4267670; J080XT
    TRAIL INTERSECTS; 11277
39.1798250 -106.4251430; J084XT
    WILLOW CREEK; 11049
39.1725040 -106.4234030; J090WT
    S WILLOW CREEK; 10848
39.1639330 -106.4142460; J100M
39.1547950 -106.4141030; J110M
39.1513320 -106.4184070; J114TH
    HALF MOON TH; 10084

SEGMENT 11
39.1513320 -106.4184070; K000TH
    HALFMOON TH; 10084
39.1460520 -106.4101640; K010M
39.1440850 -106.4075640; K013XT
    MT. ELBERT TRAIL; 10570
39.1368090 -106.4010740; K020M
39.1354370 -106.3962110; K023XT
    TRAIL INTERSECTS; 10276
39.1271260 -106.3895120; K030M

39.1243290 -106.3901780; K032XT
    INT SIDE TRAIL; 10448
39.1152150 -106.3894750; K040M
39.1094740 -106.3932470; K045XT
    MT. ELBERT TRAIL; 10617
39.1057250 -106.3948120; K048XR
    JOIN JEEP ROAD; 10517
39.0978690 -106.3778240; K060M
39.0993160 -106.3685200; K066XR
    TRAIL LEAVES ROAD; 9648
39.0980350 -106.3666380; K067XT
    CROSS CG LOOP; 9519
39.0964580 -106.3642070; K070XT; LEAVE CG; 9349
39.0935450 -106.3640010; K072XR
    UNDERPASS HWY 82; 9313
39.0946010 -106.3539970; K078FT
    VISITOR CENTER; 9288
39.0957490 -106.3321270; K090M
39.0927590 -106.3206410; K097XR
    ROAD INTERSECTIO; 9250
39.0899340 -106.3158890; K100M
39.0804260 -106.3030120; K110XT
    CROSS DAM; 9209
39.0742670 -106.3097200; K118XR; ROAD; 9212
39.0752750 -106.3317240; KK131X
    LEFT AT TRAIL INTERSECTION; 9241
39.0684090 -106.3251100; KK139X
    LEAVE OLD RD; 9727
39.0684680 -106.3320090; KK144X
    TRAIL FORKS; 9823
39.0655990 -106.3296910; KK148F
    FOREST BOUNDARY; 9917
39.0625330 -106.3252580; KK151M
39.0534430 -106.3200610; KK159X
    CROSS ROAD; 9889
39.0436300 -106.3158740; KK168X; HIT ROAD; 9810
39.0434750 -106.3136440; KK170X
    LEAVE ROAD; 9778
39.0345070 -106.3030090; KK181M
39.0341010 -106.3022060; KK182P
    JOIN POWERLINE; 9321
39.0276320 -106.3031730; KK186P
    LEAVE POWERLINE; 9439
39.0225850 -106.3045280; KK191X
    CROSS JEEP TRAIL; 9669
39.0213980 -106.3035050; KK192X
    JEEP TRAIL; 9755
39.0208960 -106.3021550; KK193X
    LEAVE ROAD; 9626
39.0193080 -106.2966230; KK201M
39.0178120 -106.2977930; KK203T; CR390; 8961

SEGMENT 12
39.0178120 -106.2977930; L000TH
    GATE CR390; 8961
39.0166420 -106.2974530; L001BR
    CROSS CLEAR CREEK; 8947
39.0158560 -106.2972510; L002XT
    TURN TO LEFT; 8945
39.0161730 -106.2962340; L0021
    RIGHT ON SGL TRK; 8957
39.0168200 -106.2904810; L005XT
    RIGHT ON TRACK; 8939
39.0150840 -106.2909120; L007GT
    LEAVE PRIVATE LAND; 8949
39.0123250 -106.2894820; L010M
39.0113480 -106.2835070; L014PL
    POWER LINE; 9349
39.0086740 -106.2832670; L018XR
    CROSS JEEP TRAIL; 9640
38.9960800 -106.2799650; L030M
38.9878700 -106.2877010; L038WT
    FLOWING SPRING; 10909

38.9809680 -106.2865740; L043WT; SPRING; 11301
38.9752270 -106.2853660; L048RT
RIDGE TOP; 11645
38.9686690 -106.2807520; L060M
38.9648600 -106.2761680; L064BR
PINE CREEK BRIDGE; 10396
38.9606240 -106.2732570; L070M
38.9540950 -106.2725480; L080M
38.9536500 -106.2720480; L081XT
RAINBOW LAKE TRAIL; 11546
38.9462330 -106.2703350; L090RT
TOP OF CLIMB; 11854
38.9388550 -106.2696660; L098WT
MORRISON CREEK; 11548
38.9363390 -106.2582650; L105XT
WAPACA TRAIL; 11502
38.9301490 -106.2536840; L110M
38.9220860 -106.2559450; L118WT
FRENCHMAN CREEK; 10986
38.9216830 -106.2544930; L119XT
FRENCHMAN CREEK TRAIL; 10969
38.9144870 -106.2462900; L130M
38.9042590 -106.2456130; L142XT
OLD MINE TRAIL; 10687
38.8950240 -106.2384290; L150M
38.8931710 -106.2396790; L152WT
ELK CREEK; 10281
38.8905240 -106.2397360; L154WT
HARVARD LAKE; 10251
38.8898880 -106.2396950; L154WB
WILDERNESS BNDRY; 10249
38.8871560 -106.2410090; L157WT
SMALL CREEK; 10157
38.8849060 -106.2408030; L159WT
POWELL CREEK; 10039
38.8798250 -106.2348830; L165XT
AU RANCH TRAIL; 9997
38.8739510 -106.2382410; L170M
38.8674220 -106.2375280; L178XT
RANCH TRAIL; 9857
38.8645050 -106.2381130; L183XR
N COTTONWOOD RD; 9431
38.8656500 -106.2403720; L185TH
N COTTONWOOD RD; 9407

SEGMENT 13
38.8656500 -106.2403720; M000TH
N COTTONWOOD RD; 9407
38.8609450 -106.2520990; M010M
38.8560440 -106.2667990; M020M
38.8522030 -106.2770830; M027WB
WILDERNESS BOUNDARY; 11242
38.8502070 -106.2812610; M030M
38.8475570 -106.2813450; M034RT
TOP OF RIDGE; 11920
38.8409380 -106.2774020; M040M
38.8277440 -106.2789670; M050M
38.8179690 -106.2779440; M060M
38.8161630 -106.2778440; M063WB
WILDERNESS BOUNDARY; 9396
38.8135960 -106.2803750; M066TH
AVALANCHE TRAIL HEAD; 9344
38.8128970 -106.2793320; M067XR; CR306; 9352
38.8121720 -106.2746890; M070M
38.8064760 -106.2583200; M080M
38.8015190 -106.2475620; M088XT
TRAIL INTERSECTION; 9006
38.8020650 -106.2468610; M089XR; CR344; 8955
38.8009700 -106.2447640; M090BR
CROSS BRIDGE; 8910
38.8042660 -106.2372840; M095XR
CROSS ROAD; 8891
38.8019030 -106.2371730; M100M; ; Allwp.txt L982

38.7994150 -106.2349020; M105XT
TRAIL INTERSECTION; 9321
38.7950930 -106.2338720; M110XT
TRAIL INTERSECTION; 9644
38.7880790 -106.2232230; M120M
38.7791820 -106.2198240; M130M
38.7753100 -106.2144930; M135RT
TOP OF CLIMB; 10035
38.7719110 -106.2104040; M140M
38.7611290 -106.2010860; M150M
38.7594440 -106.1979440; M153XT
TRAIL INTERSECTION.; 9566
38.7527910 -106.1949890; M160M
38.7480060 -106.1873180; M166XR
JOIN ROAD; 9499
38.7436740 -106.1830040; M170M
38.7399700 -106.1748340; M177XR
PASS RANCH; 8934
38.7394120 -106.1691360; M180M
38.7393200 -106.1639850; M183XR
RD INTERSECTION _ BEAR L; 8617
38.7423710 -106.1612540; M186XR
RD INTERSECTION _ BEAR R; 8552
38.7385570 -106.1564030; M190M
38.7329230 -106.1634360; M198XR
CR162 _ TURN R; 8159
38.7233890 -106.1781530; M210M
38.7220260 -106.1805630; M212XR
LEFT ON CR291; 8314
38.7178940 -106.1950780; M220M
38.7167010 -106.1995390; M223TH
CHALK CREEK TH; 8391

SEGMENT 14
38.7167010 -106.1995390; N000TH
CHALK CREEK TH; 8391
38.7156750 -106.1989490; N001XT
BOOTLEG TRAIL; 8435
38.7128180 -106.1964100; N004XR
FOREST SVC RD; 8500
38.7079640 -106.1953550; N010M
38.7082840 -106.1922500; N014RT
TOP OF CLIMB; 9315
38.7102240 -106.1810130; N021XT
FORK - BEAR R; 9024
38.7065100 -106.1817140; N024XR
CROSS OLD ROAD; 8921
38.6994640 -106.1776330; N030M
38.6893500 -106.1701840; N039XR
CROSS ROAD; 8889
38.6771600 -106.1696700; N050M
38.6699100 -106.1809700; N061XT
BEAR LEFT AT INTERSECTION; 9706
38.6666970 -106.1800020; N064WT
LITTLE BROWNS CREEK; 9542
38.6614340 -106.1787980; N070XT
WAGON LOOP; 9640
38.6512630 -106.1758670; N080M
38.6405550 -106.1812050; N090M
38.6350070 -106.1770990; N095XT
TRAIL INTERSECTION; 9598
38.6299910 -106.1790350; N100M
38.6209800 -106.1908440; N110M
38.6091110 -106.1902910; N120M
38.6020910 -106.1952370; N127XT
JEEP TRAIL; 9891
38.5989730 -106.1971660; N130XT
FORK RIGHT; 9807
38.5959930 -106.1992850; N132XR
CROSS ROAD; 9826
38.5883630 -106.2073030; N140M
38.5850940 -106.2188980; N149TH
TH NEAR CR240; 9190

38.5847250 -106.2202120; N150XR; CR240; 9175
38.5824420 -106.2208170; N152WT
    FOOTBRIDGE; 9141
38.5771380 -106.2168550; N160M
38.5771250 -106.2208730; N167RT
    TOP OF CLIMB; 9768
38.5735650 -106.2178550; N170M
38.5652030 -106.2289540; N180M
38.5651020 -106.2291620; N180XR
    CROSS ROAD; 9491
38.5547540 -106.2362140; N190M
38.5535540 -106.2374250; N192XR
    JEEP ROAD; 9336
38.5478800 -106.2403970; N198PL
    POWERLINE; 9330
38.5450080 -106.2422760; N201XR
    RAILROAD BED; 8944
38.5435900 -106.2422640; N202XR
    US HWY 50; 8864
38.5433070 -106.2419610; N203TH
    FOOSES CREEK RD; 8866

SEGMENT 15
38.5433070 -106.2419610; O000TH
    FOOSES CREEK RD.; 8866
38.5393580 -106.2516090; O010M
38.5317470 -106.2658390; O020M
38.5240410 -106.2755160; O028XR
    LEFT ON ROAD FORK; 9588
38.5228420 -106.2752060; O029TH
    PARKING AREA; 9580
38.5098220 -106.2681780; O040M
38.4961710 -106.2705080; O050M
38.4848630 -106.2769910; O060M
38.4728960 -106.2740970; O070M
38.4603270 -106.2772040; O080M
38.4545260 -106.2764960; O086RT
    CONTINENTAL DIVIDE; 11918
38.4503410 -106.2718990; O090M
38.4439460 -106.2624640; O100M
38.4422030 -106.2580130; O103FT
    SHELTER CABIN; 11503
38.4328970 -106.2550490; O110M
38.4282180 -106.2545960; O114XT
    COCHETOPA TRAIL; 11784
38.4197040 -106.2518320; O120M
38.4096420 -106.2559090; O128XR
    JOIN JEEP ROAD; 11356
38.4058180 -106.2539650; O131M
38.3948090 -106.2471350; O141RT
    MARSHALL PASS ROAD; 10841
38.3916950 -106.2461370; O143TH; 10880

SEGMENT 16
38.3916950 -106.2461370; P000TH
    MARSHALL PASS TH; 10880
38.3912760 -106.2464570; P000XT
    LEFT AT FORK; 10887
38.3825130 -106.2351660; P010M
38.3730650 -106.2379810; P020M
38.3679160 -106.2370830; P024XR
    JOIN JEEP ROAD; 11146
38.3613290 -106.2397570; P030M
38.3536340 -106.2409620; P036XT
    SILVER CREEK TRAIL; 11242
38.3509140 -106.2457190; P040M
38.3496060 -106.2570620; P047GT; GATE; 11561
38.3492280 -106.2625990; P050M
38.4834920 -106.2770610; P060M
38.3482990 -106.2839500; P066XR
    INTERSECT JEEP TRAIL; 10878
38.4786440 -106.2748370; P070M
38.3442210 -106.3051510; P080M
38.3430720 -106.3117110; P084XT; TRAIL FOLLOWS
    PIPELINE FOR 200 FEET; 10613

38.3376000 -106.3173470; P090M
38.3248880 -106.3225950; P100M
38.3141200 -106.3317210; P110M
38.3136840 -106.3325710; P111XT
    L ON TANK 7 TRAIL; 10335
38.3049710 -106.3417230; P120M
38.3057640 -106.3482840; P124XR; FS 578; 10794
38.3017490 -106.3571720; P130M
38.3011050 -106.3617300; P133XR
    CROSS LOGGING ROAD; 11108
38.3024360 -106.3664500; P136XR
    JOIN OLD JEEP TRAIL; 11220
38.2990540 -106.3712780; P140M
38.2968250 -106.3722200; P142XT
    BIG BEND CREEK TRAIL; 11391
38.2908000 -106.3780330; P147TH
    SARGENTS MESA; 11614

SEGMENT 17
38.2908000 -106.3780330; Q000TH
    SARGENTS MESA TH; 11614
38.2837170 -106.3919580; Q010M
38.2845060 -106.4074630; Q020M
38.2819340 -106.4106240; Q023XT; CAUTION TURN
    R ON POORLY MARKED TRAIL; 11167
38.2810950 -106.4131570; Q024T
    LONG BRANCH TRAIL; 11157
38.2804900 -106.4225510; Q030M
38.2839520 -106.4373840; Q040M
38.2932040 -106.4491560; Q050M
38.3037330 -106.4593700; Q060M
38.3136790 -106.4651280; Q069XT
    BALDY LAKE TRAIL -.5 MI; 11509
38.3159000 -106.4825990; Q080M
38.3146940 -106.4997830; Q090M
38.3170620 -106.5116190; Q098XT
    DUTCHMAN TRAIL; 11376
38.3059570 -106.5172260; Q108XT
    TURN L_ LEAVE CREEKBED; 10884
38.3040410 -106.5144140; Q110M
38.2919260 -106.5184380; Q120M
38.2804480 -106.5243730; Q130M
38.2682270 -106.5314160; Q140M
38.2584020 -106.5420090; Q150M
38.2534760 -106.5537270; Q160M
38.2444350 -106.5550080; Q170M
38.2399590 -106.5571450; Q178TH
    LUJAN CREEK TH; 10342
38.2410310 -106.5601310; Q180XR
    RD INTERSECTION - GO LEFT; 10328
38.2343080 -106.5736460; Q190M
38.2257650 -106.5850300; Q200M
38.2254980 -106.5850850; Q200XR
    FOLLOW HWY 114 TO RIGHT; 9738
38.2229160 -106.5908230; Q204TH
    HWY 114; 9599

SEGMENT 18
38.2229160 -106.5908230; R000TH
    HWY 114; 9599
38.2183370 -106.5990980; R006XT
    BEAR TO LEFT; 9526
38.2137100 -106.5966370; R0010R
    GO STRAIGHT AHEAD; 9544
38.2026140 -106.5974960; R018XR
    TAKE R FORK; 9704
38.2035640 -106.6040980; R030M
38.1958850 -106.6028650; R036XT
    R ON SINGLE TRACK; 9988
38.1901830 -106.6052520; R040XR
    FOLLOW FS876 LEFT; 10171
38.1776350 -106.6025120; R050M
38.1659500 -106.6106090; R060M
38.1642480 -106.6168160; R064GT; GATE; 9774

38.1612830 -106.6200060; R067XR
 FOLLOW ROAD TO R; 9729
38.1585620 -106.6168630; R070M
38.1593690 -106.6201770; R072XR
 GO L ON FS864.2A; 9620
38.1505160 -106.6208610; R080M
38.1496460 -106.6253910; R083XR
 INTERSECTING ROAD; 9745
38.1493260 -106.6384650; R090M
38.1495120 -106.6441900; R093WT
 CROSS CREEK; 9558
38.1501490 -106.6558800; R100M
38.1500440 -106.6737430; R110M
38.1484130 -106.6847290; R116XR
 FORK TO R; 9359
38.1500990 -106.6884910; R119XR
 L ON CR17FF; 9334
38.1351160 -106.6922880; R130M
38.1315110 -106.6964450; R134TH
 FS287.2D CR17F; 9520

SEGMENT 19
38.1315110 -106.6964450; S000TH
 INT. CR17FF FS287.2; 9520
38.1302650 -106.6988480; S002XT
 FORK -BEAR L; 9521
38.1245640 -106.7112650; S010M
38.1240700 -106.7154280; S012GT; FENCE; 9717
38.1226130 -106.7196590; S015XT
 INTERSECTION; 9772
38.1230570 -106.7284980; S020M
38.1220700 -106.7319510; S022XT
 RIGHT TURN; 9751
38.1243570 -106.7344680; S024XT
 MAZE OF RDS -GO WEST; 9694
38.1229190 -106.7438240; S030M
38.1174080 -106.7535880; S038XT
 L ON FS597; 9849
38.1138700 -106.7544220; S040M
38.1035760 -106.7596620; S048XR
 BEAR R AT FORK; 10186
38.0976620 -106.7702670; S060M
38.1050720 -106.7719740; S066XT
 BEAR L TO POND; 9922
38.1040980 -106.7757270; S068XT
 TRAILS INTERSECT; 9827
38.1015550 -106.7773900; S070XT
 L ON SINGLE TRACK; 9746
38.0964830 -106.7809630; S075XT
 FORK TO R; 9733
38.0896180 -106.7849420; S080M
38.0764410 -106.7915090; S090M
38.0651960 -106.7996130; S100M
38.0625830 -106.8024810; S102WT
 WADE RIVER NW; 9946
38.0628360 -106.8034140; S103WT
 W SIDE OF RIVER; 9934
38.0561550 -106.8080240; S109WB
 WILDERNESS BOUNDARY; 10040
38.0446320 -106.8197650; S120M
38.0434710 -106.8226510; S122RT
 ON SHELF ABOVE RIVER; 10202
38.0349690 -106.8318700; S130M
38.0330800 -106.8322070; S131XT
 BEAR R AT SPLIT; 10272
38.0266390 -106.8337990; S136TH
 EDDIESVILLE TH; 10308

SEGMENT 20
38.0266390 -106.8337990; T000TH
 EDDIESVILLE TH; 10308
38.0257230 -106.8351570; T001XR
 FS794 - GO LEFT; 10340
38.0235620 -106.8357420; T003XT
 TRAIL LEAVES ROAD; 10350

38.0225930 -106.8367830; T003GT; GATE; 10413
38.0151430 -106.8303670; T010M
38.0124950 -106.8271030; T013WB
 GATE - WILDERNESS BOUNDARY; 10524
38.0088320 -106.8247030; T016XT
 CROSS TRAIL; 10361
38.0030280 -106.8251960; T020M
37.9916390 -106.8344420; T030M
37.9868220 -106.8442460; T037GT; GATE; 10644
37.9843650 -106.8488070; T040M
37.9806090 -106.8646790; T050M
37.9765170 -106.8802060; T060M
37.9747780 -106.8958350; T070M
37.9755920 -106.9046600; T075XT
 STEWART CREEK TRAIL; 11749
37.9756710 -106.9053310; T076WT
 CREEK - GOOD CAMPSITE; 11750
37.9763210 -106.9129970; T080M
37.9716200 -106.9236420; T088RT
 SADDLE 12670; 12670
37.9671620 -106.9234550; T092WT
 WATER SOURCE; 12451
37.9664160 -106.9379490; T101RT
 SADDLE 12382; 12382
37.9618000 -106.9395980; T105XT
 SPRING CREEK TR; 12121
37.9626940 -106.9466940; T109WT; STREAM; 12028
37.9691810 -106.9604660; T120M
37.9697460 -106.9612580; T121RT
 CONTINENTAL DIVIDE; 12370
37.9716470 -106.9716770; T127TH
 SAN LUIS PASS; 11936

SEGMENT 21
37.9716470 -106.9716770; U000TH
 SAN LUIS PASS; 11936
37.9690150 -106.9830140; U010M
37.9646330 -106.9924660; U020M
37.9628270 -107.0021300; U026XT
 E. MINERAL CREEK TR; 11783
37.9634420 -107.0038970; U027WT
 E MINERAL CREEK; 11670
37.9627220 -107.0075180; U030M
37.9598730 -107.0093500; U033RT; SADDLE; 12163
37.9580450 -107.0184230; U039WT
 W MINERAL CREEK; 11616
37.9617160 -107.0215100; U043XT
 MINERAL CR CUTOFF; 11465
37.9623540 -107.0275710; U048RT; SADDLE; 11846
37.9576510 -107.0299890; U052WT
 SMALL STREAM; 11974
37.9538940 -107.0354730; U057RT; SADDLE; 12251
37.9512780 -107.0385040; U060M
37.9496170 -107.0416490; U062XT
 MINERAL CREEK TRAIL; 12328
37.9501600 -107.0516790; U070M
37.9532690 -107.0594310; U076RT
 BEGIN DESCENT; 12774
37.9561610 -107.0664560; U080M
37.9553890 -107.0714160; U083XT
 BEAR L DOWN TO LAKE; 12557
37.9461530 -107.0732440; U090M
37.9397910 -107.0732990; U095WT
 EDGE OF LAKE; 12300
37.9383530 -107.0775220; U097WT; STREAM; 12290
37.9388310 -107.0826040; U100M
37.9382180 -107.1005720; U110M
37.9360310 -107.1180760; U120M
37.9347770 -107.1299440; U127RT
 DROP OFF OF SNOW MESA; 12264
37.9346910 -107.1345800; U130M
37.9399550 -107.1491000; U140M
37.9401510 -107.1583990; U146TH
 HWY149; 10872

SEGMENT 22
37.9401510 -107.1583990; V000TH
    HWY 149; 10872
37.9364310 -107.1738060; V010M
37.9342550 -107.1907810; V020M
37.9291420 -107.2040890; V030M
37.9294530 -107.2212170; V040M
37.9271170 -107.2389290; V050M
37.9284850 -107.2492470; V056XT
    TRAIL JOINS JEEP TRAIL; 11707
37.9278310 -107.2558060; V060M
37.9322610 -107.2721610; V070M
37.9218640 -107.2809240; V079XT
    FORK R ON TRAIL; 12016
37.9126510 -107.2864130; V087XR
    CROSS ROAD; 11715
37.9086160 -107.2859020; V090M
37.9066000 -107.2835070; V092XR
    R ON JEEP TR; 12003
37.9052800 -107.2941300; V100M
37.8943280 -107.3033060; V110M
37.8881150 -107.3177910; V120M
37.8788600 -107.3253510; V130M
37.8714170 -107.3365670; V140M
37.8623160 -107.3436480; V150M
37.8566150 -107.3453490; V156RT
    HIGHEST PT ON CT; 13253
37.8550730 -107.3494260; V160M
37.8548580 -107.3493570; V160XT
    FOLLOW JEEP TR R; 13111
37.8557470 -107.3645330; V170M
37.8552260 -107.3652050; V171XR
    R ON JEEP TR; 12297
37.8561040 -107.3671610; V172TH
    CARSON SADDLE; 12356

SEGMENT 23
37.8561040 -107.3671610; W000TH
    CARSON SADDLE; 12356
37.8493010 -107.3684960; W005XT
    TURN R ON TRAIL; 12188
37.8483230 -107.3757500; W010M
37.8480120 -107.3924000; W020M
37.8530440 -107.4080930; W030M
37.8533710 -107.4190620; W037RT
    TOP OF RIDGE; 12929
37.8531060 -107.4240370; W040M
37.8450200 -107.4379210; W050XT
    FOLLOW L FORK; 12380
37.8378960 -107.4504980; W060M
37.8260940 -107.4598150; W070M
37.8130770 -107.4642270; W080M
37.8015820 -107.4643510; W090M
37.7905520 -107.4555170; W100M
37.7777930 -107.4609150; W110M
37.7671250 -107.4641060; W118XT
    BEAR L AT MC TRAIL; 10620
37.7618950 -107.4660160; W122TH
    STONY PASS ROAD; 10547

SEGMENT 24
37.7618950 -107.4660160; X000TH
    STONY PASS ROAD; 10547
37.7572050 -107.4669740; X005XR
    CROSS RIO GRANDE; 10427
37.7571550 -107.4752310; X010M
37.7493470 -107.4883150; X020M
37.7369330 -107.4961760; X030M
37.7245460 -107.5004320; X040M
37.7205380 -107.5060570; X045XT
    TURN R ON TRAIL; 11264
37.7237150 -107.5077650; X050M
37.7210780 -107.5151050; X060M
37.7198550 -107.5242800; X067XR
    OLD ROAD - BEAR R; 12093

37.7226150 -107.5286150; X070M
37.7258710 -107.5314260; X073XT
    INTERSECT TRAIL_BEAR L; 12451
37.7183950 -107.5354710; X079ON
    DIVIDE - GO R AND DOWN; 12682
37.7165960 -107.5460660; X091WT
    CROSS CREEK; 11764
37.7178990 -107.5598610; X100M
37.7238600 -107.5717470; X110M
37.7265630 -107.5761150; X113WT
    CROSS STREAM; 10354
37.7246580 -107.5870510; X120M
37.7215690 -107.6019140; X130M
37.7202860 -107.6173880; X140M
37.7217060 -107.6337060; X150M
37.7267460 -107.6507360; X161WB
    WILDERNESS BOUNDARY; 9095
37.7269600 -107.6510740; X162XT
    TRAIL TO ELK PARK RR STOP; 9062
37.7320340 -107.6588610; X168XR
    CROSS RAILROAD; 8907
37.7335100 -107.6604410; X169BR
    ANIMAS RIVER BRIDGE; 8922
37.7351240 -107.6609780; X171WT; STREAM; 8956
37.7394730 -107.6655780; X180M
37.7425010 -107.6700040; X191XT
    HORSE TRAIL; 10283
37.7397650 -107.6812900; X198XT
    HORSE TRAIL; 10202
37.7404950 -107.6851890; X201XT
    HORSE TRAIL; 10407
37.7437960 -107.6858500; X203XT
    CROSS TRAIL; 10499
37.7447530 -107.6875600; X204XT
    TRAIL TO MOLAS LAKE; 10574
37.7422580 -107.6909840; X208WT
    CROSS STREAM; 10509
37.7417040 -107.6938970; X210M
37.7395530 -107.6976260; X218TH
    W SIDE HWY 550; 10882

SEGMENT 25
37.7395530 -107.6976260; Y000TH
    W SIDE HWY 550; 10882
37.7416870 -107.7082940; Y007WT
    LITTLE MOLAS LAKE; 10844
37.7430990 -107.7116780; Y010M
37.7443060 -107.7218090; Y020M
37.7537310 -107.7189260; Y030M
37.7661400 -107.7260310; Y040M
37.7612900 -107.7415590; Y050M
37.7686910 -107.7529330; Y060M
37.7645970 -107.7627090; Y070M
37.7646570 -107.7764000; Y080M
37.7576880 -107.7896660; Y090M
37.7494200 -107.8029800; Y100M
37.7464440 -107.8046460; Y102XT
    ENGINEER TRAIL- GO RIGHT; 12117
37.7508080 -107.8148940; Y110XT
    TRAIL TO MINERAL CREEK; 12330
37.7493560 -107.8160430; Y112RT; PASS; 12450
37.7456350 -107.8217060; Y120M
37.7413630 -107.8323100; Y129XT
    BEAR R ON RICO TRAIL; 11450
37.7386950 -107.8423740; Y140M
37.7469290 -107.8476890; Y148WT
    CASCADE CREEK; 10794
37.7442150 -107.8497620; Y150M
37.7308780 -107.8526050; Y160M
37.7299790 -107.8654790; Y170WT; STREAM; 11173
37.7260630 -107.8628080; Y173XT
    SIDE TRAIL TO FS579; 11285
37.7188140 -107.8645510; Y180M
37.7140430 -107.8772170; Y190M

37.7178400 -107.8900420; Y200M
37.7148690 -107.9005930; Y207XT
TURN L ON SINGLE TRACK; 11139
37.7132270 -107.9028800; Y209TH
BOLAM PASS ROAD; 11081

SEGMENT 26
37.7132270 -107.9028800; Z000TH
BOLAM PASS ROAD; 11081
37.7121480 -107.9158660; Z010M
37.7160600 -107.9243450; Z016XT
AT TRAIL INTERSECTION; 11537
37.7144480 -107.9300810; Z020M
37.7061720 -107.9428520; Z030M
37.7061120 -107.9428580; Z030XT
BEGIN SINGLE TRACK; 11577
37.7055550 -107.9581220; Z040M
37.7057980 -107.9590220; Z041XT
LEFT AT SPLIT; 11752
37.6981730 -107.9676510; Z050M
37.6874820 -107.9733560; Z060M
37.6844850 -107.9797270; Z069RT
BLACKHAWK PASS; 12000
37.6754230 -107.9764210; Z080M
37.6683100 -107.9715800; Z090M
37.6614010 -107.9608340; Z100M
37.6495710 -107.9563510; Z109TH
SCOTCH CREEK ROAD; 10394

SEGMENT 27
37.6495710 -107.9563510; AA000T
SCOTCH CREEK ROAD; 10394
37.6487400 -107.9565240; AA001X
LEAVE RD TO R; 10398
37.6464410 -107.9635930; AA007T
TURN LEFT; 10391
37.6423630 -107.9611770; AA010M
37.6410350 -107.9635520; AA012X
TURN TO R; 10432
37.6409810 -107.9653070; AA013X
JOIN ROAD; 10440
37.6406380 -107.9665010; AA011
FOLLOW FS564; 10433
37.6399060 -107.9672150; AA014X
TRAIL LEAVES ROAD; 10455
37.6355950 -107.9724810; AA020M
37.6282840 -107.9814760; AA030M
37.6183800 -107.9929060; AA040M
37.6168900 -107.9930440; AA041X
CROSS ROAD; 10839
37.6160900 -107.9932350; AA042X
CROSS ROAD; 10873
37.6087730 -108.0040820; AA050M
37.6087460 -108.0041060; AA050X
TRAIL LEAVES ROAD; 10711
37.6054230 -108.0105430; AA056X
JOIN FS ROAD; 10717
37.6051030 -108.0114250; AA057X
LEAVE FS RD; 10726
37.6013950 -108.0147100; AA060M
37.5956730 -108.0139770; AA065X
BIG BEND TRAIL; 10634
37.5916210 -108.0204290; AA070M
37.5909530 -108.0218220; AA071X
JOIN LOGGING TRAIL; 10801
37.5803220 -108.0177320; AA079X
SALT CREEK TRAIL; 10899
37.5783770 -108.0194400; AA081X
JOIN OLD ROAD; 10873
37.5687610 -108.0190110; AA088X
TRAIL INTERSECTION; 10923
37.5541450 -108.0180800; AA100M
37.5432230 -108.0211610; AA110M

37.5335720 -108.0308620; AA120M
37.5335300 -108.0318050; AA123X
OVERLOOK TRAIL; 11333
37.5304860 -108.0037930; AA130M
37.5168220 -108.0329650; AA140M

37.5044530 -108.0381240; AA150X
GRINDSTONE TRAIL; 11691
37.4922350 -108.0352590; AA160M
37.4811780 -108.0331790; AA170M
37.4687530 -108.0344800; AA180M
37.4654470 -108.0330060; AA183R
SUMMIT 12308; 12308
37.4605500 -108.0343610; AA187R
2ND SUMMIT 12260; 12261
37.4594360 -108.0329730; AA190M
37.4567650 -108.0292810; AA194X
TAYLOR LAKE; 11643
37.4546160 -108.0189970; AA200M
37.4515080 -108.0105880; AA206T
KENNEBEC TH; 11645

SEGMENT 28
37.4515080 -108.0105880; BB000TH
KENNEBEC TH; 11645
37.4491710 -108.0037370; BB005R; PASS; 11698
37.4471740 -108.0014450; BB007X
TURN LEFT; 11757
37.4480400 -107.9967350; BB010M
37.4479700 -107.9955020; BB011F
SLIDEROCK TRAVERSE; 11370
37.4507880 -107.9868930; BB020M
37.4504740 -107.9836250; BB024X
ROAD TO FS543; 10390
37.4494730 -107.9789680; BB030M
37.4465990 -107.9706400; BB040M
37.4373520 -107.9702200; BB050M
37.4332430 -107.9676960; BB054F
WATERFALL; 9148
37.4332380 -107.9706510; BB057W
CROSS CREEK; 9021
37.4299410 -107.9721000; BB060M
37.4163660 -107.9723480; BB071B
BRIDGE OVER CREEK; 8546
37.4062560 -107.9696100; BB080M
37.3998360 -107.9652780; BB090M
37.3927110 -107.9671670; BB100M
37.3865270 -107.9638810; BB110M
37.3870040 -107.9602330; BB112R
TOP OF CLIMB; 9578
37.3799710 -107.9608820; BB120M
37.3694550 -107.9634640; BB130M
37.3597430 -107.9719130; BB140M
37.3559250 -107.9711050; BB146X; LEFT AT DRY
FORK INTERSECTION; 8607
37.3535700 -107.9670860; BB150M
37.3561090 -107.9513840; BB160M
37.3547190 -107.9366470; BB170M
37.3523340 -107.9346530; BB172X
HOFFHEINS CONNECTION TRAIL; 8017
37.3530270 -107.9310820; BB174F
GUDYS REST; 8032
37.3547620 -107.9290110; BB180M
37.3547970 -107.9271580; BB189B
BRIDGE OVER CREEK; 7444
37.3411030 -107.9227380; BB200M
37.3377560 -107.9193950; BB203X
ACCESS TO ROAD; 7217
37.3342750 -107.9089810; BB210M
37.3313820 -107.9020810; BB215T
DURANGO TH; 6999

Index ▲

Note:

Bolded text and page numbers indicate a Segment chapter. Page numbers in italics indicate maps.

Join with us in building and maintaining The Colorado Trail for you and the future.

✔ Yes, I want to become a "Friend of the Colorado Trail"!

Friends receive our CT newsletter, *Tread Lines*, notices of special events and summer trail crew, trek, and education class schedules.

Supporter $15 ___ Contributor $25 ___ Sustainer $50 ___
Sponsor $75 ___ Partner $100 ___ Patron $250 ___
Guardian $500 ___ Benefactor $1000 ___ Corporate $_____
I am a: Senior ___ Student ___ Individual ___ Family ___
My employer offers Matching Funds and I will apply for them ___

✔ Yes, I am ready to volunteer!

I want to work on a Volunteer Trail Crew. Please send information ___
I'd like information on the Adopt-a-Trail Program ___
I would like to help with other CT volunteer projects.
Please send information ___

Name(s):_____
Address:_____
City:_____ State:_____ Zip:_____
Telephone:_____ Email:_____

The Colorado Trail Foundation
710 10th Street #210
Golden, CO 80401-5843

Ph: (303) 384-3729 Ext 113   Fax: (303) 384-3743
Web: www.coloradotrail.org   Email: ctf@coloradotrail.org

For a FREE certificate for completing the entire Colorado Trail, contact the CTF office.

THE COLORADO TRAIL STORE

✔ **The Colorado Trail: The Official Guidebook**, 6th edition
288 pages, 29 full-color maps, 90 color photos, 6x9 format, softcover. **$22.95** _____

✔ **The Colorado Trail: The Trailside Databook**, 2002 edition
48 pages, 33 color maps, 4x6 format, softcover.   **$5.95** _____

✔ **Along the Colorado Trail**
Color photographs by John Fielder, journal by M. John Fayhee.
128 pages, 9x12 format, softcover.   **$25.00** _____

✔ **Day Hikes on the Colorado Trail**
Text and photographs by Jan Robertson.
Color photographs, 48 pages, 4x9 format, softcover.   **$3.00** _____

✔ **The Colorado Trail Cookbook**
300+ recipes, stories, 154 pages, 7x9 easel format, hardcover.   **$15.00** _____

✔ **Colorado Trail Wall Poster Map**
17x24 w/ 28 segmts. marked. Published by Trails Illustrated, 1995.   **$9.00** _____

✔ **Colorado Trail Completion Plaque**
Triangular CT sign above an engraved nameplate on wood.   **$39.00** _____

✔ **Colorado Trail Map/Completion Plaque**
CT map with list of segments in brass on wood,
9x12, with up to 30 characters engraved.   **$61.00** _____

✔ **Colorado Trail Commemorative Plaque**
CT map in brass on wood, 9x12 with up to 50 characters engraved.   **$70.00** _____

✔ **Colorado Trail Marker**
4 3/4" high triangular plastic marker used to sign the CT.   **$2.50** _____

Colorado Trail Clothing
Please contact the CTF office for color and size availability.

✔ **Colorado Trail T-Shirts**
Short sleeved, 50/50 cotton/poly blend, CT map on front,
segments on back. Jade green, royal blue, birch grey. S, M, L, XL.
Size _____ Color _____ **$11.00** _____
Long sleeved, 100% pre-shrunk cotton, with embroidered CT logo.
Heather gray, Eggplant. M, L, XL.
Size _____ Color _____ **$17.00** _____

✔ **Fleece Vest**
Forest green with black trim and CT logo. S, M, L, XL.
Size _____ **$40.00** _____

✔ **Colorado Trail Baseball Cap** Cotton, embroidered CT logo.   **$15.00** _____
✔ **Colorado Trail Embroidered Patches** CT logo or Completion.   **$2.50** _____
✔ **Colorado Trail Official Pins** CT logo, 200 mile or 300 mile.   **$2.00** _____

Subtotal _____

Shipping: $0 to $8.00 add $2.00
$8.01 to $20.00 add $5.00
$20.01 and over add $6.00
International shipping - contact office   **Shipping** _____
Tax: CO residents add 2.9% sales tax   **CO Tax** _____
Enclose check or money order   **Total** _____

Prices listed are current as of Sept. 2002. All prices are subject to change. Before ordering,
please contact the CTF office, or check our website at www.coloradotrail.org.

Colorado is waiting for you . . .
Are You ready?

THE COLORADO MOUNTAIN CLUB

MEMBERSHIP OPENS THE DOOR

The CMC is a nonprofit outdoor recreation and conservation organization founded in 1912. Today with over 10,000 members, 12 branches in-state, and one branch for out-of-state members, the CMC is the largest organization of its kind in the Rocky Mountains. *Membership opens the door to:*

Outdoor Recreation: *Over 3100 trips and outings led annually.* Hike, ski, climb, backpack, snowshoe, bicycle, ice skate, travel the world, build friendships.

Conservation: *Supporting a mission which treasures our natural environment.* Environmental education, input on public lands management, trail building and rehabilitation projects.

Outdoor Education: *Schools, seminars, and courses that teach outdoor skills through hands-on activities.* Wilderness trekking, rock climbing, high altitude mountaineering, telemark skiing, backpacking and much more . . . plus the Mountain Discovery Program to inspire lifelong stewardship in children and young adults.

Publications: *A wide range of outdoor publications to benefit and inform members.* Trail and Timberline Magazine, twice-a-year Activity Schedule, monthly group newsletters, and 20% discount on titles from CMC Press.

The American Mountaineering Center: *A world-class facility in Golden, Colorado.* Featuring the largest mountaineering library in the western hemisphere, a planned mountaineering museum, a new conference/classroom center, a 300-seat auditorium, free monthly program nights and a state-of-the-art technical climbing wall.

JOINING IS EASY

The Colorado Mountain Club
710 10th St. #200 Golden, CO 80401
(303) 279-3080 1(800) 633-4417
FAX (303) 279-9690
Email: cmcoffice@cmc.org
http://www.cmc.org/cmc

HIKING   BACKPACKING   ADVENTURE TRAVEL   SKIING   HUT TRIPS

MEMBERSHIP OPENS THE DOOR . . .

. . . TO ADVENTURE

CAMPING   TREKKING   ROCK CLIMBING   SCHOOLS   MOUNTAINEERING